THE MOSCOW ART THEATRE

The Moscow Art Theatre offers a detailed look at this famous theatre company and its founder Konstantin Stanislavsky, whose reputation as a theatre director and theoretician is unparalleled.

With descriptions of fifty Moscow Art Theatre productions between 1898 and 1917, Nick Worrall provides an account of the historical background of the company and the ways in which it ran its affairs, recruited its actors, established a repertoire and equipped its theatre buildings. He highlights the work not only of Stanislavsky and his well-known colleagues, but also the less well-known people who made an essential contribution to the artistic success and financial survival of the company. Worrall focuses in particular on four productions: Tolstoy's *Tsar Fedor Ioannovich*, Gorky's *The Lower Depths*, Chekhov's *The Cherry Orchard* and Turgenev's *A Month in the Country*.

Nick Worrall teaches English and European dramatic literature, as well as Russian and Soviet literature, at Middlesex University. He has researched widely in modern Russian/Soviet theatre, specialising in the work of theatre directors. His publications include *Nikolai Gogol and Ivan Turgenev*, and *Modernism to Realism on the Soviet Stage*.

THEATRE PRODUCTION STUDIES
General Editor: John Russell Brown
University of Michigan

There has long been a need for books which give a clear idea of how the great theatre of the past worked and of the particular experiences they offered. Students of dramatic literature and theatre history are increasingly concerned with plays in performance, especially the performances expected by their authors and their audiences. Directors, designers, actors and other theatre practitioners need imaginative, practical suggestions on how to revive plays and experiment with rehearsal and production techniques.

Theatre Production Studies fills this need. Designed to span Western theatre from the Greeks to the present day, each book explores a period, or genre, drawing together aspects of production from staging, wardrobe and acting styles, to the management of a theatre, its artistic team, and technical crew. Each volume focuses on several texts of exceptional achievement, and is well illustrated with contemporary material.

Already published:

THE MOSCOW ART THEATRE

Nick Worrall

London and New York

First published 1996
by Routledge
11 New Fetter Lane, London EC4P 4EE

Simultaneously published in the USA and Canada
by Routledge
29 West 35th Street, New York, NY 10001

*Routledge is an International
Thomson Publishing company*

© 1996 Nick Worrall

Typeset in Baskerville by
Ponting–Green Publishing Services, Chesham, Bucks
Printed and bound in Great Britain by
TJ Press (Padstow) Ltd, Padstow, Cornwall

British Library Cataloguing in Publication Data
A catalogue record for this book is available from
the British Library

Library of Congress Cataloguing in Publication Data
A catalogue record for this book has been requested

ISBN 0–415–05598–9

For
LEN ELY
(b. 1898)

CONTENTS

CONTENTS

ACKNOWLEDGEMENTS

My thanks to Professor Ted Braun of Bristol University for (I believe) recommending that I take on the task of writing this book; to the British Council for a research grant which took me to Moscow in 1988 when work on the book commenced; to Middlesex Polytechnic (now Middlesex University) for sabbatical leave which enabled me to continue the research and begin writing it; to Non Worrall for recommending the purchase of a word processor and for initiating me into its operational mysteries; to Zhenya Skvortsova for invaluable help in circumventing obstacles and for obtaining photocopied material from the Lenin Library; to staff at the STD (Theatre Workers' Union) Library in Moscow for their courtesy and help; to Professor Irina Malyutina of the St Petersburg Conservatoire for her long-standing friendship and an invaluable supply of books going back to the 1970s; to Professor Anna Obraztsova of the Moscow VNII (Institute for Artistic Research) similarly for friendship and a constant supply of irreplaceable books and for introducing me to Stanislavsky scholars in Moscow; to Professor Aleksey Bartoshevich of the STD and Milla Bartoshevicha for looking after our cats and, again, for supplying me with rare pre-revolutionary as well as more recent publications, all of which have helped a great deal with this project; and last but not least, to my editor, Professor John Russell Brown, go thanks for his advice, patience, and encouragement. Needless to say, none of the above people can be held responsible for any of the opinions expressed and some would, I know, wish to dispute them.

A NOTE ON TRANSLITERATION AND NAMES

Except in direct citations from Russian sources, Russian names are given in their accepted English forms – thus 'Meyerkhol'd' also appears as 'Meyerhold', 'Gorky' as 'Gor'kiy', and 'Stanislavskiy' as 'Stanislavsky' (as well as 'Stanislavski' where that version of his name has been used by others). The method of transliteration used in this book is based on the 'Matthews' system, with the occasional variation where a 'y' is prefixed to 'e' – so that 'Egorov' (the painter and stage designer) is transliterated as 'Yegorov', 'Epikhodov' (a character in *The Cherry Orchard*) as 'Yepikhodov', and a word like *p'esa* (a play) appears as *p'yesa*. The Russian 'yo' has not been phoneticised so 'Fedor' is not transliterated as 'Fyodor'. Soft-signs are indicated but hard-signs have been omitted from citations of pre-revolutionary sources. An attempt has been made to be consistent throughout.

It was the Moscow Art Theatre which, going against tradition, first introduced the convention of referring to actors by their initials and surnames in their programmes and publicity-handouts, rather than referring to them as Mr and Mrs which had hitherto been the norm. Unlike England, where theatre programmes refer to actors by their first and surnames, the modern convention in Russia and in the Soviet Union has always been to refer to the surname only, prefaced by the initials of the first name and patronymic of the actor concerned. Thus, an internationally renowned actress such as Olga Knipper would always feature in theatre programmes as O. L. Knipper (her patronymic being Leonardovna), just as Stanislavsky would always appear as K. S. Stanislavsky. This meant that, often, the first names and patronymics of less prominent actors and actresses were never widely known, if at all, and public references to them were by initials and surname only. For this reason the Russian practice has been observed in the notes on individual actors which appear at the end, where both the famous and the not-so-famous are identified by initials and surname only.

Part I

THE ESTABLISHMENT OF THE MOSCOW ART THEATRE

INTRODUCTION

The considerable impact of the Moscow Art Theatre, especially in Europe and North America, has largely been on the development of acting theory through the writings of Konstantin Stanislavsky, one of the Theatre's founders. However, although the Art Theatre began life in 1898, Stanislavsky did not concern himself seriously with acting theory until almost ten years later. A great deal of his theoretical work was written down during the 1930s, when his involvement in day-to-day theatre operations had ceased and the Theatre's own traditions were increasingly moribund.

Since the death, in 1943, of the Art Theatre's co-founder, Vladimir Nemirovich-Danchenko, and his successful revival of Chekhov's *Three Sisters* in 1940, the history of the Art Theatre has been undistinguished, despite attempts by disciples of both founders to sustain its values. Everything bequeathed by Stanislavsky and Nemirovich-Danchenko as an on-going legacy to be nurtured by inheritors who had acquired their experience at first hand, remains undeveloped. Despite the availability of key theoretical works (albeit incomplete), the scrupulous records of Art Theatre productions, and studies devoted to both, there is little evidence of Stanislavsky's and Nemirovich-Danchenko's positive influence on Russian theatre practice. At the time of writing, the Moscow Art Theatre is split and in crisis, and this seems symptomatic of a long-term decline, held in check and disguised by a less than disinterested, centralised state artistic policy.[1] What went wrong, and where did things begin to go wrong? It is perhaps necessary, at the approach of the Theatre's centenary, to return to its origins in an attempt to discover why the creation of the Moscow Art Theatre was such an important event and why it remains of major historical and artistic significance.

3

When the Moscow Art Theatre first visited Britain in 1958, the cultural and political after-shock was negligible compared with that of the Berliner Ensemble's visit in 1956. This was the Art Theatre's ninth overseas tour and thirteen more were made, to various parts of the world, between 1956 and 1977. However, none of these tours made any real and lasting impression on the theatrical consciousness of the countries visited. We probably have to go back to the first European tour, in 1906 (an artistic success but a financial failure) and to the American tours of 1923 and 1924, to discover what made the Moscow Art Theatre one of the world's great theatrical institutions. Moreover, the productions taken to America, whose effects proved so influential, were, in some cases, already twenty years old – and had already toured Europe in 1906. The international reputation of the Theatre seems, then, to be very specifically connected with its origins, and its historical significance with its very earliest years.

Important productions were staged at the Art Theatre between 1905 and 1917, as well as during the Soviet period, but nothing to compare in significance with those of the very first years. Who, outside Russia, can name any significant Art Theatre production staged after 1917? The international reputation of the theatre since the Russian Revolution has been almost entirely attributable to Stanislavsky's theoretical writings and, in particular, to his two-part study 'An Actor's Work on Himself'.[2] Effectively, the appropriation of the Moscow Art Theatre as a cultural instrument of the one-party state and the canonisation of its exemplary realist methods served to seal the theatre off from any influence it might have exercised on the international theatre scene, especially from the late 1920s. Its only tour abroad between 1924 and 1956 was to Paris, in 1937. On the other hand, the proliferation of Stanislavsky's theories, at first or second-hand, in translations of varying quality and accuracy, has resulted in their almost canonical status in drama schools throughout the Western world. Apart from 'The Method', however, no genuinely innovative theatrical developments have stemmed directly from these theories, only in reaction to them. Of their enlarged or extended application there is little sign, even in their country of origin where Stanislavsky's writings have been regarded as virtually sacrosanct.(The terms 'method' and 'The Method' are used to describe the American adaption of the Sainislavsky 'system' associated mainly with Lee Strasberg and the Actors Studio, which Strasberg founded in 1950.)

4

It may seem heretical to suggest that Stanislavsky's main contribution to modern European theatre was complete by 1917. But theory begins to be divorced from practice or, at least, from the daily exigencies of running a theatre, and this produced, by the 1930s, a divorce from social and political reality of a potentially disabling kind. If all that remained of Stanislavsky's inheritance was his theory (rather than both that and the record of his earlier practice) he might have gone down in history as an earnest, rather old-fashioned theoretician with a nineteenth- rather than a twentieth-century world outlook. The testing of his theories in the unreal conditions of secluded and private rehearsals (a privilege conferred by a totalitarian leader) lent public support, ironically, to the suppression of anything which appeared to challenge the premises of those theories. Stanislavsky's own 'modernist' experiments (mainly pre-1914) appear unsophisticated beside those of Edward Gordon Craig, Vsevolod Meyerhold, Antonin Artaud and others. His subsequent espousal of an apparently unproblematic notion of 'realism', based on the tangible reality of individual consciousness and emotional experience, seems both provisional and tenuous in a historical context which includes the philosophical perspectives of Luigi Pirandello, or post-modern ideas on the nature of the individual subject. When the 'humanist' elements of Stanislavsky's ideology are viewed, retrospectively, in the historical context of the inhuman, irrational politics of the *gulag* and the Holocaust, his commitment to narrow versions of realism and his immersion in theory and private rehearsal during the 1930s can seem either blinkered or complicit with a public process which had more to do with the mad-house than with nuances of psychological or emotional 'truth'.

Did Stanislavsky's fundamentally humanist theories, based on realist premises, have any relationship then with the inhumanity of the surrounding world? Did they connect with the actual practice of the Moscow Art Theatre after 1928, when he had effectively retired from day-to-day work in the theatre? What is the connection between the content of 'An Actor's Work on Himself', Stanislavsky's intense rehearsal work during his last ten years, and the life-and-death struggle being waged beyond the confines of his cloistered, state-funded rehearsal space?[3] How is it that Stanislavskyan theory could, later, be made to serve the apparently contradictory interests of unfettered individualist self-expression (in the largely American-inspired transmission of his ideas) as well as the political interests of a totalitarianism masquerading as collectivism?

Brecht's main arguments against narrow versions of 'realism' were based on the tendency of realistic methods to underwrite the 'status quo' and reinscribe the contours of a 'given' reality within the consciousness of the perceiver, rather than to awaken new ways of seeing and interpreting social reality, or challenge accepted orthodoxies. There is little doubt that the state's canonisation of the Moscow Art Theatre, and its espousal of Stanislavskyan versions of realism were devices used to underpin an orthodox promulgation of that state's self-image – ostensibly humane and considerate of individual thought and feeling – when the real world outside the theatre required definition in much more complex terms.

The problem has as much to do with the legitimisation of realist theory as with the beatification of Stanislavsky himself. In a modernist age (not to mention a post-modern one) Stanislavsky's seeming faith in a stable understanding of realism can seem culpably ingenuous. However, in his defence, it should be said that his version of realism was merely one among other, constantly evolving definitions. It fell to others to make a pernicious ideology of a single, static version – a form of 'naturalism' far removed from the idealism with which Stanislavsky sought to invest the term.

Stanislavsky's interest in late-nineteenth-century 'realist' method was, inevitably, related to the 'naturalistic' interests of others during that same period. This coloured his work at the Society of Art and Literature and his early years at the Art Theatre. But the introduction of the 'system' and Stanislavsky's dedication to the pursuit of truth in an altogether new, uncompromising humanistic and scientific vein reveal a spiritual discontent with the obsessional aspects of naturalistic disclosure. Stanislavsky's religion of realism inveighs against the reductionist perspectives of naturalism's faith in the absolutely material, against its belief in physiological and environmental determinants which reduce spirit to matter and desire to mere appetite in a spiritless universe.

When placing Stanislavsky and the Art Theatre in the context that produced them and examining aspects of Russian and European theatre history that can assist in an understanding of the Art Theatre's emergence, it is also necessary to demonstrate the inextricable connection between the ideal and the real, the elevated and the everyday. The idealistic tones of Stanislavsky's address to the band of disciples who gathered at Pushkino on 14 June 1898, to begin rehearsals for the Theatre's opening that October, appear idly high-minded if divorced from the daily round which is the lot of any theatrical enterprise. Among those who ensured that the curtain rose on the successful first night (in fact it parted in the middle) were not only luminaries such as Stanislavsky, Nemirovich-Danchenko, Ivan Moskvin, Meyerhold and Olga Knipper, but also 373 others – the total complement of staff employed by the Moscow Public-Accessible Art Theatre (as it was initially called) during its first season.

Stanislavsky and Nemirovich-Danchenko came together in the first place in order to create a theatre both 'public' and 'accessible'. For them the theatre was no idle, incidental pastime for a select few but, like the great theatres of the past – the Greek or the Elizabethan – was a fundamental part of the spiritual life, and health, of the community as a whole, as well as a profession worthy of the dedication of a lifetime's spiritual and material effort.

The first part of what follows deals with the historical background and sequence of events which led to the founding of the Moscow Art Theatre and focuses on the early years. The latter part attempts a summarising overview of the theatre's repertoire from 1898 until 1917. The total number of productions staged at the Art Theatre during this period was around seventy, which would be impossible to treat equally; therefore, four productions have been selected for treatment in detail – *Tsar Fedor Ioannovich* (1898), *The Lower Depths* (1902), *The Cherry Orchard* (1904) and *A Month in the Country* (1909) – and some justification of this particular selection seems necessary.

As well as being one of the most successful productions in the Art Theatre's history, Aleksey Tolstoy's historical drama, *Tsar Fedor Ioannovich*, was also its first. Amongst other things, it serves to illustrate the influence of the archaeological-naturalist movement in European theatre, to which Stanislavsky was exposed through contact with the Meiningen Court Theatre productions of historical plays. The historical and ethnographical authenticity which marked the production of *Tsar Fedor* were in stark contrast to the clichéd, stereotypical versions of the historical past which had been the hallmark of earlier attempts, by the Imperial Theatres and others, to stage Russian and foreign history plays. One of the most telling comments on the production of *Tsar Fedor* was made by the Imperial Theatre actress, Mariya Yermolova, who stated that, henceforth, anyone wishing to stage historical plays with any degree of artistic integrity would need to learn from the Art Theatre's example.[4]

The production was also significant in that it marked the advent of the *director* into both the Russian and, to an important extent, the European theatre. Prior to this, Russian critics and commentators invariably spoke of 'performances'; henceforth they would speak of 'productions', with all the implications this had for ensemble, unity of intellectual conception and aesthetically integrated, effective *mises-en-scènes*. With this production, Stanislavsky might be said to have been making a deliberate bid for a place in theatre history in a manner conscious both of his own and its historical significance. He was not merely following in the footsteps of Ludwig Chronegk as a stager-of-crowd-scenes, but staking a claim for the importance of the role of the director as overall organiser of the production.[5]

Tsar Fedor not only proved to be the most popular production during the Theatre's first season but was also immensely popular in the long-term, despite undergoing many structural alterations and changes of personnel. It was given its 700th performance in 1944 on the occasion of the actor Ivan Moskvin's 70th birthday, when he repeated the performance as Fedor which he had first given forty-six years previously. The production was even to outlive Moskvin himself and record one thousand performances – perhaps not many by London West End standards but a considerable number in terms of the Russian repertory system.

The choice of a play by Maxim Gorky, and *The Lower Depths* in particular, may not seem to justify itself so clearly. However, its production needs to be seen in the context of a history in which Gorky was not only a romantic modifier of the naturalist tradition, but also the first Russian 'proletarian' playwright. Moreover, this production was staged at a theatre which had christened itself 'public-accessible' with the specific aim of appealing to working-class audiences. Somewhat ironically, by the time it staged *The Lower Depths* the Art Theatre no longer carried the phrase 'public-accessible' as part of its title and audiences in its new, 1902, premises were drawn from an increasingly affluent constituency.

Although Gorky became the 'house playwright' (the Art Theatre was officially named in his honour in 1932), this obscures the fact that the Theatre did not stage a single one of his plays between 1905 and 1933, despite ample opportunity. Moreover, the Theatre's relations with Gorky had cooled as a result of rows over the rejection of *Summerfolk* and controversy surrounding productions of work by Dostoyevsky, of whom Gorky disapproved.[6] Most characteristic of the Art Theatre's relationship with the plays of Maxim Gorky during the author's own lifetime was its meagre involvement with their staging.

The conferral, in the 1930s, of a 'special relationship' with Gorky was officially promulgated to endorse the Art Theatre's exemplary realist methods, now offered as models for general imitation at a time when an ideological war was being waged against 'modernism' and 'formalism'. The elevation of Gorky to 'socialist realist' status was both a political and an aesthetic promotion. It followed his decision to turn his back on 'bourgeois' Europe and opt for permanent settlement in the Soviet Union. Prominent among the official welcoming party on his return, in 1931, was Stanislavsky, whose last association with Gorky had been his production of *Children of the Sun*, in 1905, as a vehicle for élitist rather than socialist propaganda.

The association with the work of Gorky, once established, became persistent. Beginning with productions of *The Merchant Class* and *The Lower Depths* in its fourth and fifth seasons, the Art Theatre went on to stage a further ten of Gorky's plays between 1933 and 1976, including excellent productions by Nemirovich-Danchenko of *Yegor Bulychev and Others* (1934) and of *Enemies*, in 1935. Following Gorky's return, it became customary to confer retrospective ideological respectability on his earlier works. This was inevitably the fate of his novel *Mother*, with its clearly defined socialist theme of which Lenin approved, but it was also the case with an otherwise apolitical-seeming play like *The Lower Depths*.

By the mid-1930s, Stanislavsky's official status in the Soviet theatrical pantheon had begun to rival that of Lenin and Stalin in Soviet politics. Some attempt to explain this phenomenon is offered as part of the conclusion to this book and may be seen to derive, in part, from the ideology implicit in many of Stanislavsky's own productions, and from his deliberate espousal of realism. Moreover, it had been the (ostensibly bourgeois) Art Theatre which originally gave 'the first proletarian writer' a theatrical hearing and had been prepared to descend with him into 'the lower depths' of life. From these same depths Satin's hymn to 'Man' in Act Four had rung out like a socialist clarion call – a paean delivered originally by Stanislavsky himself. A canonical work of socialist realism was seen to have been given a canonically realist interpretation. Gorky's play and its production, as well as Stanislavsky's performance, became hagiographic reference points for Soviet theatrical culture. Hence the retrospective significance of that 1902 production, however pragmatically the Art Theatre may have embarked on its staging.

The importance of Chekhov in the history of the Art Theatre is well-known. Precisely what his fate as a dramatist would have been had not the Theatre championed his cause is uncertain. What seems clear is that, had the 1898 production of *The Seagull* been a failure, Chekhov would probably have kept his vow never to write another play so long as he lived.[7] Thus, the generally accepted view that Chekhov is one of the most important dramatists of the last hundred years depended, crucially, on the public rehabilitation of *The Seagull* after the debacle of 1896. This then generated the writing of *Three Sisters* and *The Cherry Orchard*. Despite being one of Chekhov's most frequently performed plays, the original production of *The Cherry Orchard* is one of the least well-documented. *Uncle Vanya* has possibly an equal claim for attention but, unfortunately, the production score remains unpublished. As distinct from *Uncle Vanya*, however, which is a re-working of an earlier play *The Wood Demon*, the importance of *The Cherry Orchard* is that it is a completely original play which, like *Three Sisters*, was composed specifically for the Art Theatre with known actors in mind.

Another original feature of *The Cherry Orchard* is its rather unusual form. Written at a time when Chekhov was interested in the work of Maurice Maeterlinck, the play can be seen as one of his most abstract and symbolic, where conventional reality (of character and situation) is questioned. This was never a major problem in staging *Three Sisters*, although disagreements existed between the Theatre and Chekhov over questions of mood and genre. These disputes were more pronounced in the case of *The Cherry Orchard*, which Stanislavsky read as a 'tragedy', Meyerhold thought was a Maeterlinckian 'Dance of Death', and Chekhov described as a 'farce'. Although Chekhov never saw the final production in its entirety, his letters leave little doubt that the reports he received led to his feeling that the Theatre, and Stanislavsky in particular, had 'ruined' his play.

The three productions mentioned above belong to the first five years of the Art Theatre's history and, in differing ways, are striking examples of the Theatre's predominantly naturalistic approach during this period, although the nature of some of the production scores can seem to challenge this straightforward definition. The choice of a later production, from 1909, has been dictated by a number of factors. Most importantly, Stanislavsky's production of Ivan Turgenev's *A Month in the Country* marked his first major attempt to move away from acting technique inspired by external

10

fidelity to character and milieu to concentrate, instead, on inner psychological mood. It is ironic that, almost at the precise historical moment that modernist artists were moving away from a view of human character imagined 'individualistically', or conceived as ontologically 'real', Stanislavsky attempted to resuscitate the notion of a meaningful human psychology and a humanly knowable 'truth'. His method was to explore the inner life of the living actor, viewed as a creature reducible to flesh, blood, nerve and sinew, in the investigative spirit of a forensic, scientific naturalism, but, equally, as a being capable of transcending these reductionist definitions.

Where modernists were contriving to suggest something un-knowable, relativistic, metaphysical, abstract, or myth-laden about humankind and, in the process, were devastating the ground of nineteenth-century artistic practice, it was precisely here that Stanislavsky chose to pitch his ideological tent – on terrain which the modernists had not only abandoned but had identified as fundamentally unstable. Stanislavsky sought to negotiate the flux, the relativity, the contingency of human reality and to found it on some inner, psychological and ascertainable 'truth', convinced that this was no idealist mirage or spiritual fiction. This was the reason for the development of his 'system' and for his choice of Turgenev's play for experimental purposes.

This raises questions about the nature both of this particular play and of plays in general. If 'truth' was not discernible in an actor's performance, Stanislavsky was in the habit of crying 'Ne veryu!' ('I don't believe it!'). But could the 'system' make intellectual and dramatic sense of any worthwhile play if what the work itself imagines, or constitutes, is not a single, verifiable truth at the level of a traceable human psychology, but is actually engaged in the production of 'meanings' which are either contradictory or ex-tremely complex and which may diverge to produce simultaneously different and equally valid levels of 'reality' or 'truth'? Is drama, as a genre, more like Greek tragedy or Jonsonian comedy than it is ever like a naturalistic play or a play interpreted as if it were a version of a nineteenth-century novel? Does even a 'novelistic' play, like Turgenev's, defy any attempt to have the categories of a Stanislavskyan 'system' imposed upon it? These are questions which go beyond the limits of this study, which simply aims to make available some of the material on the basis of which such questions can be asked. It therefore attempts to describe how the Moscow Art

Theatre came into being, how it was managed and financed during its formative years, how its productions were staged and how audiences and critics responded to them.

1

HISTORICAL BACKGROUND

As we approach 1998 and the centenary of the Art Theatre's opening, there has been a return in the former Soviet Union to the kind of market conditions which gave rise to the Theatre's original foundation. In many respects, its origin is similar to that of The Theatre, constructed by James Burbage in 1576 and run on shareholding lines. There are other historical parallels between the two events. Just as England was experiencing the rise of capitalism and the decline of feudalism at the end of the sixteenth century, so a similar process was occurring in Russia towards the end of the nineteenth. The spread of entrepreneurial activity was centred in Moscow, whilst St Petersburg remained the bureaucratic centre of a crumbling Empire, whose tsar was to lose absolute feudal authority under the impact of new historical pressures exerted by a rising merchant class.[1] The revolutions and civil war of 1905 and 1917 can, in this context, be seen to have a parallel in the rise of middle-class power and the resultant revolution/civil war in mid-seventeenth-century England. Just as, in England, the conflicts and tensions of the period were anticipated and reflected in revolutionary theatrical practice and in innovatory dramatic writing, so the theatre of Stanislavsky and Nemirovich-Danchenko also mirrored the innovativeness and social awareness of its Elizabethan/Jacobean counterpart and acquired its own 'Shakespeare', or in-house dramatist, in the person of Chekhov.

From the mid-nineteenth century, a class of capitalists began to emerge in Moscow amongst whom were many with 'progressive' attitudes. Not unlike Elizabethan London, Moscow produced a group of wealthy benefactors (in this case factory owners and merchants) who were prepared to vie with one another in the foundation, construction and provision of hospitals, schools, printing presses, churches, theatres and people's leisure centres. Some were exceptionally enlightened patrons of the arts, who collected art works and provided generous subsidies for artists. Others were more actively involved, such as Savva Mamontov, who created the first private opera in Russia and managed to attract several talented stage designers and many foreign singers.[2] Chaliapin made his debut on the Mamontov stage in 1896. Stanislavsky was a friend of Mamontov's and took part in his productions. The Art Theatre's chief designer, V. A. Simov, gained his first working experience with Mamontov.[3]

The theatrical situations in Moscow and St Petersburg were comparatively distinct, although the repertoire of the Aleksandrinskiy Theatre, in St Petersburg, was similar to that of the Malyy, in Moscow. Aleksey Suvorin's private, commercial theatre, founded in St Petersburg in 1895, was in many ways similar to that of Fedor Korsh in Moscow, founded in 1882.[4,5] On the other hand, traditions in 'the theatre of Ostrovsky' – Moscow's 'second university', as the Malyy was called – tended to be more democratic than at the Aleksandrinskiy, where the tastes of the aristocracy still held sway. The situation in Moscow thus seemed more susceptible to reform although, at the end of the 1880s and the beginning of the 1890s, the professional stage did not present a very encouraging picture. Perhaps because of this, theatrical amateurism developed apace.

By the 1890s, 80 per cent of the industrial enterprises in Moscow had been established in the period since 1861, following the abolition of serfdom. The textile industries led the way in turning Moscow into a major banking centre, bringing increased political power to the merchant class. Pavel Tret'yakov, in addition to art collecting, which became the basis of the Moscow gallery named after him, was also a member of the Moscow City Council, as was Mamontov.[6] Referring to the 'rapprochement' between art and capital, Chekhov noted in 1897 that: 'the intelligentsia goes to meet capital and capital is not averse to meeting it halfway' (Chekhov 1974–83: vol. 6: 297). People like Savva Morozov, so influential in supporting the Art Theatre financially, also founded schools, hospitals and libraries. From this group were to emerge great patrons of the arts such as S. I. Shchukin and A. A. Bakhrushin.[7,8] Nemirovich-Danchenko was an astute businessman, and tales of Stanislavsky's comparative commercial naivety do not square with the kind of business acumen which, by the end of the century, had helped to place his family firm of gold- and silver-thread manu-facturers at the forefront of world markets.

Moscow in the 1890s, like London in the 1590s, was a city of merchants, traders and entrepreneurs as well as emergent groups of artisans and university-educated intellectuals. Other parallels involve comparisons between both cities in the nineteenth as well as the sixteenth centuries. Just as a Patent House monopoly existed in England between 1660 and 1843 (reinforced by the Licensing Act of 1737), so a similar monopoly existed in Russia, imposed by the Court in the eighteenth century, when public theatre first came into existence, and surviving under increasing challenge until its repeal in 1882 (the historical equivalent to the repeal of the Patent monopoly in England in 1843). The consequences of the repeal were similar for both nations – namely, the spread of commercially inspired theatrical enterprises designed to appeal to predomin-antly middle-class taste and directed, with some notable exceptions, towards the commercial exploitation of a public demanding straightforward entertainment. Where enterprises like those of Anna Brenko, Korsh and the Art Theatre differed, was in their efforts to cultivate serious-minded audiences with a taste for classic plays, as well as the new naturalist drama, which not only reflected social problems but also challenged conventional values.[9]

Historically, the advent of the Moscow Art Theatre was not a uniquely Russian phenomenon but part of a European commercial and artistic movement which brought the new drama to new audiences. The parallels here are with the Théâtre Libre in Paris, the Freie Bühne in Berlin, the Independent and Court Theatres in London, the Abbey Theatre in Dublin and even the Intima Teatren in Stockholm. Just as these enterprises turned their backs on the unrealistic world of romantic comedy or extravagant melodrama with which Patent Houses such as Drury Lane and Covent Garden, or the Malyy and the Aleksandrinskiy, were associated, so the Moscow Art Theatre, like these other serious commercial theatrical enter-prises, turned its back on the routine methods of nineteenth-century Russian theatre epitomised by the work of the Imperial Theatres.

The appeal of naturalism and the naturalist drama, for Stanis-lavsky as for others, lay in its uncompromising pursuit of truth. In comparison with its down-to-earth, forensic interrogation of the ordinary and everyday, earlier dramatic forms and preceding theatrical practice appeared unreal, exaggerated and fundament-ally untruthful. It was Chekhov, in his correspondence, who saw dunghills as having as respectable a place in the landscape as flowerbeds and suggested that dramas which concerned someone's departure for the North Pole, whilst the abandoned lover committed suicide from a belfry, were not in the least like life. Nineteenth-century Russian theatre practice was characterised by its carelessness in matters of verisimilitude, its lack of artistic integrity and a general disregard for the theatre as a serious art form with a social mission.

V. A. Nyelidov, who worked in the offices of the Moscow Imperial Theatres in the 1880s and 1890s, and who was generally sympathetic towards the work of Imperial Theatre *rezhissery*, described their methods in the following manner:

> Having received the play he [the director] distributed the parts. [. . .] Furthermore, the director wrote the 'montirovka' [the staging], i.e. filled out a form with the headings: 'Actors, décor, furniture, costumes, wigs, props, effects' (headings 1 to 10). Under the heading of, say, 'décor', he wrote: 'prison, forest, drawing room', etc., nothing more. Under 'furniture', the words 'poor', or 'rich'. Costumes were defined as 'metropolitan' or 'historical'. Wigs were 'bald', 'grey' or 'red-haired'. All this was carried out by the office. The director and the actors frequently did not see any of these details before the dress rehearsal or even sometimes before opening night, for it was considered that, once they knew the plan of the stage, i.e. that a door would be here and a writing table there, everything was fine. Rehearsals were conducted in the simplest manner. They would arrive on stage with script in hand, read the role from it and 'decipher' places, i.e. arrange that 'x' stands here and 'y' sits there. The greatest number of rehearsals would be from 12 to 14. After the third rehearsal, scripts were taken away. The role had to be learned by heart, for which one, two or three days were set aside for learning, depending on the size of the role.[10]
>
> (Nyelidov 1931: 108–9)

In 1900, the St Petersburg dramatist and critic, P. Gnedich, invited his readers to:

> Go to the theatre – a nice, cultivated drama theatre – take a seat in the stalls or in a box and simply take stock of everything you see without any preconceptions. The room depicted is

the usual four-cornered one. Its dimensions are those of a decent-sized theatrical auditorium, even if what is being represented is Khlestakov's room under the inn stairs.[11] A drawing room in a middle-class house or the office of a Petersburg official are always equal in size to a square in any Italian trading town. The furniture in the room is set out in the strangest fashion: the chairs are on one side facing the audience. If it is daytime, it is brighter in the room than in the sunlit street outside. If it is evening then, despite the single burning lamp, the entire room is evenly lit in every corner and, significantly, from below floor level by means of the footlights. Even if a garden or field is represented, then all the light strength emanates from below, from ground level, illuminating the throat, the nostrils and the upper parts of the actor's eye sockets. . . . It sometimes happens that doors in the most ordinary dwelling apartments are left ajar, – on stage, however, in the majority of circumstances they are kept, and held, shut. The actor does not open a door by means of a doorhandle as the handle is more often than not painted on, but simply opens both halves of the door with both hands which, following his exit, slam together again by means of some mysterious force.[12]

(*Mir iskusstva*, 1900, no. 3: 52)

In this context, it is possible to appreciate the genuine innovativeness of the Art Theatre's staging of Act One of *The Seagull* when, in the name of truth-to-life, the actors sat along the line of the footlights with their backs to the audience whilst watching (like the audience observing them) the play-within-the-play.

As regards stage furniture and properties, the typical nineteenth-century situation is summarised by this description of the Aleksandrinskiy Theatre in the 1860s:

for decorating the walls there are only two paintings, one of the Aleksandra Waterfall and the other of the repentant Mary Magdalen. These were an eyesore for audiences who were forced to contemplate them three or four times a week. As for the remainder of the furnishings, for example the door curtains and window hangings – either dark red or green – these are generally soiled, faded and discoloured as well as unspeakably crumpled. They have no fixtures – usually a piece of metal is stuck up and a curtain unceremoniously

suspended from it. The less said about the furniture the better
– three changes (one green and two red) totally inadequate.
The style of this furniture is old and vile. . . . Pitiful vases
and no less pitiful flowers complete the furnishings. Only in
1866 did there appear new 'pavil'ony' and furniture 'with
seven slip-covers'.

(Vsevolodskiy 1929: 183)

The mid-century move towards what the Russians called *pavil'ony*
was away from conventional painted hangings and involved the
introduction of what the Germans called the *geschlossenes Zimmer*
(literally 'closed room' or interior setting). This move towards a
more realistic presentation of predominantly domestic milieux was
characteristic of the emerging naturalist drama and replaced the
palaces, mountains, castles, forests and other similar settings of the
romantic theatre. These domestic interiors, whether depicting
peasants' cottages, merchants' drawing rooms or the humble
dwellings of office clerks, tended to be displayed in a geometrically
regular box-shaped unit front-on to the audience. Eventually this
format began to be broken up through the introduction of niches,
embrasures, recesses, etc., some even placed at an angle to the line
of the proscenium arch in a manner anticipated by Strindberg in
his famous preface to *Miss Julie* (1888). It is interesting to look at
photographs of interiors for Art Theatre productions of Chekhov's
plays. Most go out of their way to break up the line of the square box-
set and, in *The Cherry Orchard*, explore the possibilities of construction 'on the diagonal'.

Stanislavsky was the first in the history of the Russian theatre fully
to appreciate the role of the director. Hitherto, that role had been
performed by various people including prominent actors, the
dramatists themselves, the designer or, more often, the prompter.
Russian theatre historians tend to give pride of place to Charles
Kean and Heinrich Laube when it comes to estimating which
Western European directorial innovations most influenced the
course of Russian theatre, and where the example of the Meiningen
Court Theatre was to prove so important.[13,14] At the beginning of
the nineteenth century, 'directors' were already being introduced
into Russian theatres, although their duties were restricted to
administrative and technical matters. At this stage, there was little
sense of an acting 'ensemble' or any evidence of the need for scenic
unity in all aspects of a production.

The effects of 'archaeological naturalism', associated with the work of Charles Kean, were evident in the Russian theatre as early as the 1860s. As part of a 'scientific' drift, it became fashionable to invite 'experts' from disciplines outside the theatre, such as architects and archaeologists, to oversee productions. Critics became increasingly concerned with authentic stage representation. Until the late nineteenth century, Griboyedov's comedy *'Tis Folly to be Wise* (*Gore ot uma*) had always been acted in contemporary costume, or costume of mixed period, rather than in that of the period in which it is set (the 1820s). Critics devoted articles to authentic staging at the Aleksandrinskiy Theatre and, increasingly, demanded accuracy of both costume and décor. According to A. Sokolov, there were only two settings at the Aleksandrinskiy, a dark red and a dark green *pavil'on*, which were used to represent both aristocratic Petersburg salons and the country homes of humble landowners, as well as the rooms of impoverished officals. He also complained of the fact that historical productions tended to use one and the same setting irrespective of whether the play was set in the ninth, fifteenth or sixteenth centuries (Vsevolodskiy 1929: 175–7).

At the same time, P. Bazhenov noted improvements between 1862 – when he described scenery for a production as 'distinguished neither by successful perspective nor good taste' – and 1865, when he characterised the décor and costumes for Alexander Ostrovsky's *Voyevoda* ('The War Lord') as 'faithful to the period' and the production as having been 'quite carefully' staged.[15] Generally speaking, however, productions of historical plays tended to be a mixture of 'the faithful, the unfaithful and the dreamed-up' (179). The 1860s marked an increasing tendency for costumes, accessories, furniture, etc., to be more or less faithful to period, but the degree of authenticity which characterised the Art Theatre's opening production of Aleksey Tolstoy's *Tsar Fedor Ioannovich* still struck with the force of revelation.

The stage conditions which prevailed, and which the Art Theatre sought to replace, are well characterised by Stanislavsky:

> In other theatres of the time the problems of scenery were solved very simply: there was a backdrop and four or five wings in arched form on which were painted a palace hall with entrances, passages, an open or covered terrace with a view of the sea and so on. In the centre of the stage – a smooth, dirty stage floor and a few chairs, according to the number of

actors. In the spaces between the wings one could see a whole crowd of stage hands, extras, wig-makers, tailors, wandering about or gawping at the stage. If a door was necessary, it would be placed between the wings; no matter if this left a hole above the door, a gap. When necessary, a street would be painted onto the backdrop and wings in deep perspective, and with a huge town square, painted fountains and monuments, devoid of people. Actors who stood near the backdrop were much taller than the houses. The dirty floor of the stage was completely bare, and provided the actors with every opportunity to stand near the prompter's box which, as is well known, always attracts the servants of Melpomene. [...] We replaced the painted 'pavil'on' with wall-papered walls, stuccoed cornices and ceilings. We covered the floor with decorated canvas ... We 'planted' trees on the forestage to allow actors to roam among them. . . . Usually there was just one room on stage. We showed whole apartments of three or four rooms. [...] We would make use of the most unusual cross-sections of rooms, corners, small areas with furniture placed right on the forestage with its back to the audience, thereby suggesting a fourth wall. [...] It is conventional to act on a lit stage; we staged whole scenes (and very often important ones) in complete darkness.

(Stanislavskiy 1988: vol. 1: 255–6)

According to K. Rudnitskiy, it was Heinrich Laube who first made directing an independent profession.[16] Laube's role did not consist in what, for example, Ostrovsky did – which was to give instructions solely during rehearsals of his own plays. Instead, Laube sought to achieve artistic unity in the production of plays by other authors (Rudnitskiy 1989: 8). Ostrovsky's undoubted influence on the Art Theatre's founders was less as a director than as one who espoused the idea of a National Theatre both popular and accessible. As he wrote in his 'Note on the Situation of Dramatic Art in Russia at the Present Time' (1881):

A national theatre is a sign of a nation's maturity. . . . Possession of one's own native theatre and pride in it are desiderata for the whole people, [...] A Russian theatre in Moscow is needed primarily by merchants, therefore merchants should build it. [...] Aided by specialists in dramatic art and experts at scenic work, the Russian theatre in the hands of an enlightened merchantry will become firmly grounded in Moscow and will gradually arrive at perfection.

(Senelick 1991: 400–1)

Earlier in the century, Nikolay Gogol had also seen the theatre as a focus for social unity when he wrote: 'The theatre is by no means a trifle, or a petty thing . . . . It is a kind of rostrum from which much good can be spoken to the world' (Zagorskiy and Stepanova 1952: 386). Both he and Turgenev expressed concern about the staging of their plays, the latter being unique in the extent to which he incorporated detailed stage directions within the play text. In indicating very precisely the position of windows and doors, virtually supplying a complete plan of the stage, Turgenev anticipated by nearly fifty years the methods employed by Stanislavsky in his prompt-books. Gogol, too, provided sketches of his characters, costumes and settings for *The Government Inspector*, in 1836, and felt that matters of staging were so important that they should be the special province of someone whom he refers to as the 'actor-artist' – a version of the Russian *rezhisser*, a term borrowed from the French (*régisseur*) which was first used around 1825.[17]

The two visits to Russia paid by the acting troupe led by Georg II, Duke of Saxe-Meiningen, and his stage director Ludwig Chronegk, were important events in nineteenth-century Russian theatre history. Attitudes among Russian theatre researchers are divided as to the extent of the Meiningen influence on the Moscow Art Theatre, some undoubtedly affected by Ostrovsky's hostile reaction to the German company's first tour, in 1885, when they presented plays by Schiller and Franz Grillparzer and three by Shakespeare – *Julius Caesar*, *The Winter's Tale* and *As You Like It*. Even before the tour had begun, Ostrovsky was comparing them unfavourably with native theatre troupes and complaining about the overt hand of the director which restricted actors of talent and feeling and which resulted in the staging of mere *tableaux vivants*. In Ostrovsky's opinion, authors who supervised the production of their own plays were infinitely superior to so-called 'directors' as far as 'observing the strictness of rehearsals and the external accuracy of the production' were concerned (Ostrovskiy 1973–80: vol. 10: 297). Whether Stanislavsky was influenced by this view is uncertain, but there is no record of his having attended any productions or recorded any impressions of this first Russian visit by the Meiningen company.

21

In fact, the most informed criticism of this visit came from Nemirovich-Danchenko who, on 28 March 1885, addressed an open letter to the editor of the journal *Theatre and Life* in which he took issue with the way the company had interpreted *Julius Caesar*. He was especially critical of the production's tendency to romanticise Mark Antony, whom Nemirovich saw as a 'cunning, talented, amoral pragmatist' and a skilful manipulator. He also criticised those textual cuts which served to detract from an idealised conception of the characters, especially Brutus. The letter is especially interesting in the light of Nemirovich's own attempt to stage *Julius Caesar*, in 1901, employing archaeologically realistic, Meiningen-style methods.

It was the Saxe-Meiningen company's second visit, in 1890, which attracted Stanislavsky's attention at a time when his work at the Society of Art and Literature was beginning to show evidence of a high standard of professionalism. He attended six productions, five of which had been toured in 1885, plus *The Merchant of Venice*. Stanislavsky's personal archive includes an entire album devoted to the productions and consists of detailed notes and some drawings. It is possible to trace a connection between this attention to detail and Stanislavsky's prompt-books for early Art Theatre productions:

> *The Maid of Orleans*, Act 2 Sc. 3: Troops cross the stage without a word in complete darkness. The gleam of chain mail is visible and the sound of armour. Thanks to the darkness the illusion is complete.
>
> In the battle, the greatest illusion is produced by the sound of distant trumpets. On stage only two or three fight.

> *The Merchant of Venice*, Act 2 Sc. 4: Street before Shylock's house. Gondolas run very smoothly on rails. One gondola floats off and is stopped from a bridge; it returns. Conversation passes between those standing on the bridge and those sitting in the gondola. The participants all appear in gondolas for the most part. The finale is a carnival. Those in the gondolas are showered with bits of paper [*bumazhki* – possibly paper money].

> *Fiesco*, Act 4 Sc. 7: A courtyard in Fiesco's palace. Darkness on stage. Four torches are brought in and then affixed to the wall. To the extent that the light produced by these four

torches dwindles, no further light is introduced ... Each new person's entry is effectively realised. First a distant knock is heard off-stage – in the distance the bass voice of a guard demands that the newcomer announce himself. The reply is heard, and then the command of the officer to permit him entry. The noise of the chains of a drawbridge being raised or the sounds of a gate opening, a grating sound. You can hear how the chains drag along the stone floor. A pause. The characters enter. The noise of the gates being closed. The impression is intensified by the fact that those on stage are constantly listening in silence to whatever is happening off-stage.

(Vinogradskaya 1971: vol. 1: 128–9)

In addition to surface detail and atmosphere, the Art Theatre also adopted the Meiningen troupe's strict adherence to company discipline. The Meininger were the first to adopt the practice of collective play-reading and to institute rehearsal periods which lasted for months rather than weeks. They were also the first to hold dress rehearsals and 'closed previews' ('intimate performances' in German) – a practice which the Art Theatre took over.

The influence of the Meiningen company on Art Theatre productions was matched by that of European Naturalist theatre. It seems certain that Stanislavsky read P. Boborykin's article 'Antoine as Actor and Troupe Leader' published in 1894, as the French theatre director's work was widely publicised in the Russian press.[18] However, although Stanislavsky visited Paris on five occasions between 1888 and 1897, there is no mention of Antoine, nor of the Théâtre Libre, in any of his published letters. He also visited Berlin, and there is no mention of Otto Brahm or the Freie Bühne, although recent French research has established that he attended the première of Maeterlinck's *Pelléas et Mélisande* at Lugné-Poë's Théâtre de l'Oeuvre and may well discover that he attended performances at the Théâtre Libre as well (Rudnitskiy 1989: 25).

2

THE SOCIETY OF ART
AND LITERATURE

Prior to the creation of the Society, Stanislavsky made frequent appearances on his own, domestic, stage as well as on amateur stages in Moscow. Hitherto, his role had been as performer rather than director, and included appearances in opera with the Musical-Dramatic Circle who performed in the building where Anna Brenko's short-lived Pushkin Theatre had its base and where the Society of Art and Literature was soon to establish itself. He also acted at the Ermitazh (Hermitage) Theatre, which was to become the Art Theatre's first home *(Moskovskiy Khudozhestvennyy teatr* 1914: 10).

Stanislavsky had already made the acquaintance of A. F. Fedotov, husband of the actress Glikeriya Fedotova, and, in January 1887, was preparing the role of Ikharev in Gogol's *Gamblers* with Fedotov, whom he considered 'a genuinely talented director'.[1,2] According to Stanislavsky, Fedotov was 'to lay in me the first bricks of a new understanding of the theatre' and came a close second, in terms of his influence on Stanislavsky's theatrical education, to Fedor Komissarzhevskiy (11).[3] During work on the production of *Gamblers*, there was talk of creating a new drama group with the purpose of staging 'genuinely artistic' productions. It was at this point that Stanislavsky became a director of the family firm upon the death of his uncle. With his first year's dividend of 1,020 roubles he established, together with Komissarzhevskiy and Fedotov, the Society of Art and Literature, where he acquired his first experience as a director and where his acting also brought him to the attention of a wider public.

The aims and objectives of the Society were formulated as follows:

The Moscow Society of Art and Literature aims to encourage among its members a broad acquaintance with areas of art and literature and stimulate the development of cultivated taste whilst providing the possibility for the stage appearance of musical, literary and artistic talents and facilitating their growth. With this in mind, the Society aims to sustain, with appropriate permission, a musical-dramatic school. . . . Moreover, whilst observing generally approved governmental rules and regulations, the Society will arrange stage, musical, literary, artistic and domestic mornings and evenings, picture exhibitions, concerts and plays.

(Stanislavskiy 1962: 535)

The constitution was approved by the Ministry of the Interior and Stanislavsky began to search for suitable premises whilst rehearsing the part of the baron in Aleksandr Pushkin's *The Miserly Knight*, with Fedotov, for the opening production. He rented Anna Brenko's Pushkin Theatre on Tverskaya Street, not far from where the Art Theatre was to have its second home, and set about forming a troupe and looking for staff for the proposed theatre school. He worked out the cost of renovating and refurbishing the building as well as the costs of a school where dramatic art, the history of costume, make-up, drama, Russian literature, aesthetics, fencing and dancing were to be taught. He was twenty-five years old at the time and had spent so much of his own money that, he realised later, he could not subsidise the Art Theatre in its hour of need as he would have wished.

In September 1888, the Minister of Education was informed of the rules and regulations of the school, which opened in October. That same month, the directorate of the Society of Art and Literature was formed, consisting of a president, Komissarzhevskiy; a vice-president, Fedotov; an administrator, Stanislavsky, as well as musical, literary, artistic and financial representatives. Meanwhile, Stanislavsky had found time to visit Berlin and Paris where, in July, Komissarzhevskiy asked him to discover as much as he could about rehearsal procedures at the Comédie Française, how they maintained stage discipline, etc. He also requested that he familiarise himself with the 'pedagogical procedures' of the Paris conservatoire, including the amount of time devoted to each discipline. To this end, Stanislavsky attended drama classes at the conservatoire during August and September.

The official opening of the Society of Art and Literature, on 3 November 1888, was followed by its first performances on 8 December. As well as acting leading roles, Stanislavsky was involved in recruiting personnel to join the group, many of whom later became founder members of the Art Theatre. Mariya Lilina was invited to join that October and acted opposite Stanislavsky in Schiller's *Love and Intrigue* the following April before marrying him in June 1889.[4] Vasily Luzhskiy, a key member of the Art Theatre company, joined the Society after seeing Stanislavsky perform in a vaudeville by Fedotov, *The Rouble*.[5]

Stanislavsky's first significant work as a director was in March 1889 when, in the absence of Fedotov, he took charge of the latter's work on a production of Peter Gnedich's *Burning Letters*. His account clearly points the way towards methods employed at the Art Theatre:

> During the read-through I asked people not to be shy about pauses so long as they were full of feeling; I also asked that they speak in their own, unforced voices and avoid gestures. At points I made lively demonstrations.
>
> (Efros 1924: 63)

Referring to audience reaction to his directorial debut, Stanislavsky noted:

> we introduced a new manner of acting previously unseen on the Russian stage. The intelligent, sensitive public felt this and went wild with excitement, while the traditionalists pro-tested. . . . The task of the actor is to educate the public and, although I do not consider myself strong enough for the task, nevertheless I do not wish to submit to its taste and will cultivate subtle acting in my own person based on gesture, pauses and the absence of false, theatrical gestures. I will perfect this side of things. Perhaps, one day, this will be valued; if not . . . then I'll give up the stage. It is not worth acting in any other way.
>
> (Stanislavskiy 1954–61: vol. 5: 108–9, 111–12)

Nemirovich-Danchenko gained his first impressions of the Society when, in company with Chekhov, Fedotova and others, he attended a costume ball arranged by the Society in February 1889. Although he was not introduced to Stanislavsky, he subsequently saw him act the tragic role of Anany Yakovlev in Pisemskiy's *A Bitter Fate*, on 29

November, and was full of praise for his performance.[6] This was two days after the opening of the Society's second season with another Pisemskiy play, *Despots* (*Samoupravtsy*), in which Stanislavsky acted the leading role of the tyrannical Prince Imshin. In preparing the part, Stanislavsky tried to avoid clichéd, stereotypical images of evil-doers, which gave rise to his famous and oft-quoted apophthegm: 'When acting the part of an evil person, seek out the good in him.'

The spring and summer of 1890 saw a reorganisation of the Society. Because of expenses and accumulated debt, it was forced to rent a more modest building, and the Pushkin Theatre was taken over by the Russian Sporting (Okhotnyy) Club, where the Society undertook to give productions and arrange artistic evenings, an agreement which the Art Theatre was to inherit and honour in its first year.[7] Following the destruction of the Pushkin Theatre by fire, the Sporting Club's activities were transferred to the German (Nemetskiy) Club and it was here, on 8 February 1891, that a production of Tolstoy's *The Fruits of Enlightenment* was given, described by Stanislavsky as his first, totally independent work as a director.

By the beginning of 1891, Stanislavsky had already assumed responsibility for both repertoire and direction. On 29 January, the newspaper, *Novosti dnya*, announced that a new play was being prepared 'very carefully' and that there had already been as many as ten rehearsals. Seven of the roles were performed by members of the Society who subsequently went on to become members of the Art Theatre, including Lilina, Sanin, Artem, Luzhskiy and Samarova.[8,9,10] The cast also included Vera Komissarzhevskaya and Stanislavsky himself.[11] Nemirovich-Danchenko attended the first night and reviewed the production enthusiastically:

I declare that I have never seen such an immaculate performance by amateurs ... the comedy was acted with such ensemble, such *intelligence*, as is not to be found even at Korsh's theatre.

He was especially impressed with Stanislavsky's performance:

If I was a theatre reviewer I would have devoted an entire article to him, as well as to several of the others, so many subtle and characteristic details did he insert into the role of Zvezdintsev.

('Goboy' [Vl.I. N-D], 'Interesnyy spektakl', *Novosti dnya* 1891: 10 November)

This impression was echoed by Chekhov who, writing to Suvorin about the première of the same play at the Malyy on 12 December, compared it unfavourably with that of the Society (Chekhov 1974–83: vol. 15: 329–3).

In March 1892, prior to a provincial tour with actors of the Malyy, Stanislavsky rehearsed the role of Bogucharov in a comedy by Nemirovich-Danchenko himself – *Schastlivets* ('The Fortunate Man'). He was subsequently invited to partner the Malyy actress, Mariya Yermolova, in Ostrovsky's *The Dowerless Bride* on tour in Nizhniy Novgorod. With the departure of Fedor Komissarzhevskiy, in April, a new directorate of the Society was formed and Fedotova was invited to become president. In May, Stanislavsky was again in Paris, where he expressed disappointment with theatrical standards apart from those at the Comédie Française. Meanwhile, he was rehearsing the role of Rostanyev in Dostoyevsky's *Stepanchikovo Village* – a part which was to cause him sorrow and travail when revived at the Art Theatre, under Nemirovich's direction, in 1917.

Rehearsing Ostrovsky's *The Last Sacrifice* in February 1894, Stanislavsky began for the first time to prepare a prompt-book. By the autumn, when working on Karl Gutzkow's *Uriel Acosta*, he was writing an extended directorial commentary on the entire play, paying particular attention to crowd scenes. In August, he wrote a letter to the directors of the Sporting Club setting out the conditions under which the Society would assume responsibility for staging regular productions at the Club during the forthcoming season and listing a number of demands connected with reforms in theatrical practice. Stanislavsky asserted that a theatre could only produce the desired results 'in conditions of good administration and strict discipline' and asked

> is it possible to act any kind of serious role when a few metres away from an inspired actor a door squeaks every second or the shuffling feet of latecomers drown his voice? Is it possible to convey mood when at a distance of a couple of feet from the actor, people are making a noise with their boots, whispering or muttering unconstrainedly or when there are even drunken stagehands?
>
> (Stanislavskiy 1954–61: vol. 8: 86)

The première of Gutzkow's *Uriel Acosta*, in which Stanislavsky also played the leading role, had been preceded by painstaking rehearsals, during which he resorted to the dictatorial methods derived from the Meininger (which he was later to regret). One V. Marov, recalling a rehearsal he had witnessed, described it thus: 'The first 10 – 15 minutes were absolute torture. Not one word was spoken without criticism, every gesture was analysed, every intonation "placed" as if these were born singers, rather than members of an amateur dramatic society'. (*Vecher*, St Petersburg 1908: 14 October). However, the impression made by the actual production on 9 January 1895 was powerful. Nikolay Efros recalled an impact which lingered in the mind:

> in it there was the spirit and colour of the epoch, of the seventeenth century, Amsterdam, and not only in the details of a carefully reproduced historical picture of everyday life. You felt [. . .] the Jewish law subjugating and engulfing the personality, the fettering power of age-old traditions, the religious and national fanaticism.[12]

(Efros 1924: 68–9)

In preparing his next production, of *Othello*, Stanislavsky followed the ethnographical lines of an archaeological naturalism inaugurated by Charles Kean and perfected by the Meiningen Company. In addition to a director's score, he constructed a precise model of a Cypriot town, emphasising its exotic Eastern quality, including complete thoroughfares, houses with flat roofs and with washing hanging out to dry, Turkish rugs slung over balcony railings, etc. Whilst in Paris, and with the *Othello* production in mind, he bought books on the history of costume, on ancient weapons and on tapestries. He hunted for costume materials, for shoes and hats and, after an encounter with a North African in a Paris restaurant, attempted to imitate the physical mannerisms of a real 'Moor'. He then travelled to Venice, went the rounds of museums and made sketches for costumes.

According to one reviewer, the production, which opened on 19 January 1896, was reminiscent of the Meininger 'from an external point of view' and was a 'tremendous success' (*Novosti dnya* 1896: 23 January). It was admired by a visiting Italian tragedian, Ernesto Rossi, and by a young law student who, under its influence, gave up his studies and joined Nemirovich-Danchenko's acting classes at the Moscow Philharmonic School, before becoming a founder member of the Art Theatre. 'Stanislavsky is a powerful talent', noted the young man. 'The ensemble is splendid. Each one of the crowd lives on stage'. The young man was Vsevolod Meyerhold

(Meyerkhol'd 1976: 17). Later that year, Stanislavsky directed Gerhart Hauptmann's *Hannele* (*Hanneles Himmelfahrt – The Assumption of Hannele*) with professional actors. The Art Theatre actor, L. M. Leonidov, recalled the scene in which a group of beggars staggered downstage in the half-light as the Angel of Death bent over Hannele, its wings nearly filling the stage.[13] Meyerhold was cast as the Angel of Death in the revival scheduled for the Art Theatre's opening season, but the Orthodox Church stepped in and banned it.

Already Stanislavsky's thoughts were turning towards the organisation of a professional theatre with broad appeal. He proposed describing the venture as an 'Accessible' Theatre, with modest seat prices and designed to appeal to a different kind of audience. He began to imagine possible collaborators and backers, his attention turning first to M. V. Lentovskiy, a successful entrepreneur and manager of the Hermitage Pleasure Gardens.[14] Efros gives an account of a conversation with Stanislavsky concerning the establishment of such an Accessible Theatre:

> The initiator of the business ... does not see matters in terms of money, as many believe, but in terms of the reorganisation of backstage life. 'It is necessary to discipline future actors, get them to unlearn previous on-stage and backstage provincial habits, and lure their consciousness with the tremendous seriousness of the matter in hand.' The first season Stanislavsky proposes playing in a small theatre where new cadres of stage workers need to be prepared, costumiers, stage painters, props people. ... Only when thus equipped will it be possible to open the doors of a broadly accessible theatre.
> (N. Efros, 'Obshchedostupnyy teatr v Moskve', *Novosti dnya* 1896: 8 April)

During the early months of 1897, Stanislavsky was preparing to transform the Society of Art and Literature into a professional theatre company, with the intention of staging daily productions. He requested the Society's resident designer, F. N. Navrozov, to obtain information about the dimensions of Moscow stages. He studied the architectural plans of contemporary Russian and foreign theatre buildings and drew up provisional budget estimates. Following a performance of Erckmann-Chatrian's *The Polish Jew*, in which Stanislavsky played Mathias the burgomaster, the Meiningen actor, Ludwig Barnay, prophesied: 'You are destined to play a role in the history of theatre art . . . . In life there are always ninth waves. You are fortunate in having risen on this wave of Russian theatrical life' (Efros 1918: 63–4).[15]

3

THE CREATION OF A NEW THEATRE

There was much talk of the need to establish a new theatre. As early as February 1897, Fedor Shekhtel', a friend of Chekhov's and the architect destined to build the Art Theatre's second home in 1902, was already proposing the construction of a People's Theatre along the lines previously suggested by Ostrovsky.[1] On 1 March 1897, Chekhov informed Suvorin:

> At the actors' conference you'll probably see the plans for the huge people's theatre we are planning. *We* means the representatives of the Moscow intelligentsia . . . . A theatre, auditorium, library, reading room and buffets, and so on and so forth, will be gathered under one roof in a neat attractive building. The blueprints are ready, the constitution is being drafted and the only thing that is holding us up is a paltry half million. There will be stockholders, but it will not be a charitable organisation. We are counting on the government.
>
> (Chekhov 1974–83: vol. 6: 297)

Needless to say, these were not the first plans to be based fruitlessly on hope of government support.

Planning the Society's work for 1897, Stanislavsky anticipated much of what was to be included in the Art Theatre's repertoire in 1898 including *Tsar Fedor, The Merchant of Venice* and *The Mistress of the Inn.* He began negotiations with the entrepreneur Ya. V. Shchukin over the lease of the Ermitazh Theatre on Carriage Row (Karyetnyy ryad) where he proposed that the Society give regular performances for two-and-a-half months.[2]

Why was Stanislavsky so confident that he could succeed where others had failed? In the first place, he was neither as naive nor as impractical as many have suggested. He had had experience of accountancy and clerical work, having been employed in the offices of the family firm from the age of nineteen. It was he who, together with a talented engineer, A. Shamshin, set about modernising the company and broadening its interests. He was among the first in Russia to introduce technology into the production process, thus extending the enterprise into world markets and enabling it to overtake its competitors. Stanislavsky's organising abilities and technical know-how were highly valued. He was elected president of the directorate of the Amalgamated Company, to which the Alekseyev factory belonged, and it was his initiative which led to the company's decision to diversify, vastly increasing its operations and its profits. He was also among the first in Russia to introduce bonus schemes for the company's workforce. He also catered for their creative needs by building a small theatre within the factory for workers' performances. In addition to this and his work at the Society of Art and Literature, he was treasurer of the Russian Musical Society, where his contributions to various committees had attracted the approving notice of no less a person than Tchaikovsky. It also needs to be remembered that, notwithstanding his commitment to the Art Theatre after 1898, Stanislavsky maintained his manufacturing interests in the family firm until 1917.

However, becoming a theatre-owner was a risky business. Because of the subordination of the Imperial Theatres to the Palace Ministry, theatres were shackled generally by laws regulating the activities of state institutions. A commission established by the Palace Ministry characterised the situation thus:

> The complete authority of the director is only possible when he also happens to be the owner of the theatre building. In such cases, if the director also happens to be a gifted administrator, then all permanent and extraordinary expenses are covered by audience receipts. However, if the director is not so capable, then he has to pay out of his own pocket. Such is not the case with the Imperial Theatres. The public is not their paymaster and only contributes towards half the cost of the productions through the box-office. The larger proportion of the running costs is paid out of the Imperial purse. There is no expenditure of others' private money and, in the case of Imperial monies, that is to say the public exchequer, the government may not leave matters to the arbitrary whim of a single person.
>
> (Orlov 1989: 66)

Thus, in order to be fully in control of a theatre it was necessary to own the building. Except in rare cases, it was far too expensive for an entrepreneur to build at his own cost. Sometimes the town council would construct a theatre and hire it out. Town council control usually meant the imposition of a ceiling on the theatre's gross receipts to ensure that it remained broadly accessible to the local populace. Because of this, the council had to take a share of the expenses for sustaining the theatre's operation, including general maintenance of the building, in order to ensure its survival as a going concern.

The demands placed on an entrepreneur by the town council through the agency of a civic theatrical commission severely limited a theatre's independence. The commission could impose conditions regarding the number of productions, the number of premières in a season, the gross takings per performance and the order in which productions were to be staged. Each year, the commission would oversee the constitution of the troupe and the repertoire. Any deviation from what was agreed could result in a fine. In the circumstances it is regrettable, but hardly surprising, that the Art Theatre founders found it necessary to appeal to the Moscow City Council for a subsidy.

A number of instances could be cited of individuals trying to work under these conditions. The only successful example, prior to the Art Theatre, was that of Fedor Korsh who exercised an important influence on the development of theatre in Moscow. The example of other serious undertakings in the provinces might also have encouraged Stanislavsky and Nemirovich. N. N. Sinel'nikov had pioneered staging reforms in Kazan' and Rostov during the 1880s.[3] His memoirs describe a particular interest in *mise-en-scène* and a desire 'to discard all ... clichés ... stereotypes that set one's teeth on edge, and exchange them for a natural, beautiful, truthful arrangement of persons and objects on stage' (Senelick 1991: 399).

The comparable efforts of P. M. Medvedyev pre-dated the rescinding of the Imperial monopoly.[4] He ran a successful theatre in Kazan' during the 1860s, switching to opera during the 1870s. He was particularly successful in staging classic plays to a high standard and paid particular attention to the importance of ensemble. His company included a whole 'pleiade' of acting talents and, although forced to abandon his activities in 1889 for financial reasons, this was a result of poor management rather than a consequence of artistic failure.

Stanislavsky was very conscious of the failure of Anna Brenko's enterprise. She had been granted permission to set up a theatre in Moscow in 1880, before the abolition of the Imperial monopoly. Like ingenious thespians before her, she evaded the letter of the law by terming the company's productions 'readings of dramatic scenes in costume and make-up' and, for two years, staged plays from the classic repertoire with a first-rate troupe. In 1882 Brenko's Pushkin Theatre ran out of funds and went into liquidation.

More encouraging was the example of Korsh, who was the first to take advantage of the lifting of the Imperial monopoly when he took over the theatre in the Lianozov house on Gazetnyy (Kamergerskiy) Lane – in the very building which the Art Theatre was to convert to its own use in 1902. Here, he surrounded himself with a strong company, headed by V. N. Davydov, staging a première every Friday.[5] Through astute management he managed to include both classic and new plays, offering special-priced matinées for students. Not only was he responsible for the first production of Chekhov's *Ivanov*, he also staged Ibsen. He even managed, eventually, to build his own theatre which survived until it was nationalised after the revolution.

In March 1897, Stanislavsky attended the First All-Russian Congress of Stage Workers when the state of the theatre and matters concerning theatrical training, criticism and censorship, actors' welfare, etc. were discussed. Yevtikhiy Karpov, in a keynote speech, addressed the question of making theatres 'accessible' (*obshchedostupnyy*) to a broader public:

> The basic repertoire of a people's theatre should consist, in my opinion, of the dramatic works of Russian authors and foreign classics, precisely because this is a *Russian people's theatre.* [...] I cannot understand why some fear that the people will not grasp such plays as *Hamlet, King Lear, Othello, The Robbers* and so on. [...] The productions of these plays should be distinguished by assiduous historical accuracy and artistic taste.[6]

His conclusion was that: 'a people's theatre at popular prices in Moscow will probably have an enormous success' if led by 'an incorruptible director' (Senelick 1991: 408–9).

Nemirovich-Danchenko had arranged to come to Moscow in May 1897 for talks with the director of the Moscow Imperial Theatres, Pavel Pchel'nikov, to whom he had proposed large-scale reforms of the Malyy.[7] Anticipating his likely response, Nemirovich simultaneously sent a note to Stanislavsky suggesting a meeting on the same day. Stanislavsky telegrammed his acceptance. Nemirovich left an unproductive meeting with Pchel'nikov, whom he eventually met on 22 June, for a pre-arranged rendezvous with Stanislavsky in a private room at the Slavic Bazaar restaurant. The historic meeting continued overnight at Stanislavsky's parents' country estate at Lyubimovka, lasting altogether eighteen hours. The range of topics they discussed established the essential basis for the future organisation of the Moscow Art Theatre.

Nemirovich's attraction to the theatre was of long standing. He had written plays, sketches and stories while at school and had then acted briefly in the provinces with both amateur and professional companies. Moving to Moscow, he took part in a number of productions staged by the Moscow Artistic Circle before embarking on a literary career, writing for journals and newspapers as humorist, belletrist and occasional theatre critic. More significantly, in the course of twenty years (1881–1901) he wrote eleven plays, all of which were performed at the Malyy Theatre. Not only was he close to the Malyy and familiar with its methods, he also sat on its repertoire committee. Although a great admirer of the talents of Imperial Theatre actors, Nemirovich was highly critical of the Theatre's directorate and of its repertoire.

For example, the neglect of Chekhov seemed to him little short of scandalous. So strongly did Nemirovich feel on this score that he protested against the award of the Griboyedov prize to his own play, *The Value of Life* (*Tsena zhizni*), which he thought should have gone to Chekhov's *Seagull*. He was to repair this deficiency by persuading Chekhov to let the Art Theatre stage the play in its first season. In the autumn of 1891, Nemirovich began teaching drama at the school of the Moscow Philharmonic Society. The course included the study of theatre history and dramatic theory as well as practical work. The talents which the school attracted included Olga Knipper, Vsevolod Meyerhold and Ivan Moskvin.[8,9,10] In 1896, one of the school's examination productions was of Ibsen's *A Doll's House*. During its first twenty years, largely because of Nemirovich's enthusiastic promotion, the Art Theatre was to stage more productions of plays by Ibsen than by any other dramatist.

The results of the meeting between Stanislavsky and Nemirovich were as follows: Stanislavsky wished to found the future company on the basis of the Society of Art and Literature, with the first season opening at the Sporting Club. His idea then was to hire a large theatre, flesh out the amateur company with new blood and, gradually, transform it into a professional unit. In support, he pointed to the Society's existing reputation and the degree of public goodwill it had accrued. Nemirovich disagreed. He did not want to associate the new business with Stanislavsky's amateur experiments and proposed forming a troupe based in a large provincial town and uniting the best of the Society's actors with his own hand-picked students. There, they would work to achieve an ensemble before going on tour. Having conquered the provinces, they would advance triumphantly on Moscow. Stanislavsky begged to differ.

A good deal of time was spent in deciding whether or not the Theatre should be a privately financed company, a collective of shareholding actors, or a joint-stock venture. Already in 1895, Stanislavsky had devised the rules and regulations for the last of these and, on 8 August 1897, sent Nemirovich a draft of the Theatre's charter. Stanislavsky's arguments, set out in a further letter of 19 August, sought to convince Nemirovich that their efforts would be best served by a Moscow-based, firmly established joint-stock company and not by a provincially based, privately financed enterprise as favoured by Nemirovich, who clearly imagined Stanislavsky financing it with his own capital. Stanislavsky insisted:

> A joint-stock enterprise is essential at the outset, at the moment of greatest risk, for material support; such a joint-stock company is also necessary for the continuation of the business along the lines which we establish, after we are no longer here. . . . Moreover, it seems to me that Moscow will not trust a purely private enterprise and won't even pay attention to it; and even if it does, it will be when it's too late, when our pockets are already empty and the doors of our theatre boarded up.
>
> (Stanislavskiy 1954–61: vol. 7: 123)

To win public respect, a joint-stock company had to have enlightened aims. Stanislavsky was concerned by the fate of Mamontov, who was accused of being a mere dilettante – a millionaire and powerful magnate who just happened to have founded an excellent opera company. Stanislavsky feared that his own financing of an exclusively private enterprise would be construed by the

Moscow public, citing the example of Mamontov, as 'the petty tyranny of a merchant' (123).

He also believed that the creation of an 'accessible' theatre on a joint-stock basis would appeal to powerful businessmen who, although not patronising the theatre on principle, could be persuaded to dig their hands into their pockets in support of a worthwhile artistic cause. However, neither he nor Nemirovich would agree to the theatre being named 'after some Maecenas or other' (124). Nemirovich thought that founding the theatre on the basis of Stanislavsky's own money would provide stability in the first instance. Only subsequently, within a space of two years or so, did he contemplate inviting wealthy shareholders. Only thus, thought Nemirovich, could the Theatre guarantee its creative and ideological independence.

Stanislavsky rejected this idea. Most of his own money was tied up in the family business and was not easily accessible. Moreover, his experience at the Society of Art and Literature had not been such as to encourage confidence in the new Theatre's financial success. Indeed, both men were to discover that artistic success and financial reward did not necessarily go hand-in-hand, the first years of the Art Theatre's operations being dogged by financial crises.

It was eventually agreed to create a shareholding company/syndicate (*tovarishchestvo*). By the time the Theatre had earned public confidence it might be possible to proceed without shareholders, especially since there was always the risk that the latter might tend to prioritise material, rather than artistic, factors. The advantage of a joint-stock company in the first instance, 'at the moment of greatest risk', was that this risk would be spread evenly among the sharers.

Nemirovich rapidly set about trying to persuade wealthy Muscovites to enter for a share. His approaches were met with some suspicion, as what was being offered was a pig in a poke or, in his own phrase, 'a cat in a sack'. In an interview given in January 1898, Nemirovich insisted on the modesty of the undertaking. They had no intention of building their own theatre. They would simply hire one temporarily and only after a year or two might they consider acquiring a theatre of their own.

During the first months of 1898, they set about raising money (Nemirovich estimated that they would need an initial capital sum of 28,000 roubles). They proposed establishing a Syndicate for the Establishment of a Public-Accessible Theatre in Moscow with the dual aim of raising private capital and obtaining a civic subsidy. Nemirovich approached Varvara Morozova, a member of the celebrated family associated with the textile industry, who turned him down. This forced him to approach the Moscow City Council for an annual grant of 15,000 roubles. Meanwhile, Stanislavsky was petitioning Prince Dmitry Golitsyn, the Council President. Finally, they placed a report before the Council, the basic argument of which was that Moscow, with a population numbering millions, most of whom were working class, needed a popular-accessible theatre more than any other Russian city. The repertoire would consist of plays of high artistic quality whose staging would be exemplary. The distinguishing feature of an accessible theatre would be the comparative cheapness of its seats.

The report was compiled under four headings: (1) the Theatre's aim; (2) the repertoire and its implementation; (3) the Theatre's feasibility; and (4) the Theatre building and the decentralisation of its operations. The report began by complaining about the lack of cheap theatre seats, going on to dispel prejudices about what constituted a 'popular' theatre. This was not to be a home for *lubok*, nor for versions of *féerie à la* Lentovskiy, nor for narrowly tendentious plays, nor for boulevard melodrama, but a home for the work of classic Russian and foreign plays, as well as for contemporary drama.[11] Theatre was, first and foremost, entertainment but the spectator needed to take away 'a particle of goodness and truth'. Plays would be put on daily, the total number of performances in any season, apart from the first, to number 210. Prices would be approximately equivalent to those charged at the Korsh and for morning performances at the Malyy, i.e. from two roubles maximum to ten kopecks minimum. Special charity performances would be staged at higher prices while others would be given, free of charge, for schoolchildren (Nemirovich-Danchenko 1952: 63–71).

The City Council eventually considered the report towards the end of 1899 and, despite the poor financial state of the Art Theatre at the end of its first season, turned a deaf ear to its plea.

Having grown impatient of the Council's dilatoriness, the decision was taken to establish the Theatre without public money. Nemirovich turned his attention to the directors of the Philharmonic Society one of whom, the head of a chemical firm, was persuaded to buy 4,000 roubles' worth of shares. Other industrialists, company directors and friends of the Society of Art and

Literature soon followed with sums of between 1,000 and 2,000 roubles. In March 1898, an agreement was concluded which laid the basis for a Syndicate for the Establishment of a Public-Accessible Theatre in Moscow. This empowered Stanislavsky and Nemirovich to manage the business at their own discretion. In case of disagreement, Stanislavsky would possess the power of veto in matters relating to staging and Nemirovich would have similar powers on the literary side.

The members of the syndicate included the brothers Savva and Sergey Morozov, who contributed 5,000 roubles each, on condition that the Theatre did not seek higher patronage.[12] This did not trouble Stanislavsky or Nemirovich but worried those shareholders who had joined for snobbish reasons. The enterprise had attracted the interest of Grand Princess Elizaveta Fedorovna, wife of Moscow's Governor-General, who could not be expected to have such limits imposed on her. The Theatre's dependence on the Governor-General was a very real factor. The ban on *Tsar Fedor*, which had been lifted for a production at Suvorin's theatre in St Petersburg, was only lifted in Moscow as a result of a petition to the Princess and a resulting appeal to the Minister of Internal Affairs by the Governor-General himself (Kholodov 1987: 255–6).

Thirteen sharers concluded an agreement on 10 April 1898. Nemirovich and Stanislavsky were each offered annual salaries of 4,200 roubles. The enterprise was to belong to the sharers, not to the acting company, whose interests were to be represented by both co-founders. Neither, at this stage, had contemplated the possibility of an actors' co-operative; rather, the model was that of the Comédie Française, whose organisational system Stanislavsky had studied, and where control lay in the hands of 'sociétaires'. The long-term aim, however, was to transfer control of the Theatre to the acting troupe itself.

The agreement was to extend for twelve years, during which time none of the signatories could repossess his capital unless losses amounted to 75 per cent of the original sum. Decisions would be taken by majority vote but would take account of each member's initial outlay. Thus, two people whose joint holding came to 10,000 roubles could out-vote four whose holding totalled only 8,000. A problem then arose in the case of Nemirovich, who had had no capital to invest but whose voice needed to count in decision-making. This was resolved by making his vote the theoretical equivalent of his having entered for an initial sum of 5,000, i.e. on a par with Morozov and Stanislavsky. An Artistic Council was established as an advisory body on all key decisions, consisting of nine close colleagues of Stanislavsky and Nemirovich, and including Lilina, Knipper and Meyerhold. This lent flexibility to the way in which the theatre was run and, in various forms, was retained during the first twenty years of its operations.

The first shareholders' meeting took place on 12 May 1898, when Nemirovich reported on proposed seat prices, rehearsals, actors' contracts and the repertoire. Seventeen premières and 160 performances before Lent were proposed (the season began in October and ended in February) as well as student matinées (in fact, morning performances) and charity benefits. He concluded by announcing an estimated budget for the first year of 98,000 roubles, estimated receipts of 88,300 and a four-month rehearsal period. The bulk of the budget, 20,800, or 21 per cent of the total, was for production costs alone. In fact, the overall budget was exceeded and the first season saw a deficit of 46,000 roubles. Further financial backing was sought during the summer of 1899 when, eventually, Savva Morozov advanced an additional 21,000 roubles and persuaded the remaining shareholders (dividend-less after the first season's operations) to re-engage themselves for sums equivalent to the initial outlay of each. The third season was to cost Morozov alone some 120,000 roubles (Amiard-Chevrel 1979: 41).

For a season to consist of merely three or four productions (as later became quite common) was, at this time, unheard of so the Theatre had to prepare for considerably more. According to preliminary calculations, of the 160 performances during that first winter season, seventeen needed to be 'first' performances, which meant more or less weekly premières. More than a quarter of the total number of productions was reserved in advance for charitable societies and for the Sporting Club. Also earmarked were twelve low-priced 'accessible' performances and twenty 'scientific-artistic mornings for young people', which needed to be preceded by lectures given by 'the best professors and outstanding critics'. As this left only about thirty performances for so-called 'gala' evenings, it was decided to renovate some of the productions previously staged at the Society of Art and Literature in order to make up the required number of performances. In addition, Hermann Sudermann's *Magda* (*Heimat*) and V. A. Dyachenko's *The Tutor* (*Guverner*) were to be got up in a week for three or four performances only. It was also planned to select new works dealing with 'problems which severely exercise the thoughts and feelings of the contemporary spectator' and to present these in a double-bill with a comedy. This is how they came to stage Emil Mariott's *Greta's Happiness*. The first season was also to include single performances of Turgenev's one-act comedy *Lunch With the Marshal of the Nobility*, Ostrovsky's *Late Love*, and a vaudeville by Aleksey Yakovlev, *Feminine Curiosity*.

The 28,000 roubles capital was needed to cover the rehearsal period, the preparation of sets, and the first instalment on the hire of a building. Some idea of comparative costs can be gained from the fact that, at the state theatres, more than half the annual expenses were met through subsidy. Even deficits were compensated by the Palace Ministry. At the end of the nineteenth century, annual expenditure on Imperial Theatres amounted to more than 2 million roubles on a total of just four theatres. The sum spent on secondary education throughout the whole of Russia amounted to only 6.5 million in 1900. The hire of the Shelyaputinskiy Theatre, to act as a 'filial' for the Malyy and the Bolshoy, cost the palace exchequer 450,000 roubles in 1898. As Nemirovich noted in a letter to Lenskiy, whilst the government was exercising financial economies which imposed restraint on his own ability to get a private theatre off the ground, a royal box being built at the New Theatre (the former Shelyaputinskiy) was 'costing 60,000 roubles, more than half of my entire budget!!' (Nemirovich-Danchenko 1979: 131).[13]

There remained the problem of a theatre to perform in. Possibilities included the renting of unoccupied premises or venues where an existing tenancy was coming to an end. The Omon (Lianozov) Theatre (where they finally settled in 1902) was a possible choice. Another was the Paradiz, or 'International' Theatre, formerly run by George Paradiz and which the Art Theatre later hired for a production without décor of *The Seagull* for Chekhov's benefit, and where they occasionally rehearsed. It had been modernised, electric lighting had been installed and, although it was leased out for the forthcoming season to touring groups from abroad, the Art Theatre could occupy the building in those weeks which remained free. Eventually it was agreed that they would hire a decent building in the city centre, on Theatre Square, the aforementioned Shelyaputinskiy (named after its proprietor). Unfortunately, they were pipped at the post by the Court Ministry who requisitioned it for the New Dramatic Imperial Theatre (the New Theatre).

In the spring of 1898, V. A. Telyakovskiy replaced Pchel'nikov at the offices of the Imperial Theatres in Moscow.[14] Unlike his predecessor, he seized on the reformist ideas of Lenskiy, who proposed organising a new theatre to serve as a branch of the two Moscow Imperial Theatres, the Malyy and the Bolshoy. To this end, Telyakovskiy requisitioned the best building in town from under the nose of the Art Theatre. The opening of the New Theatre, so close to that planned for the Art Theatre, constituted a serious threat. The question then became whether it would be better to open before, or after, the New Theatre. Nemirovich wrote to Telyakovskiy on 8 March 1898, pointing out that the existence of the New Theatre would make things more difficult for himself and Stanislavsky but declaring that they would not be deflected from their course. After discussion, it was decided to open the Art Theatre in October. The New Theatre opened on 1 September with Tchaikovsky's *Eugene Onegin*. Two days later, they performed Gogol's *The Government Inspector* in Lenskiy's own production. This was competition with a vengeance.

On 19 April, Stanislavsky had assumed responsibility as Principal Director of the Moscow Public-Accessible Theatre (the 'Art' element was added later as almost an after-thought of Nemirovich's). In this capacity, he contracted to hire the Ermitazh Theatre on Carriage Row for one season, with an option on extending the contract for two years. The building was uncomfortable, ugly and impractical with a cramped auditorium and only 815 seats. Its advantages were a degree of intimacy and good sightlines. However, it was inconveniently situated at some distance both from the city centre and from densely populated areas. This put the notion of 'accessibility' into question at the outset, but there was no alternative.

It now became necessary to assemble a company and begin rehearsals. Stanislavsky attended productions at the Philharmonic School with an eye for potential recruits (Knipper reported seeing him in the audience at a performance of Carlo Goldoni's *Mistress of the Inn*). All in all, twelve members of the School joined the company (30 per cent of the troupe) including Nemirovich's favourite pupils – Moskvin, Knipper, M. G. Savitskaya and M. L. Petrovskaya-Roksanova, as well as Meyerhold, his sister-in-law E. M. Munt, A. L. Zagarov, L. V. Aleyeva and I. A. Tikhomirov.[15-20] Stanislavsky brought fourteen actors with him from the Society of Art and Literature (35 per cent of the troupe) including his wife

Lilina, M. F. Andreyeva, A. A. Sanin, V. V. Luzhskiy, G. S. Burd-zhalov, M. A. Samarova and I. A. Krovskiy.[21,22] It was decided to strengthen their forces by inviting from outside A. L. Vishnyevskiy, who happened to be a former classmate of Chekhov's, and M. E. Darskiy, a classical actor.[23,24] Together with other young invitees, who included V. F. Gribunin from the Malyy Theatre School, S. N. Sud'binin, A. I. Adashev and V. A. Lanskoy, the permanent acting company eventually numbered thirty-nine, made up of twenty-three men and sixteen women.[25,26,27,28]

As the Theatre's plans included crowd scenes, it was considered desirable to create a permanent cadre of 'walk-ons' (twenty-nine in all). These were to be augmented by twenty or so students from the Philharmonic School, among whom was the young Alla Nazimova.[29] V. A. Simov was invited to become chief designer and the young composer V. S. Kalinnikov chosen to direct the orchestra.[30] Ya. I. Gremislavskiy was put in charge of make-up and wigs, a role he had performed at the Society, and a further staff of seventy-eight were appointed as stage-hands, carpenters, scene-shifters and administrators – the entire complement, including orchestra and chorus, totalling 323.[31] A repertoire had been worked out during the spring. Among the new productions – of *Tsar Fedor Ioannovich*, *The Seagull*, *Antigone* – were some which had already been put on by the Society or at the Philharmonic School – Pisemskiy's *Despots* and Goldoni's *The Mistress of the Inn*.

> On 14 June 1898, in Pushkino near the station of the same name on the Moscow-Yaroslavl line, thirty-three versts from Moscow, in a hastily constructed building which could hardly be termed a theatre as it consisted of just one stage with a small adjoining room and veranda, situated in a private park belonging to the barrister's assistant, Nikolay Nikolayevich Arkhipov, a member of the directorate of the Society of Art and Literature, here the Public-Accessible Art Theatre began its activities.
>
> (Ryndzyunskiy 1899: 3)

Thus G. D. Ryndzyunskiy began his detailed account of the Theatre's activities during its first season.[32] The Ermitazh had been hired for the summer by a third party and so was unavailable until September. When the company gathered at the barn, which looked like a small cricket pavilion, every effort had been made to render the space as much like a theatre and as congenial as possible. The interior walls had been covered with hessian and wallpaper; the exterior boards had been painted and curtains hung at the windows and along the newly constructed, roofed veranda where the actors drank tea and awaited their calls. Separate dressing rooms had been provided for men and women and a stage 'on tall trestles, quite large, not high', with a curtain 'made out of the sort of material peasants use for their shirts', had been built in the small 'auditorium' with footlights made out of kerosene lamps (Benedetti 1991: 22).

Stanislavsky kept a day-book in which he recorded the company's activities – which play was being rehearsed and those involved; the names of absentees and latecomers, with accompanying explanations. The summer was hot. The building had a metal roof which intensified the heat. There were ten productions to prepare.

Most of the actors lived in a dacha at Pushkino, about twenty minutes' walk away. Stanislavsky stayed at his parents' estate nearby at Lyubimovka and came to rehearsals every day, usually on horseback. The first meeting on 14 June began with a short religious service. Stanislavsky then made a speech, 'of great warmth and beauty', according to Meyerhold, who reported the first day's events in a letter to his wife (Meyerkhol'd 1976: 18) in which he stressed the theatre's 'public-accessible' and high-minded ideals:

> we have taken upon ourselves something which does not have a simple or a private but a social character. Do not forget that we are striving to bring light into the dark lives of the poorer classes, to give them joyful aesthetic moments amidst the gloom which envelops them. We are striving to create the first rational, moral and public-accessible theatre and we dedicate our lives to this high goal.
> (Stanislavskiy 1954–61: vol. 5: 175)

The speech was greeted with loud applause, after which the actors took tea. At the meeting which followed, greetings-telegrams were read out (including one from Nemirovich who was away in the Crimea finishing a novel). Roles were then distributed and the new Theatre's regulations, the Corporate Rules, ratified.

Rehearsals began at mid-day and usually lasted until 4.00 p.m. The company reassembled in the evening and continued rehearsing from about 7.00 onwards, sometimes concluding as late as midnight. Two rehearsal sessions meant that two plays could be rehearsed each day. Often, rehearsals were held in tandem – one in the Theatre, another somewhere in the surrounding woods or in the field where the barn was situated. A daily 'monitor' ensured that rehearsals were conducted in an orderly manner, that the rehearsal room was swept, meal tables laid and the samovar permanently on the go. During the second half of June, Stanislavsky rehearsed *The Merchant of Venice, Antigone, Hannele, Despots* and *The Tutor*.[33] Reading round the table became an integral part of the rehearsal – either of the entire play, or whole sections, or individual acts and scenes, not just once or twice but several times, analysing, commenting, discovering a style, the general tone, vocal colouring, etc. Only when this had been done did rehearsal on stage begin – in an attempt to flesh out the work with speech and gesture. This was something altogether new. Another novelty consisted in re-hearsing small chunks and scenes instead of, as was customary, the entire play at one go.

Stanislavsky had spent most of May and the beginning of June in Rostov-Suzdal'skiy finding material for *Tsar Fedor*, immersing himself in Russia's medieval past. Together with Sanin, Simov and Burdzhalov, he kept a special album in which he made drawings of costumes, footwear, window gratings – anything, in fact, which helped to convey a sense of the period. They hunted down and bought ancient ornaments and tableware. Even if some of the items were not historically accurate, Stanislavsky strove to ensure that the general effect should be one of complete, even exaggerated, authenticity. If sleeves were worn long and broad in the sixteenth century, then he insisted on the longest and broadest. If hats were tall, then he wanted the very tallest. A characteristic detail of the setting for *Fedor* became the extremely low entrances which compelled the actors to stoop. This had the effect of, not only emphasising the architectural features of ancient buildings, but also encouraging a sense of subjugation which communicated a feeling for the political mood of the period. To this was added atmospherically gloomy lighting from icon lamps, with bleak shafts of light filtering through the narrow slits of thick-walled, 'medieval' buildings.

Working closely with Simov, Stanislavsky prepared a prompt-book as well as models of sets for both this play and *The Merchant of Venice*. When these were unveiled, Meyerhold especially was full of excited praise and, within a fortnight, was already hailing Stanislavsky as 'a director-teacher of *genius*' (Meyerkhol'd 1976:

19). Work on *Tsar Fedor* began on 7 July. Stanislavsky read the play and displayed his director's plan. Suvorin, who was staging it in St Petersburg, dropped in on a rehearsal together with members of his company. Nemirovich reported:

> They're all wild about the way you're staging *Fedor*. Suvorin calls you 'a genius'. And can you imagine, their Petersburg version is *almost ready*, after only six rehearsals; moreover they start rehearsing at 11.00 a.m. and have finished *the entire tragedy* by half-past one (all eleven scenes). Can you imagine it?
>
> (Nemirovich-Danchenko 1979: 155)

The running-time of *Tsar Fedor*, as indicated on the posters, was from 7.30 p.m. until midnight, i.e. a whole two hours longer than the running-time of Suvorin's production.

In late July, Nemirovich rejoined the company and began rehearsing the role of Tsar Fedor with Moskvin, who had finally been selected from among six other potential candidates. By 9 August, *The Merchant of Venice* was ready and *Antigone* and *Despots* were being given their final rehearsals. On 10 August, Stanislavsky left for his brother's estate, near Kharkov, in order to write the director's score for *The Seagull*.[34] A read-through of the play had been held, by Nemirovich, who reported to Chekhov on 21 August that the first discussion with the actors had lasted for more than four hours and had only dealt with the first two acts (144). On 1 September, Nemirovich received Stanislavsky's plan of the first three acts followed, on 10 September, by the plan for Act Four. The latter rejoined the company on 18 September, less than a month before the season was due to open.

With the onset of the autumn rains the company left their barn in Pushkino and moved to Moscow. The Ermitazh summer season was still in full swing, with performances in the theatre and popular songs being sung for the delectation of patrons sitting at tables outside. Rehearsals, accompanied by the noise of refurbishment, began in the company's new home on 15 September.

As Stanislavsky had foreseen, delaying the opening beyond that of the New Theatre had had the effect of arousing people's curiosity. Despite pessimistic prognoses in the daily press and articles entitled 'A Chimerical Project', *Novosti dnya* announced, on 13 October, that 'the public is laying siege to the box-office and literally fighting for tickets'. In fact, tickets were still available on opening night. Success had been predicted if they opened in mid-week; 14 October happened to be a Wednesday. It also marked the seventy-fourth anniversary of the opening of the Malyy Theatre.

4

THE HERMITAGE
THEATRE ON
CARRIAGE ROW

The Ermitazh Gardens on Carriage Row (Karyetnyy ryad) where the
Hermitage Theatre stood are frequently confused with the Ermitazh
Pleasure Gardens – a kind of Muscovite Tivoli Gardens managed by
the impresario M. V. Lentovskiy, which boasted an open-air theatre.
The former were opened in 1894 by the ubiquitous Ya. V. Shchukin,
who owned the theatre which backed on to them facing Carriage
Row, where the Miniature Theatre (Moskovskiy Teatr Miniatyur)
stands today. The name of the theatre derived from its garden setting
and meant, literally, 'a recluse's shelter' or 'hermitage'. At the time
when the Art Theatre company moved in, it had been run more like
a music-hall than a monastery. Stanislavsky's reminiscences capture
the atmosphere of a rather seedy venue:

> The Ermitazh in Karyetnyy ryad was in a terrible state, dusty,
> uncomfortable, unheated, with the smell of beer and some
> sort of acid that had remained from the summer use of the
> building. There was a garden and the public was entertained
> with various divertissements in the open air, but in inclement
> weather the entertainment would be carried over into the
> theatre. The furnishings of the theatre had been intended for
> garden audiences and were tasteless. This could be seen in the
> choice of colours, in the cheap decorations, in the miserable
> attempt at luxury, in the posters hung on the walls, in the stage
> curtain with its advertisements, in the uniforms of the ushers,
> in the choice of food in the buffet and in the entire insulting
> character of the building and the disorder of the house.
>   We had to get rid of all this, but we had no money to create
> an interior that would be bearable for cultured people. We
> painted all the walls and the posters on them white. We

covered the rotten chairs with decent material; we found carpets and spread them in the corridors which bordered on the auditorium, so as to deaden the sound of footsteps which would interfere with the performance. We removed the nasty curtains from the doors and windows; we washed the windows and painted their frames, hung tulle curtains and covered the worst of the corners with laurel trees and flowers, giving a somewhat cosy appearance to the auditorium. [...] Our worst problem was heating the theatre.

(Stanislavskiy 1988: 268–9)

Stanislavsky had appeared here in the 1880s with the Musical-Dramatic Circle when he and Artem – a future colleague both at the Society of Art and Literature and at the Art Theatre – had found the cold in the dressing rooms so intense that they used to change in the intervals at the house of Stanislavsky's sister, who lived around the corner on Sadovaya (*Moskovskiy Khudozhestvennyy teatr* 1914: 10).

The problem of naming the new theatre exercised Stanislavsky's imaginative ingenuity and a number of possibilities were entered in his notebook. These included 'The Public-Accessible Theatre'; 'The MOIL Theatre' (The Moscow Theatre of Art [Iskusstvo] and Literature); 'The Allcomers (Vsesoslovnyy) Theatre'; 'The Philharmonic Theatre'; 'The Moscow Theatre'; 'The Inexpensive (Deshevyy) Theatre'; 'The Accessible (Dostupnyy) Theatre'; 'The New Theatre'; 'The Literary Theatre'; 'The Russian Theatre'; 'The Experimental (Probnyy) Theatre'; 'The Theatre on New Lines' (Na Novykh Nachalakh); and, semi-seriously, 'The First and Last Theatre' (Teatr v Pervyy i Posledniy Raz) and the 'In Memoriam Theatre' (Teatr v Pamyat' . . .) (Stanislavskiy 1986: 117).

The problem was solved by Nemirovich's ultimatum: 'We can't wait any longer. I propose we call our theatre the Moscow Public-Accessible Art Theatre. Do you agree – yes or no? We must decide at once.' Stanislavsky gave his consent 'without thinking' but became concerned when he saw the advertisements in the newspapers 'for I realised what a responsibility we had taken upon ourselves with the word "Art". I was deeply worried' (Stanislavskiy 1988: 270). In fact, he ought to have been more concerned about the currency of the term 'Public-Accessible', which the Theatre was obliged to drop from its masthead in its third season because of the need to increase seat prices.

Working conditions at the Ermitazh were inadequate. The auditorium was too narrow and the roof was in a bad state of disrepair. Apart from a lack of rehearsal space the dressing rooms were poor and storage space limited. The stage was too small, the wings virtually non-existent, the lighting and heating systems antediluvian. The fact that sets had to be constructed at some distance from the building and then transported and that costumes, properties and flats had to be stored in dilapidated barns where they deteriorated more rapidly, also contributed to increased costs. A number of settings had to be destroyed as there was no space to store them, which meant that their materials could not be recycled.

The main problems were the size of the stage and the limited number of seats. Although only 815 were fixed, a maximum capacity of over 850 was recorded for some performances of *Tsar Fedor*. Thirty-seven, including twelve in the boxes, were reserved for dignitaries. The success of *Tsar Fedor* led to the addition of a further twenty seats in the front stalls, which were reintroduced for other popular productions such as *The Seagull* and *Hedda Gabler*. Additional seating was also provided 'on demand' on ninety-one occasions during the first season when, for example, people had travelled long distances 'on spec' from outside Moscow.[1]

The best seats cost a lot in comparison with what was then the average. However, it was possible to sit in the gallery for as little as twenty kopecks, although only fifty-eight seats were provided at that price. To describe a seat costing between twenty and fifty kopecks as 'cheap' needs to be seen in relation to the best stalls seat, which cost 3.5 roubles, or a seat in a box at a gala performance which could cost anything between twenty and twenty-six roubles. During its first season, the average price of a ticket was only slightly less than that at the Malyy. By the second season they were virtually on a par, 1.5 roubles at the MAT (see p. 226) and fractionally more at the Malyy. Boxes at the MAT were considerably more expensive – from six to twenty roubles during their first season, as opposed to 4.4 to 15.4 roubles at the Malyy. Tickets for stalls and circle were somewhat cheaper. On average, however, the price of a ticket for the MAT was higher than that in the private theatres of St Petersburg and Moscow and much higher than in provincial theatres. In comparison with the cost of living at the time these sums were not inconsiderable. For example, in Moscow and St Petersburg at the end of the century, a kilo of lamb cost 17 kopecks and a kilo of butter 45. A nourishing two-course meal at a metropolitan eating house, which included a meat dish, could cost as little as five kopecks; even less in a provincial town. Other items of food, oatmeal for example, were very cheap and fruit and vegetables cost a mere one or two kopecks.

Measured on an entirely different scale, the Theatre's working capital of 28,000 roubles was still an extremely small sum. All future expenses were predicated on box-office turnover. Salaries during the first season amounted to 64,000 roubles (by the third season this had risen to 100,000). The second most expensive item was production expenditure. Rent for the the building was 15,000 roubles in the first, and 20,000 in the second season (very reasonable when compared with the 450,000 which Lenskiy was paying for the Shelyaputinskiy). By the end of the first season, the cost of salaries, new productions and building hire stood at more than 80 per cent of the total budget (approximately 117,000 out of a total of 144,400 roubles). Other payments included those to authors (around 5,000) and a slice due to the Society of Russian Dramatic Writers – 1,700. Box-office receipts amounted to 106,000 which, together with the return on share investment, came to 136,000 roubles. The total deficit of more than 10,000 had to be met somehow. Stanislavsky, Nemirovich and Sanin offered to waive their salaries but it still became necessary to borrow. The idea of increasing seat prices to cover losses seemed, at this stage, to run directly counter to expressed policy.

With its declared intention of trying to attract members of the poorer intelligentsia, most performances reserved 60 seats in the circle and gallery for Moscow University students. A further thirty were reserved for students of the Imperial Moscow Technical School.[2] Overall, approximately one hundred student seats were reserved on any one day until 8.00 p.m., when those unclaimed would be sold off. Posters for the opening production announced: 'Advance tickets can be purchased between 10.00 a.m. and 8.00 p.m. Those reserving seats need to collect tickets before 4.00 p.m. on the evening of the performance, after which time uncollected tickets will be put on general sale.'

In view of the 'special educational interest' of *Antigone*, the theatre sent out circulars to over one hundred educational establishments, offering advance booking facilities for three, reduced-price, morning performances.[3] The take-up was so great that the Theatre had to add a fourth performance. Because of the size of the auditorium, it was not possible to offer similar arrangements for *Tsar Fedor*, despite numerous requests.

Although the theatre employed an orchestra, it abandoned the practice of providing music during the intervals. Benefit performances were also done away with and members of the public were not permitted backstage or into the actors' dressing rooms. Art Theatre posters and programmes dropped the appellation 'Mr' and 'Mrs' and designated the cast by initials and surnames only. Before long, the public was not allowed to enter the auditorium after the performance had begun. Where traditional stage curtains tended to be made of red plush with elaborate tassellated designs and rose from the stage floor, the Art Theatre curtain was of plain, dark-green material and parted in the middle – a singular innovation at this time.

One hundred and thirty-eight performances were presented during the first season, of which fifteen were morning shows. Ten were given at the Sporting Club and the remaining 113 were normal evening performances. Five of the latter were given for charity. Two performances of *Tsar Fedor* were given with increased seat prices. Notice of five morning productions at reduced prices was given to local factories but the take-up rate was not very high.

The average attendance for the season was 756 per performance or 92.6 per cent of total capacity. The busiest month was January (97 per cent capacity) and the slackest December (80 per cent). The most popular production was *Tsar Fedor*, which was given 57 performances to more than 100 per cent capacity (through the introduction of extra seats) – an average audience of 826. The second most popular production was *Hedda Gabler*, despite being given only four performances, followed by *The Seagull* (eighteen performances to an average audience of 804). The least popular of the twelve productions was *Greta's Happiness*, performed only three times to average houses of 416 (51 per cent of capacity). *Antigone* and *The Sunken Bell* were next in popularity after the top three, with *The Merchant of Venice* a disappointing eighth, with average audiences over ten performances of 582 (71.1 per cent of capacity). The popularity of *Hedda Gabler*, which was badly mauled by the critics, might have had something to do with the fact that all four performances were given during the Shrovetide holiday.

The theatre had a single chief stage director, Stanislavsky, and three other directors – one of whom was managing director of the company, Nemirovich, and two who were also company actors – A. A. Sanin and V. V. Luzhskiy. Each director had two assistants, whose job it was to conduct rehearsals and keep a diary. These two divided the work between them but, following the departure of Kh. S. Zolotov, nearly all the burden of rehearsal fell on the shoulders of N. G. Aleksandrov.[4,5]

One hundred and twenty-one rehearsals were held at Pushkino between 16 June and 25 August before work transferred to the Sporting Club (38 rehearsals) and then, from 12 September, to the Ermitazh. By opening night, five of the season's productions had been prepared, four of which were re-stagings of work previously shown at the Society of Art and Literature or at the Philharmonic School. Apart from *Tsar Fedor*, two other new productions were almost ready by opening night – *Antigone*, which only needed the chorus and crowd scenes to be added (they had been rehearsed separately) and *The Seagull*, which still needed a few alterations. *The Tutor* and *Late Love* were also nearly ready. The remaining plays were rehearsed during the course of the season.

After 12 September, there were a further 159 rehearsals in the theatre, plus another five elsewhere, making a grand total of 323 occupying 1,100 hours. The average rehearsal length was three hours and the average number of rehearsals per production, twenty. The rehearsal graph shows that *Tsar Fedor* (74) was given more than twice as many rehearsals as *Antigone* (36) and *The Merchant of Venice* (35), and three times as many as *The Seagull* (26) and *Hedda Gabler* (24). Stanislavsky's work involved rehearsing nine plays, of which five were newly prepared versions of previous productions.

A saying coined by Stanislavsky and Nemirovich during their first meeting, which was postulated as a norm for the typical actor of the proposed 'star-free' theatre, ran something like this: 'Today Hamlet, tomorrow a spear carrier, but even when carrying a spear, the actor must still be an artist.' It became a rule that any actor could be called upon to play any role and understudying was adopted from the outset, not simply so that principals could be covered in the event of illness, but in order to give 'minor' actors in the company experience of acting 'major' roles. In the case of *Tsar Fedor*, because of the sheer number of rehearsals, it was discovered that almost every actor knew every other actor's part and all could have stood in for each other in almost any circumstances.

Because of the importance of crowd scenes as part of a general notion of 'ensemble', approximately seventy extras were drafted in to supplement the existing cohort of twenty-five supernumeraries. Crowd rehearsals were held separately until the state of preparedness was sufficient for integration into the production proper. Main responsibility for rehearsing the crowd scenes was given to A. A. Sanin, with the help of A. S. Solov'ev and two student crowd leaders.[6]

V. S. Kalinnikov, a teacher at the Philharmonic School who was appointed chief conductor, had the task of assembling an orchestra. This eventually consisted of forty musicians. In addition, there was an accompanist and a chorus director for those plays which demanded choral forces as well as solo performers. A children's and a male-voice choir as well as students of singing at the Philharmonic School and other musical-dramatic schools, plus a professional singer, were also enlisted.

The Head of Design, V. A. Simov, had his own private workshop and another which was rented for him. Some settings were hired from the Society for those productions which had already been staged there. Other sets, such as those for *The Sunken Bell*, were Simov's own work. There was also some 'doubling-up' of settings. For example, the set for Act Three of *The Seagull* was also used for *Greta's Happiness*.

The work of the costume department was especially onerous, as new costumes had to be made, or found, for a number of first-time productions. In his trips to the provinces when preparing *Tsar Fedor*, Stanislavsky proved himself an astute hunter-down of costumes and purchaser of materials. In this he was ably assisted by N. G. Stepanov-Zarayskiy. The directorate concluded a deal with the latter, who had his own costume workshop and was employed as the Art Theatre's chief costumier. He was engaged on fixed terms, according to which he was paid for each specially made costume. He was also required to hire out costumes from among his spare resources and use the money to hire, in turn, costumes for crowd scenes. This was especially necessary for productions such as *Tsar Fedor* which contained scenes, like the one on the Yauza river, in which dozens of extras needed to be kitted out. Work on costumes for that production was aided significantly by the needlework of Lilina, Knipper and others. Property items were also assiduously collected by Stanislavsky and those who accompanied him on his forays into the Russian countryside. These found their way into Stanislavsky's own personal collection and included old-fashioned weapons, ornaments and utensils.[7]

Responsibility for overseeing the repertoire and rehearsal schedules, the economic–administrative side of things and the functioning of both the theatre and the box-office was that of the Managing Director. Responsibility for the upkeep of the building, for the welfare of theatre staff, and for ensuring the orderly running of the house during performances, was that of the theatre's superintendent, Colonel L. A. von Fessing.[8] Specific individuals were responsible for making minor cash payments, keeping the books, posting details of rehearsals and issuing publicity hand-outs. It was the task of others to design posters or, in the case of G. D. Ryndzyunskiy, to keep an account of the theatre's activities during the season.

Posters and programmes were produced in the typographical style employed by the Imperial Theatres so that Art Theatre posters differed little from those produced to advertise plays at the Malyy or the Bolshoy. The distinctive, scroll-like Art Theatre motif at the top was the work of one of the actors, S. N. Sud'binin, who later became a sculptor. By special arrangement with the Theatre's owner, programmes were printed at the programme-sellers' own expense, and they were then allowed to keep the proceeds. The programme for *Antigone* included notes contributed by Sanin and Ryndzyunskiy designed to explain the nature of Greek theatre to the uninitiated. Programmes for productions given at the Sporting Club were financed by the club.

One striking thing about the history of the Art Theatre is the extent of its photographic record. It was the directorate's wish that a permanent record be kept of each production and that photographs be made available to the public. Through an agreement with the photographer, P. P. Pavlov, photographs of characters from *Tsar Fedor*, *Antigone* and *The Sunken Bell* were offered for sale in the theatre foyer with 20 per cent of the takings going to the theatre. The photographs of *Tsar Fedor* were used to produce a sheet of drawings offered for sale at twenty kopecks a sheet. The hundreds which were made sold out very rapidly.

Apart from the banning of *Hannele*, which had already been staged elsewhere and whose prohibition therefore seemed inexplicable, there were few problems with censorship during the first season. Nevertheless, permission was needed to stage *Tsar Fedor*, which had already been staged by Suvorin in St Petersburg.

Permission was also needed to stage *Antigone*, which had never previously been performed in Russia. In a number of instances, petitions to the city administration had to be made before even minor organisational decisions could be implemented. For example, permission was obtained from the Chief of Police to add extra rows of seats for charity performances as well as to sell photographs in the foyer. Similarly, the Governor-General had to be petitioned to allow children to take part in productions (on two occasions). Permission had to be granted by the Trustees of the Moscow Educational District before lectures by experts in connection with particular productions could be given.

On 13 October 1898, *Novosti dnya* announced that the Ermitazh Theatre had been completely transformed. The foyer, corridors and vestibules were a mass of tropical plants, doors had been removed and portraits put in their place. By the following week, all the furniture in the stalls area was to be replaced by plush seating ordered from Warsaw. A visitor from St Petersburg spoke of how

> You enter the theatre and are surprised. The first thing that strikes you is the curtain, unlike that of any other theatre, parting in the centre and made of soft, dark-green material decorated around the edge with a gold design. . . . The walls do not have the customary mouldings and gilt trimmings. Everything is painted in a grey hue of barrack-like coldness. It is true that to sit in the auditorium is a fairly awesome and uncomfortable experience, but the entire surroundings seem to demonstrate to the spectator that he is not here simply for amusement, and that his attention should be concentrated on the stage.
>
> (Belyayev 1902: 217)

5

ACTORS, SALARIES,
CONDITIONS OF
SERVICE

As late as 1902, the theatre historian and critic, Petr Morozov, was criticising traditional methods of Russian acting and particularly its dependence on notions of *emploi*: 'When a play is produced, each of the performers selects a role according to his "emploi" and essentially acquaints himself with his own part whilst concerning himself very little with the content of the play as a whole' (*Obrazovaniye* 1902: No. 33: 103–4).[1] Nemirovich and Stanislavsky rejected the standard definitions of 'hero', 'lover', 'fop', 'simpleton', etc., which produced narrow specialisation and reinforced clichéd acting styles. Stanislavsky noted that narrowness of *emploi*: 'depends on low intelligence in the actor. Thanks to narrowness of feeling and thought, these actors are deprived of subtlety and insight' (Stanislavskiy 1954–61: vol. 5: 180). In a letter to Suvorin, Nemirovich made the point that the contemporary repertoire demanded a different kind of actor: 'For example, if you were given permission to stage two of the most interesting plays in Russian drama – *The Power of Darkness* and *Tsar Fedor Ioannovich*, then you would need to find actors and actresses for these plays rather than lovers, ingenues, grandes dames, etc.' (Nemirovich-Danchenko 1979: 80).

The ideal actor was someone like Moskvin, who could move Stanislavsky to tears as Tsar Fedor and excite laughter as Yepikhodov in *The Cherry Orchard*. After graduating from Nemirovich's drama school, Moskvin had worked in the provinces and was already into his second season at the Korsh Theatre where he was being paid 100 roubles a month. Roksanova, another graduate of Nemirovich's and one of his favourites, had worked in Vil'no and Kiev, for 250 roubles a month. An 'outsider', like A. L. Vishnyevskiy, gave up an engagement of 500 a month to join the Art Theatre.

The Art Theatre's attitude towards its actors was commercially hard-headed and unsentimental, judging from the tone of Nemirovich's correspondence on the subject: 'To speak of an actor needing talent is as much as to say a pianist needs hands', he wrote to Chekhov. 'Why else did I select only eight from among seven groups of graduates from my school (out of a total of 70) and Alekseyev only 6 of all those he has worked with over the past ten years . . .' (Nemirovich-Danchenko 1979: 152). Nemirovich's attitude to his own 'brood' – Moskvin, Meyerhold, Knipper, Savitskaya, Roksanova, Kosheverov – was business-like:[2]

> The best of my brood continue to assert that they will act for us half-price. We must establish a yearly salary and then the figures would express themselves quite unlike those which we projected. Contracts for a minimum of three years. For example:
>
>   Moskvin: 1,200, 1,200 and 1,500 (1st, 2nd and 3rd years)
>   Petrovskaya [Roksanova]: 1,500, 1,800 and 2,100 (ditto)
>   Kosheverov: 1,200, 1,500 and 1,800 (ditto)
>
> These are high rates. The second rate will be – 600, 600 and 900. These rates will apply to a Dorine [i.e. the important role of a domestic servant in a Molière play] or to an actress playing a servant role.
>
> (90–3)

When debating whether to employ a certain V. V. Charskiy *or* Vishnyevskiy, Nemirovich suggested acquiring both, not as talented actors but as investments.[3] Of Vishnyevskiy, he wrote:

> he is an ideal premier, who would cost 5,000 but who will go on for 1,800. [. . .] I would even go further: both Vishnyevskiy and Charskiy! What do we risk? 3½ thousand. What do we gain? Freedom of action, peace of mind, substance in the troupe, great economy of forces and all this together is 3½ thousand returned with interest.
>
> (125)

He then suggests sending Vishnyevskiy the following matter-of-fact telegram:

> I would find your presence in our troupe very beneficial. All I can offer is 1,800 roubles in your first year with an increase, according to our rules, of 25% in your second and third years.

59

Salary on tour is half as much again, plus bag and baggage, rail fares at our expense.

(126)

When dealing with lesser fry, or with members of the orchestra, yet another tone obtrudes:

> Fessing and Snigirev are able to take part in our productions.[4,5] So, for the time being, I've offered them each 25 roubles a month (after all some of the extras each receive 25 roubles a month). Besides these, I've taken on Tarasov . . . who's on the same course as Kosheverov.[6] He has a fine figure, a strong bass voice and a handsome face. But he is rather immobile (although much better than Sud'binin). For 60 roubles a month. [. . .] Kalinnikov has already assembled an orchestra. His initial plans have exceeded all possible estimates. It turns out that we have to retain almost an entire opera orchestra, which is totally senseless. Even without the conductor's and harpist's salaries he won't get by for less than 9,000 roubles, which is a pointless and unnecessary luxury. Now we have to put down the following markers. (1) 6 – fully qualified, experienced musicians. (2) Upwards of 20 students of senior status. [. . .] They will come to us on single engagements, which will involve no more than 35 to 40 roubles a month [. . .] (3) Permanent harpist (for all plays). Thanks to this combination we can get by with an orchestra for not more than 6,000.

(146–7)

Two days later Nemirovich writes that he has found a workshop for Simov at a monthly cost of thirty-five roubles, compared to one found by Simov himself for 4,000 a year. He goes on: 'Yesterday I concluded an agreement with the chorus master of the famous (best in Moscow) Vasil'yev choir, which often takes part in Bolshoy productions, 20 singers for *Antigone*, for which he asked 60 roubles (I offered him 50)' (150).

Some actors, like M. E. Darskiy, were hired with particular roles in mind – in his case, Shylock. As a fully-fledged professional with some years' experience, Darskiy was furious at Stanislavsky's rehearsal methods, which involved his having to repeat the same thing time and again. Meyerhold, after his initial enthusiasm, also came to complain of the dictatorial methods employed by both Stanislavsky and Nemirovich (Meyerkhol'd 1976: 20–3).

From the outset, those who joined the company were interested in its co-operative aspect and accepted salaries which were certainly less than they would have received in more fashionable theatres. Not a season passed without the company's personnel changing, but there remained a solid kernel of permanence at the heart of the theatre, denoted by the fact that the company list for 1917 contained twelve names of those who were there on day one – Adashev, Burdzhalov, Vishnevskiy, Gribunin, Luzhskiy, Moskvin, Knipper, Lilina, Nikolayeva, Rayevskaya, Samarova and Khalyutina.[7,8] V. N. Pavlova, who joined in May 1899, was still on the production staff.[9] There were also other, long-standing members, who were not founder-members, such as V. I. Kachalov (joined 1900) and L. M. Leonidov (joined 1903).[10] Savitskaya had died in 1911 and Artem in 1914.

When the Art Theatre opened with a permanent company of thirty-eight, the Malyy troupe consisted of 118 (fifty-one actors and sixty-seven actresses), many of whose services were never called upon. In 1900, the Aleksandrinskiy troupe numbered 100.[11] During subsequent years, when the MAT troupe did not exceed forty-three, numbers at the Malyy fell slightly but, nevertheless, remained high. At the turn of the century, the Korsh Theatre employed a permanent company of between twenty-five and thirty. During the second season, the Art Theatre's complement of actors increased to forty-two and the overall number of performers rose to 170. Working on the scenario of the final act of Ibsen's *Pillars of Society*, Nemirovich proposed bringing on a crowd of 128 (Nemirovich-Danchenko 1979: 274). In a letter to Stanislavsky in July 1903, he refers to a crowd scene in the first act of *Julius Caesar*, involving 154 people (335). During the 1906–7 season, an attempt was made to regularise matters and co-opt extras as 'associate artists'. They eventually numbered forty-six. The Theatre also retained a supernumerary group of thirty-six, which meant that the company was operating with an acting complement of around 100, later reduced to ninety-three, two-thirds of whom were men (Orlov 1989: 27).

Whenever an actor or actress seemed ideal for their purposes, Stanislavsky and Nemirovich would make strenuous efforts to acquire his or her services. L. M. Leonidov was wooed from the Korsh Theatre in 1903 and paid the then unheard-of sum (in Art Theatre terms) of 4,200 roubles a year (he had been earning even more at the Korsh). Both men were prepared to 'tighten their belts' to the extent of offering Komissarzhevskaya 10,000 a year, despite the fact that the top female earners in the company, Knipper and Andreyeva, were only on 3,000. However, Komissarzhevskaya's demands were such – five major roles in a season – that the Theatre did not feel it could meet them. To have done so would have marked a return to the 'star' system and would also have threatened to infringe freedom of repertorial choice.

From the outset it was decided not to adopt the widely accepted form of written contracts. Despite the fact that, within ten years, the disadvantages of non-contractual service had become apparent, Nemirovich still stuck to his original position. As he stated in a letter to V. A. Telyakovskiy:

> In my own case, I have never entered into an agreement with anybody, my experience being that, if an actor wants to break away, then it isn't worth retaining him. Anyone working for the theatre is of interest to it in so far as, and just so long as, he is himself enriched by the theatre.
>
> (Nemirovich-Danchenko 1954: 284)

However, a consequence of engaging actors without contracts sometimes gave rise to financial loss. Having invited an actor to join the company whose contract to another theatre had not expired, the Art Theatre was obliged to pay compensation. Such was the case with one Kuznetsov, for whose services the theatre had to pay M. F. Bagrov, proprietor of a theatre in Odessa, a substantial sum in compensation. Likewise, if an actor left the MAT at a moment's notice and joined another company, the Theatre was not paid a kopeck in compensation, which could have contributed towards the hire of a replacement.

Contracts and conditions of service at the Art Theatre were matters of verbal agreement and corresponded to the ethical norms which prevailed. 'Agreements' obtained for three years rather than, as elsewhere, for one. Remuneration was calculated in advance for either two or three years, the Theatre retaining the right to either increase or decrease salaries, depending on individual effort. At the outset actors and other staff at the Theatre were paid modest salaries in comparison with other theatres. The maximum – 2,400 roubles a year – was earned by Darskiy and Kosheverov. This was higher than the women's maximum of 1,800. Roksanova, Sanin and Luzhskiy each earned 1,500 and five other salaries touched

1,200 a year. A significant number of the company were on annual salaries of between 660 and 900 roubles. Supernumeraries each received 360 and members of the orchestra from 715 to 900 roubles. Props-makers, costumiers and stage-hands received between 122 and 336 roubles a year.

On the production side two categories of worker were employed: (1) permanent, with an annual salary, and (2) seasonal. A few of the seasonal workers were taken on from year to year and so became, effectively, permanent members of staff (they were still paid seasonal rates, however). Between seasons, those on yearly rates were employed in the preparation and repair of settings for the next season's productions. When the company returned for the start of a season, supplementary workers were hired on specific terms for a certain number of months. For example, by 2 October of the seventh season, the theatre had fifty workers on its books, which reduced to twenty at the end of the season and prior to the period of touring. As a result, productions taken on tour tended to be 'economy' versions of those staged in Moscow and the settings were not so complicated or of so high a standard.

The first season revealed a lack of experienced, permanent stage staff with the result that, in the second season, their number was doubled to thirty-two. Staff numbers in the costume department were also increased by one-third. The design section, which was mostly involved in the building of sets, had grown to fifty by the tenth season and included painters, paper-hangers, modellers and wood and metal craftsmen. By 1918, even the properties department numbered as many as eighteen, largely as a result of more complicated sets and the invention of new effects. Lighting technology also improved dramatically over the period, the number of technicians increasing twofold by the tenth season, and swelling to fourteen by 1916.

Despite a limited budget, the Art Theatre attempted to attract the kind of actors it needed. Nemirovich wrote to Stanislavsky on this score as follows:

> You may meet with stubbornness on my part when it comes to expending spare thousands of roubles on painting the theatre, but at no time will you encounter obstacles to the invitation of a useful actor, or the removal of a useless one.
>
> (Nemirovich-Danchenko 1979: 92)

Beginning by paying relatively modest sums, the Theatre strove to increase remuneration over the years. Moskvin's original salary of 1,200 had risen to 3,000 by the second season, largely on account of his phenomenal success as Tsar Fedor. It was sometimes necessary to offer financial inducements to retain the services of a wanted actor, as occurred in the case of Uralov during the 1907–8 season.[12] To retain the services of Kachalov, the Theatre planned to pay him even more than he could earn at the Imperial Theatres – 10,000, rising in annual increments of 1,000 to 12,000.

By 1910, Art Theatre salaries were starting to keep pace with those at the Imperial Theatres. This had the unfortunate effect of reinforcing the discrepancy between the salaries of established actors and those starting out on their careers. Salaries for Knipper and Vishnyevskiy in 1911–12 were 5,400 roubles with an annual increment, for Knipper, of 300. Moskvin was to receive 7,500 for the same period rising to 8,100 over two seasons. In comparison, an actor starting out on his or her career could expect to receive something in the region of 900. In the 1911–12 season, when Alisa Koonen first appeared on the Art Theatre stage, playing Masha in Tolstoy's *A Living Corpse*, she was paid an annual salary of 1,500 roubles, a factor which may have contributed to her decision to leave.[13] The average annual wage for a working man with a family at the beginning of the century was around 350 roubles; that of a Moscow University professor, around 3,000.

Financial incentives included overtime – e.g. for a stage-hand who put in a couple of extra hours – and there were also rewards for 'extra effort'. The Theatre's designer was frequently not included in salary planning exercises as, in addition to his salary, he received regular increments for every stage-set which was ready ahead of or on time. Complaints at the lateness with which Simov carried out his work are constantly to be found in Stanislavsky's and Nemirovich's correspondence, alongside acknowledgement of his outstanding talent. One-off payments were also recognised rewards for effort. In the Theatre's first season, a cloakroom attendant, M. P. Grigor'yeva, and director's assistant, N. G. Aleksandrov, received such rewards. Non-financial rewards included honorific ones, such as the gold medals given to eleven members of the cast of *Tsar Fedor* on the occasion of its fiftieth performance. The other side of the coin was the administration of financial penalties. During the first season, for example, these were imposed on three occasions, amounting to a total of 62 roubles 50 kopecks – all of which was given to charity. Two of the fines must have been quite small as

Stanislavsky himself was fined 50 roubles for missing a rehearsal in December (Nemirovich-Danchenko 1979: 164).

The idea of creating a school attached to the Theatre was first mooted by Nemirovich in 1897. There had been a move since the beginning of the nineteenth century to introduce theatrical education into specially designated theatre schools. After 1856, which celebrated the centenary of the first Court Theatre, there was an increasing separation of operatic training from the balleto-dramatic. This in turn led, between 1880 and 1888, to the separation of dramatic education from the balletic. After 1888 (the year in which Stanislavsky founded the theatre school attached to the Society of Art and Literature) total differentiation in the various types of training was instituted.

The first major step towards improving theatrical education was taken in 1867 by E. Voronov, a director at the Aleksandrinskiy Theatre. He instituted the study of drama and the theory of stage art, aesthetics and rhetoric in addition to the study of expressive movement. It was felt that would-be actors also needed to learn singing, pantomime, dancing and fencing. Voronov began teaching in 1868 and was assisted by the appearance of a number of books, the most important of which were P. Boborykin's *Teatral'noye iskusstvo* ('Theatre Art', 1872), S. Kaftyrev's *Pervoye znakomstvo so tsenoy ili kratkoye rukovodstvo k izucheniyu dramaticheskogo iskusstva* ('First Acquaintance With the Stage or A Short Guide to the Study of Dramatic Art', 1873), F. Altman's *Prakticheskoye rukovodstvo k iskusstvu grimovat'sya* ('A Practical Guide to the Art of Make-up', 1873) translated from the German, and N. Svedentsov's *Rukovodstvo k izucheniyu tsenicheskogo iskusstva* ('A Guide to the Learning of Stage Art', 1874 and 1877). A number of private theatre schools were opened during this period and, in 1883, drama schools became attached to the Society of Stage Amateurs in St Petersburg and to the Philharmonic Society in Moscow, where Nemirovich taught. Ostrovsky was largely instrumental in establishing guidelines for theatre courses. These tended to be of three years' duration and were a mixture of preliminary, artistic-practical and scientific-theoretical training (Vsevolodskiy 1929: 184–99).

The establishment of a theatre school had been a theme of Nemirovich's speech to the All-Russian Conference of Stage Workers in 1897. In 1901, a class in 'dramatic art' was established within the Art Theatre under the direction of both founders, designed to prepare students for work in this theatre and no other.

A would-be applicant gave an audition, consisting of a verse and a prose text chosen by the candidate, before an Admissions Committee. On acceptance, the new recruit took morning classes in diction, declamation, singing, recitation, dance and juggling (the last to cultivate gesture and muscular agility). In the afternoons, he/she attended rehearsals and might take part in evening productions so as to become familiar with stage discipline.

The course was free of charge, the cost being compensated by non-remuneration of pupils for participation in current productions. Some took two years to reach the stage; others four. In her memoirs, Alisa Koonen describes improvisation sessions, which included waltzing with a stool; being your own grandmother; or pretending to be both a small and a large German who ran a beauty parlour and who talked to a client on the phone. Reading a poem in the manner of a schoolchild was yet another exercise. The first group of graduates staged extracts from various plays, including Ostrovsky's *Wolves and Sheep*, Nemirovich's *Gold*, Chekhov's *The Seagull*, Hauptmann's *Michael Kramer* and Turgenev's *A Month in the Country*.

Despite the flood of candidates, only a handful were admitted in any one year. The first intake, in 1901, was the most sizeable and consisted of ten male and twenty-seven female students. By contrast, in 1903, only seven were admitted; in 1905 only nine; in 1907 six, and in 1908 a mere five. Of sixty-eight applicants in 1906, only one was admitted. At the end of three years' training only the strongest, and most gifted, survived – the rest having been winnowed along the way. In 1902, the year in which Meyerhold left the Theatre, ten first-year students left the school to follow him. Of the seven students admitted in 1903, only three completed their final exams and of nine who entered the school in 1905, only four survived, among whom was Koonen.

The training course, which lasted either two or three years, involved the students' participation in main house productions, principally in crowd scenes. The more talented were rewarded with walk-on parts. The students also went on tour, as this was felt to contribute to their maturation as artists. From 1907, the principle of 'active participation' was fully introduced and all who passed the entrance exam were immediately included in crowd scenes with no practical exercises at all being undergone in Year One. Instead, the students received a monthly salary like everyone else. Each student's progress was monitored on a daily basis before he or she was finally accepted.

In May 1902, Stanislavsky wrote to V. V. Kotlyarevskaya:

> The first year's efforts of the school produced amazing results. Thanks to the practical tasks, the students in the first year act more interestingly, artistically and with more experience than any graduates in the final year classes of other institutions.[14]
>
> (Stanislavskiy 1954–61: vol. 7: 234)

A month later he wrote to the same correspondent:

> I would like to try and establish something in the nature of a manual for actor-beginners. I have a vague idea of some kind of grammar of dramatic art, a sort of coursebook of practical exercises. I will try it out at work in the school.
>
> (241–2)

In February 1904, Stanislavsky proposed creating a branch section of the troupe for permanent work in the provinces and for the dispersal 'among the broad mass of the people' of the cultural and artistic principles of the Art Theatre. These branch organisations were to ensure the 'practical development' of graduates of the MAT School and to serve as a source of recruitment to its main company (Stanislavskiy 1954–61: vol. 5: 207–10). The plan was unrealised.

There is little doubt that work in both the Theatre and the school added considerably to the load of both founders. In a letter to Chekhov of 7 November 1903, we find Nemirovich complaining:

> At 12.30 I have a lesson. At 2.00 another lesson. At 3.00 a rehearsal of two scenes from *Lonely Lives*. At 4.00 a meeting of the directorate. At the same time I have [...] interviews with 10 people who are of no use to anyone. That's my day for you.
>
> (Nemirovich-Danchenko 1979: 352)

6

SAVVA MOROZOV AND THE LIANOZOV THEATRE

Production costs in the Theatre's third season had risen to 100,000 roubles, nearly double those of the first. As a result, a decision was taken to renege on the idea of 'accessibility' and increase seat prices. If a full house recouped 950 roubles during the first season then, by the third, this had become 1,450 and, by the fourth, 1,550. Despite this, the Theatre faced financial crisis with losses of 52,500, plus a deficit from the previous season of 27,500. The situation was saved by one of the major shareholders, Savva Morozov, who stumped up the entire sum needed. None of the other shareholders was in a position to help, as their entire capital had been expended. At the end of the fourth season there was not even enough money in the kitty to pay for running expenses.

The Morozov family had made its money in cotton, expanded into railways and controlled two important Moscow banks. It employed 8,000 workers during the 1890s. Savva Morozov was a chemist by training and had received his practical education in England. Unusually for a wealthy capitalist, he was sympathetic to the Russian revolutionary movement and felt especially attracted to Gorky, whom he bailed out of prison in 1905 for 10,000 roubles. Gorky subsequently included aspects of Morozov's personality in his portrayal of powerful capitalists with contradictory natures, such as Yegor Bulychev. Morozov also admired Lenin, lending support to the Social Democratic Party and to its newspaper, *Iskra*. During the 1905 strike, much to his family's consternation, Morozov offered his workers a share of the firm's profits. Having entered the Syndicate for the Establishment of a Public-Accessible Art Theatre, in company with his brother, he became the most powerful member of the shareholding group and was largely responsible for ensuring the Theatre's survival. His relations with the Theatre, and especially with Nemirovich, were not always smooth and the latter's rejection of Gorky's *Summerfolk* combined with other factors to cause Morozov to break with it. However, this was not before he had financed, singlehandedly, the reconstruction of the Lianozov (Omon) Theatre on Chamberlain Lane (Kamergerskiy Pereulok) which, from 1902, became the Art Theatre's permanent home.[1]

In *My Life in Art*, Stanislavsky wrote warmly of this 'remarkable man' who was able not only 'to bring material sacrifice to the altar of art, but who could also serve art faithfully, unselfishly and without any love of self, ambition or thought of personal gain' (Stanislavski 1988: 316). Morozov undertook the supervision of stage and auditorium lighting at the Ermitazh, throwing himself heart and soul into the work, dressed in overalls and working alongside the electricians, much as he was to do when assisting with building work on the new theatre in 1902. Stanislavsky considered him 'touching in his enthusiasm, in his unselfish devotion to art, in his overwhelming desire to help the theatre in every possible way' (316).

Faced with financial crisis in November 1901, the Theatre was forced to work out a new pricing system which, had it been introduced, would have made it the most expensive in Russia. Nemirovich proposed introducing five classes of season ticket, the gross receipts from the most expensive being 4.5 times greater than the gross receipts of a full house in the first season. It was also proposed that maximum receipts for an evening performance be increased to 2,300. Such proposals were self-defeating, as their introduction at this stage would have priced the Art Theatre out of the market. Morozov's solution was to buy out all the other shareholders, becoming joint controller of the Theatre, alongside Stanislavsky and Nemirovich.

The latter objected strongly to this *fait accompli*. As early as February 1900, he had been writing to Stanislavsky in terms which suggested that Morozov's interest in the Art Theatre did not meet with his approval: 'I began this business with you, not in order for some capitalist to come along and make me into some kind of . . . what shall I say – secretary?' (MAT Museum, N-D Archive no. 1157). To which Stanislavsky countered:

> Morozov and you either cannot or will not come to terms. As is evident, quarrels and misunderstandings will occur and I will have to stand in the middle and receive the blows. No, that must not happen, as my nerves certainly won't be able to

stand it. Without you I do not wish to remain in this business. . . . Without Morozov, I am unable to remain – *not under
any circumstances.*

(Stanislavskiy 1954–61: vol. 7: 167–8)

However, once Morozov had expressed interest in Nemirovich's
play *In Dreams,* the latter reluctantly began to accept the idea of
the Theatre henceforth being run by a triumvirate.

The significance of Morozov's involvement lay in his capacity to
strengthen the financial basis of the enterprise: 'When the theatre
was materially exhausted, along came S. T. Morozov, bringing with
him, not only material security, but labour, cheerfulness and faith',
noted Stanislavsky in 1909 (vol. 5: 385). However, power relations
in the newly formed triumvirate were unequal, and Nemirovich
began to feel himself being sidelined as what he termed 'the Gorky
element' made its presence felt more strongly. Whilst informing
Gorky that *The Lower Depths* was a roaring success, Nemirovich
simultaneously expressed doubts to Chekhov, hinting that 'too
much Gorky' was dangerous. The 'backstage dirt', which Efros had
warned about, had become a fact of life now that Morozov had
assumed *de facto* control of the Theatre. Gorky, despite reservations,
was of the Morozov faction:

> When I see Morozov backstage at the theatre – covered in dust
> and anxious about the success of the play – I am prepared to
> forgive him all his factories, which he does not really need –
> and love him because I feel almost palpably in his peasant-
> like, mercantile, money-grubbing soul, a disinterested love
> of art.
>
> (Gor'kiy 1949–56: vol. 28: 133)

Chekhov did not share these feelings:

> Morozov is a good man but he should not be allowed too close
> to the essence of the business. He is capable of judging actors,
> acting and plays much as the public does, but not like a
> manager or a director.
>
> (Chekhov 1974–83: vol. 11: 280)

True to the ideals of the Theatre's founders, Morozov did not in
fact assume a dominant role but, instead, took the magnanimous
step of establishing the basis of a new shareholding company. After
prolonged deliberation, fifteen shareholders were nominated,

drawn principally from among members of the troupe. Apart from the triumvirate, they included Lilina, Aleksandrov, Vishnyevskiy, Andreyeva, Luzhskiy, Moskvin, Chekhov, Knipper, Samarova, Simov, Artem and one other outsider apart from Morozov – A. A. Stakhovich.[2] Excluded from the shareholding group, much to Chekhov's annoyance, was Meyerhold; as was Sanin – a fact which contributed to their joint decision to leave. Nemirovich tried to prevent Sanin's departure and wrote to Stanislavsky in the strongest terms:

> Sanin *must not be allowed to leave the theatre.* [...] such a worker as he is *so rare as to be virtually non-existent and certainly won't exist in the future.* We will lose an enormous backstage talent! [...] In the final analysis, Morozov could not care less, which is not the case with us. I consider it my sacred duty to the Art Theatre to utilise every available means.
>
> (Nemirovich-Danchenko 1979: 247)

Stanislavsky failed to prevent Sanin's departure, much to his regret. However, he was glad to be rid of the 'troublemakers', as he described Meyerhold and his followers.

Released from its debts by Morozov's munificence, the Theatre found itself with accumulated assets in the form of 100,000 roubles' worth of stage furniture, costumes, sets, properties and other items collected during the course of four years' work. However, the changed conditions still required working capital and not all shareholders possessed the ready means. Once again, Morozov took it upon himself to finance the company, lending various sums on credit for a three-year period. Thus, Stanislavsky was lent 15,000, Luzhskiy 6,000, and the others anything up to 3,000 each. In case of seasonal losses, Morozov offered to extend his credit to facilitate the topping-up of share instalments. He himself became the principal shareholder, owning shares worth 14,800 thousand roubles. Next came Stakhovich with 9,000. Stanislavsky's initial stake was 4,200, that of Luzhskiy, 4,000. With the 3,000 per capita of the remaining members, the sum of working capital was raised to 65,000 roubles – more than twice the amount of the original shareholding group.

The following year's work in the newly forged circumstances turned out to be the Theatre's first without a deficit. For the first time in five years, income was greater than expenditure. A third of the profits was distributed to the shareholders as dividend in proportion to the extent of their holdings. The remainder was ploughed back. Matters continued in this fashion for the next two seasons. Moreover, not only did the arrival of fresh capital permit the Theatre to continue its work, there were other important circumstances which enabled it, at a stroke, to increase the number of seats by about one-third, with a corresponding increase in the gross evening's receipts. The circumstances in question involved the acquisition of a new theatre building.

In the summer of 1901, Nemirovich had entered into negotiations with building firms for the construction of a purpose-built theatre. However, the lack of working capital and the colossal sums involved meant that the project was deemed unrealisable. Once again, Morozov came to the rescue. Out of his own pocket he financed the capital reconstruction of the Lianozov Theatre on Chamberlain Lane, just off Tverskaya Street (later Gorky Street) at the heart of Old Moscow which was also its commercial centre, a stone's throw from Theatre Square where the Malyy and the Bolshoy were situated and only a few minutes from the university.

The original building had been constructed by Prince P. I. Odoyevskiy, after the Napoleonic invasion, as a private residence. It was an imposing structure with a Greek portico front supported by six columns and flanked by two extensive wings. The building was purchased, in 1851, by a privy councillor, S. I. Rimskiy-Korsakov, son of a famous Muscovite noblewoman. He was responsible for remodelling the façade between 1852 and 1858, removing the columns, together with the single-storey building on which they stood, and constructing a third storey above each wing. In 1872, he sold the building to two merchants, M. A. Stepanov and G. M. Lianozov, who, in the course of the next ten years, decided on a general reconstruction of the building in order to accommodate a theatre within it. To this end, they invited M. N. Chikagov, one of a famous family of architects, to draw up plans for the conversion.

The new Lianozov Theatre, as it became styled, was then hired out to various private enterprises and, in an important sense, became a theatre of 'debuts'. Here, on 30 August 1882, as a direct result of the winding up of the Imperial Theatre monopoly, Fedor Korsh's Russian Drama Theatre opened with a production of Gogol's *The Government Inspector*. Inheriting the talented nucleus of the disbanded Brenko company, but lacking a rich patron or a civic subsidy, Korsh was obliged to appeal to a broadly popular audience to ensure reasonable receipts. To this end he introduced cut-price morning performances of classic plays and the plays of Ostrovsky. He also allotted a certain number of free tickets for schoolchildren and, on non-performance days, held literary-musical evenings. After three successful seasons, the theatre ran into financial difficulties and Korsh was forced to give up the Lianozov building.

He was followed by Mamontov's private opera company, which opened on 9 January 1885, with Aleksandr Dargomyzhskiy's *Rusalka*, this theatre having been chosen because it was the only one which possessed electric lighting. Mamontov was succeeded by a company led by Ye. N. Goryeva, whose tenancy was short-lived (1889–91).[3] She was followed by the future doyen of the Russian operatic stage, Leonid Sobinov, who later became an enthusiastic devotee of the Art Theatre, being especially taken with the soft sound of the gong which signalled the beginning of each performance and which had 'a pleasant, very special timbre' (Shestakova 1989: 37–8).[4]

The next period of the Lianozov Theatre's history, from 1 October 1891 until the arrival of the Art Theatre in 1902, was not especially distinguished. A certain 'Solomon' – 'a French citizen from Algiers', better known by his pseudonym 'Charles Omon', opened a *café-chantant*, the closure of which was frequently advocated (*Teatr* 1, 1984: 87–90). Stanislavsky attended a performance at the Omon Theatre (as the Lianozov became known) whilst doing the rounds of theatres which the company thought might serve its purposes. He was quite taken with the foyer but fairly appalled by the goings-on on stage (Stanislavski 1954–61, vol.7: 225).

The remodelling of the building was commissioned from F. O. Shekhtel'. The actual designs were produced free-of-charge and, because of the urgency, many had to be drawn up on the spot. Elaborations, such as the incorporation of a large decorated panel on the front of the building composed of iridescent blue-brown ceramic tiles crowned by an enormous theatrical mask, were never carried out. The transformation of the interior of the building was completed for a total of 300,000 roubles. Extensive work, lasting three months, continued during the spring and summer of 1902, supervised by Morozov, who not only worked but virtually lived on site. Apart from financing the reconstruction he also completely refurbished the interior, introducing the very latest in Western European lighting equipment, a revolving stage and many other refinements. Thus, the Theatre was able to open its fifth season, in October 1902, in a virtually new building equipped with the very latest stage technology.

The stage, with its seventeen-metre diameter revolve, continued to be equipped after the Theatre's opening, when the expertise which Morozov had acquired in lighting the Ermitazh stage came into its own. In 1903, a virtual power station of lighting equipment was installed, costing him an additional 59,000 roubles. A further wing was added containing a separate rehearsal stage and, for the first time, it became possible to rehearse in proper surroundings whenever the main house stage was occupied.

The new auditorium had a capacity of around 1,200 but one of the conditions which Morozov imposed was that normal gross receipts should not exceed 1,750 roubles, so that the Theatre retain some of its 'accessible' character, despite having abandoned the title. He hired the building out to the company at a comparatively low cost – 15,000 a year, the same as that charged by Shchukin for the hire of the Ermitazh. The building did not, in fact, belong to Morozov but to Lianozov, from whom Morozov had leased it for twelve years.

Shekhtel's plans were far-reaching and included remodelling the façade and refurbishing the interior – from the design of the stage curtain down to the shape of the house-lights, the style of the windows, and the lettering of the signs over the doors. The stage was brought closer to the auditorium to retain some of the intimacy of the Ermitazh and sightlines were improved so that even the cheapest seats were afforded a more ample view of the stage. The orchestra pit was filled in and the proscenium arch widened to approximately twenty-one metres so that it extended virtually the width of the auditorium. In the dispositioning of the seating, advantage was taken of the existing tiers and the open circle, without the usual divisions into boxes. The striking arc-shape of the proscenium opening, surmounted by a highly original and ornately painted frieze in *style moderne*, when set against a background of the subdued décor of the entire auditorium, had the effect of focusing the spectator's attention on the stage. The whole amounted to a unique example of organic co-operation between the artistic directorate and the theatre architect (Anisimov 1984: 50).

An article in *Russkiye vyedomosti* described the alterations. The façade of the old building had been retained but redecorated. It was now pierced by doors of original design and ornamented with wrought-iron awnings above each. The main building now had three entrances – the right, and nearest to Tverskaya Street, led to the gallery; the central entrance led to the stalls, and the left-hand entrance (nearest to Dmitrovka) led to the circle and boxes. The central entrance also afforded access to the ticket offices. The restructured auditorium had one level fewer than before, the stalls now occupying the space where the circle had been. The auditorium consisted of stalls (eighteen rows), with an aisle and, at the rear, an additional five rows of seats shaped to fit the horseshoe pattern of the auditorium. Rather unusually, another two rows of seats extended around the walls, facing the side aisles and side-on to the stage. The article continued:

> The auditorium has a very elegant appearance; the woodwork is painted dark, olive-green. The elegant design of the wooden seats is in the same tone with leather uppers. The lighting is in the form of cube-shaped lanterns, of pale-pink opalescent glass, disposed in discrete clusters along the sides of the boxes and fixed to the ceiling in the form of a circle, in place of the conventional chandelier.

The auditorium ventilation was innovative as were the spotlights above the proscenium arch – 'overhead footlights', which supplemented the usual forestage ones. For the convenience of the audience, two foyers had been provided, the décor of each being both simple and elegant with a complete absence of any pretentiousness or conventional theatrical plushness. The stalls foyer had been done out in dark wood with portraits of Russian and foreign writers hung on the walls, around the base of which plain benches had been placed at intervals. The men's and women's dressing rooms were on separate floors backstage, each furnished with a couch, writing-table, make-up stool and mirror, a marble washstand and a large wardrobe (Shestakova 1989: 49–50).

Other commentators added to some of the details mentioned above. The ventilation consisted of several apertures built into the floor which could admit either hot or cold air. In winter, hot air was calibrated to the required temperature and, whilst the system pumped this into the auditorium, it also expelled spent air into the street through underfloor vents. There was also another kind of ventilation system of regulated *fortochki* (small windows) placed throughout the building, which could add to the supply of fresh air without the disadvantage of draughts which conventional *fortochki* produced.

The interior doors and pillars were decorated with patterns of blue-green majolica. The upper halves of the dark-polished doors consisted of rows of small glass panels in mica-like material. The leather door-handles were fixed diagonally on panels lightly encrusted with zinc. The lower sections of the entrance doors were done in *style moderne* coloured-glazed tiling in a pattern which was repeated in the designs of the transoms in the upper halves of both the doors and the windows, made up of square segments of stained glass. Stylish bronze handles were fixed to the main entrance doors, and the lanterns on the building façade were of elegant, cubic design suspended from elaborate consoles.

The walls of the auditorium were painted pale-grey with a dark-olive frieze around the top, of non-figurative design, art nouveau or *style moderne* in appearance and reminiscent of the strings and curlicues of a cellist's fretboard. Below this was a bold floral motif consisting of a single, open-petalled flower spaced around the walls at regular intervals. The tip-up seats, the balcony and circle fronts were in polished oak, without any ornamentation. The house lights, consisting of opalescent cubes disposed in groups of three, were fixed to decorated plaque mountings at regular intervals around the front of the gallery and the circle, and hung from short bronze chains. The curtain consisted of a large grey serge cloth, with a brown frieze at the base, designed by Shekhtel', which formed a gentle and regular stylised wave pattern. In the centre, where both halves of the curtain met, were two darker, gold rectangles placed at about head height containing within them the white, stylised emblem of a seagull, or storm petrel, in flight. This sign, like a trademark, found its way on to all objects associated with the Theatre. At the front centre of the stage was the hood of the prompter's box and directly above it the 'overhead footlights' which hung from a stylishly wrought, ornamented iron bar extending the width of the proscenium. The lights were suspended from this on elegant chain supports, each designed of nine square links connected by nine rectangular ones.

The large, round metal frame of the central 'chandelier' was fixed to the ceiling with zig-zag pivots, which lent a sharp, dynamically agitated aspect to the ceiling ornamentation. This consisted of approximately forty silver-grey lines painted horizontally, some culminating in a zig-zag, 'lightning' effect, and depicted with such tension that they seemed to echo both the musical motif in the upper frieze and that of natural forces in the wave-pattern motifs. The rhythm of these lines was then repeated in the flowing and jagged forms above the proscenium arch. The darker colours tended to be in the lower section of the auditorium, gradually lightening as the gaze moved upwards, 'producing a juxtaposition of the "earthly" and the "airy" characteristic of the gothic style of the 1890s'. (Kirichenko 1973: 80–1).

The design of the vestibules, foyer, galleries and buffets served as a kind of prelude to the main auditorium. The muted ornamental murals, the small opalescent lights, the simple furniture, the soft carpeting – everything seemed anticipatory of the atmosphere which awaited the spectator in the auditorium. The vast public foyers were disposed on three sides of the auditorium, all with chevroned parquet floors, and containing a buffet salon as well as a smoking room and another buffet serving alcoholic drinks.

The theme of waves, symbolic of natural forces, was featured in A. S. Golubkina's sculpture, entitled *The Swimmer* which was added some months after the Theatre's opening and which came to dominate the Dmitrovka entrance.[5] Above the double door a large awning was suspended from chains beneath which was a sculpted relief of scattered human heads being engulfed by a stormy sea, topped by a large wave which threatened to overwhelm the head and upper torso of a powerful swimming figure. The swimmer's raised left arm, poised to take the next stroke, seemed to hold suspended the wave about to swamp both the swimmer and the heads of the other figures which emerged from the bas-relief above and around the upper halves of both doors. Hovering above the swimmer's head and the threatening tidal wave, the outline of a seagull or storm petrel was discernible. The hair on the swimmer's head and the foam of the overwhelming wave seemed to merge into one. The other human heads projected, in seemingly mute appeal, from the encircling lava-like, petrified wave-mass, resembling Pompeiian victims anticipating either burial or release, as if their ability to be freed depended on the efforts of the swimmmer to remain buoyant.

Looking at the sculpture today, the image of the swimmer appears an exceptionally powerful, muscular, quasi-heroic figure. This has the effect of making the wave appear also like a burgeoning tree, the trunk of which supports the swimmer's left pectoral, whose own extended arm then comes to form a thick, knotted branch of the tree whose overarching canopy of leaves are simultaneously a protective canopy as well as an engulfing deluge. It would seem to represent a synthesis of the 'art versus nature' motifs which run throughout the design of the building and which are a very precise reflection of key elements in the thought of the period deriving, amongst other things, from naturalist philosophy and the Idealist thought of those who admired Nietzsche. It is also interesting to note how, throughout the period of its early operations, Art Theatre productions were frequently of plays which, however neutral in themselves, tended to be given a slant in which much was made of the contrast between the world of ordinary mortals and that of enlightened or superior individuals – usually artists, social outcasts or quasi-supermen who could endure isolation or do battle with the elements, like the swimmer in the mural. This symptomatic (invariably male) figure, representative of some transcendent typicality or ideal, tended to be shown in contrast to the ineffectual average person or group, constantly threatened with inundation by the 'tidal waves' of Life, who are seen to be generally representative of spiritual nullity.

The first season in the new building opened on 25 October 1902, with a production of Gorky's *The Merchant Class*, which was preceded by tributes to Shekhtel' and Morozov. The newspaper *Kur'yer* reported that, in the new theatre, 'taste and simplicity go hand in hand' and, whilst recognising that one of the hands was 'the helping hand of a Maecenas', considered that what had been created was 'a masterpiece'. *Moskovskiy listok*, whilst regretting that there had been no curtain-call for the builders, considered that:

> An impression of thoughtfulness and taste lies over all. Everything is both severe and stylish. Nowhere do you find loud tones or colours. You immediately feel that you are entering the ante-chamber of a genuine 'temple of the arts'.

The atmosphere of the auditorium with its soft and unostentatious lighting, the curtain which parted soundlessly and ceremonially, all contributed 'in the fullest sense to the beauty of an artistic production . . . in which each detail retained the spirit of the whole and where there was nothing, including the brightly beautiful, to destroy the general harmony' (*Teatr* 1, 1984: 87–90).

Ironically in these circumstances, relations within the company worsened, largely as a consequence of disagreements over the extent of Morozov's influence. Nemirovich considered quitting the Theatre and Stanislavsky began to think that he himself would be forced out. The conflict was a logical consequence of the growing power of Morozov, whom Stanislavsky respected but Nemirovich did not trust. The Theatre seemed to be dividing into opposing camps. On one side, Nemirovich saw Morozov and Andreyeva (which also meant Gorky). On the other he saw himself and Stanislavsky (although their own relations were far from smooth), Lilina, Knipper and Vishnyevskiy. Where Luzhskiy and Kachalov stood he did not know (Nemirovich-Danchenko 1979: 316–20).

Nemirovich felt that the alliance between Morozov, Andreyeva and Gorky threatened to disrupt, if not destroy, the Theatre. In November 1903, he was talking of backstage 'Morozovitis', which was nervously debilitating but had to be endured (352). Andreyeva and Knipper were squabbling over parts, with the result that Andreyeva began to intrigue against Nemirovich who, she suspected, supported Knipper. Morozov was thought to be sowing dissension between Stanislavsky and Nemirovich. 'The merchant is just waiting for Alekseyev and Nemirovich to fall out', wrote Knipper to Chekhov (Knipper-Chekhova 1934: 317).

In February 1904, Andreyeva announced her intention to leave. In a letter to Stanislavsky, she declared that she had ceased to respect the Art Theatre's work: 'I believe in your talent. I do not believe in you as a person. You are not what you were' (Andreyeva 1961: 55). She signed a contract with Nyezlobin and went to work in Riga.[6] Soon, another rupture developed when Gorky's play, *Summerfolk*, was turned down by Nemirovich. Suddenly, Morozov announced that his feelings towards the Theatre had cooled. He left the group of shareholders and resigned his directorship. At the same time, he agreed not to withdraw his share of around 15,000 roubles but categorically refused to exercise his right to a decisive voice in the Theatre's affairs (Stanislavskiy 1954–61: vol. 7: 702). Shortly afterwards, the newspapers reported plans to open a theatre in St Petersburg, also designed by Shekhtel', whose artistic council would consist of Andreyeva, Gorky, Komissarzhevskaya and other prominent artists. Nobody doubted whose money lay behind the venture. However, all came to nothing when news arrived of Morozov's suicide whilst abroad in France, in Nice, on 13 May 1905. Within a week, Andreyeva announced that she wished to return to the fold and Gorky offered the Theatre his *Children of the Sun*, on condition that Nemirovich had nothing to do with staging it.·

Coupled with Chekhov's death the previous year, Morozov's departure and subsequent suicide were severe blows to the Theatre's fortunes. The revolutionary year of 1905 also plunged it once more into financial crisis. The three-year agreement concluded with Morozov ran out on 15 June 1905. A new joint-stock company was formed, to last for a further three-year period. Its members included most of the previous shareholders, with the exception of Andreyeva and Simov. They were replaced, semi-symbolically, by relatives of the deceased – Chekhov's nephew, Michael Chekhov, and Morozov's widow.[7] Somehow the company managed to raise working capital to the tune of 70,000 roubles, each shareholder contributing an equal amount of 5,000. The Theatre began to lose money. Wages and production expenses rose sharply. The total production budget for the first season had been 38,000, the bulk of which was spent on *Tsar Fedor* with its complicated sets and huge crowd scenes. By 1901, a comparatively straightforward production, such as *Three Sisters*, cost 25,000 whilst *The Snow Maiden*, with its elaborate sets and costumes, cost even more in the same year. In the sixth season, two very different kinds of production – *Julius Caesar* and *The Cherry Orchard* – cost exactly the same to stage – around 25,000 roubles each.

The first six seasons had seen costs more than double. However, the sixth season, in comparison with the fourth, showed a 43 per cent rise in costs. Prior to the 1904–5 season, thanks to Morozov, the Theatre had covered its losses and had managed not to exceed the gross receipts ceiling of 1,750 per performance which he had stipulated. However, with Morozov's departure, not only was his financial support lost in the long term, but the rent on the building was suddenly increased from 15,000 to 53,000 roubles. There was also the additonal cost of the building's upkeep, which Morozov had previously met. In 1907, the Theatre managed to secure Morozov's widow's agreement to lower the annual rent on the building to 30,000 but when, in 1914, the lease on the building ran out, it reverted to the original owner, Lianozov, who promptly re-established a yearly rate of 53,000.

It soon became apparent that a rise in seat prices was inevitable and, during the eighth season, gross receipts for a single perform-ance rose to 1,800 roubles. At this point, Nemirovich reverted to his previous idea of a season ticket system. Those who bought 'first-class' season tickets would buy the right to attend every première; 'second-class' season ticket holders bought the right to see all second performances of new productions; third-class holders, the third performance, and so on. Each season ticket also permitted the holder to see productions from previous seasons. A production attended by season ticket holders only generated gross receipts of 2,200, or 20 per cent higher than normal. Higher seat prices enabled the Theatre to end its seventh season in the black.

Signs of revolution grew throughout 1905. On 14 October, in the middle of a dress rehearsal of Gorky's *Children of the Sun*, all the lights in the theatre went out. A general strike had begun. The Theatre's expenses were cut to the level of their second season, with the result that workers were laid off and salaries lowered. Average gross receipts per performance in October and November only just topped the 1,000 mark. A crisis decision was taken to embark on a foreign tour. At the beginning of February 1906, an acting company of twenty-seven, headed by Stanislavsky and Nemirovich, accompanied by eighty-five others, set out to give sixty-two performances in eleven Western European cities during the course of three months. The critical acclaim was considerable and the tour was an artistic success. Despite the accolades, however, it proved a financial failure. On this occasion the Theatre was bailed out, to the tune of some 30,000 roubles, by Nikolay Tarasov and Nikita Baliyev.[8,9]

Still more money was needed to open their ninth season. It was decided to increase the number of shareholders and invite Tarasov and Baliyev to join, plus other newcomers, on the basis of 5,000 roubles each. Another means of raising money was devised through encouragement of small investments and, by the eighth season, the Theatre was receiving 67,000 roubles from outside investors alone. However, most of the working capital had been eaten up during the 1905–6 season and, despite income exceeding expenditure at the end of the ninth, the Theatre still found itself 35,000 short of the capital sum needed for its continued operations. Once again, prices were increased. The evening gross receipts which averaged 2,100 in the ninth season had risen to 2,300 by the tenth. The price of first-class season tickets was increased so that a full house at premières grossed as much as 3,000 roubles, later rising to 4,850.

Despite Nemirovich's call for economies, only one production cost less than 28,000 during the tenth season. The cost of staging Maeterlinck's *The Blue Bird*, in the eleventh, was 26,000, half of which went on the music composed by Ilya Sats.[10] There was also an author's payment to Maeterlinck of a further 16,000. The settings alone for *Hamlet*, in the 1911–12 season, cost 43,000 and Craig had been paid a total sum, since November 1908, of 14,500 roubles. This last was more than the entire cost of *The Brothers Karamazov* (11,500) which ran over two evenings. What is more, it was given eighty-three performances to *Hamlet*'s forty-seven, the former grossing twice the receipts of the latter.

Instead of being the most accessible, the Art Theatre was rapidly becoming the most expensive in Russia. The years of the First World War saw further price increases, this time at the behest of the government, which increased the tax on theatre tickets by an average of 30 per cent from 22 November 1915. Only tickets below thirty kopecks remained exempt. The Art Theatre consequently increased its proportion of cheap seats and decreased the number costing betwen twenty and twenty-five roubles. This had the effect of lowering the overall takings but retained the level of gross receipts for a single performance at around 2,700. In the meantime, the price of heating and electricity had risen to five times that of the first season.

It was not until 1911 that an agreement between the shareholders was drawn up in anything like an official, legal form. The result was a complicated document running to fifty-two paragraphs, designating the owners of the firm called The Moscow Art Theatre Ltd to be K. S. Stanislavsky and Vl. I. Nemirovich-Danchenko, whilst its assets remained at the disposal of the group of shareholders, whose membership had increased from sixteen to twenty. The largest share, of 23,500, belonged to Stakhovich. Responsibility for the Theatre's overall direction was given, by unanimous vote, to Nemirovich and he was simultaneously assigned a salary, over and above his dividend, of 18,000 roubles a year, about the same as the then prime minister.

In 1916, both founders took the decision to hand the firm known as The Moscow Art Theatre Ltd over to the shareholders on a permanent basis and, in April 1917, a new group of shareholders was created who re-christened themselves a 'co-operative'. How practically effective this new form of co-operative ownership would have been is uncertain, as the October Revolution intervened and the Theatre was brought under state control.

Part II

THE MOSCOW ART THEATRE REPERTOIRE 1898–1917

7

FIRST SEASON:
1898–1899

The Theatre's output, play by play, during the period 1898–1917 gives an impression of both development and exploration. It also shows how responsibility was shared and how uncertain achievement and popular success could be. Either as actor and/or director Stanislavsky is associated with the Theatre's major successes, but he was also responsible for many failed productions. In addition, Nemirovich-Danchenko contributed to successful productions such as *Three Sisters* and *The Lower Depths* as did Sanin, Luzhskiy and the two assistant directors.

TSAR FEDOR IOANNOVICH

As late as May 1898, no firm decision had been taken as to which play would open the first season. Nemirovich's preference was for Sophocles' *Antigone*, followed by *The Merchant of Venice* and with Aleksey Tolstoy's play as the third première of the season. However, by the time rehearsals began in June, a decision had been reached to begin with *Fedor*, which Stanislavsky clearly saw as the trump card in his directorial pack. He wrote the bulk of the score, with the exception of the key scene on the bridge over the Yauza, during June, and rehearsals began on 7 July. The director's score for the Yauza scene, which proved so successful with the public, was not ready until 12 September, a mere four weeks or so before opening. The scenes involving representatives of the Church were still included at this stage and, only on 24 August, when Nemirovich reported the censor's permission to perform the play, did it become apparent that one of the conditions imposed included omission of all the religious characters. This entailed wholesale alterations when the play had already been in rehearsal for over a month.

Stanislavsky made the first of three excursions to the Russian countryside in search of material for the production at the end of May 1898. In Rostov-Suzdal'skiy he visited churches and museums and collected various property items. Here he sketched plans of a restored palace and its treasures, spending a night there by candle-light so as to absorb the atmosphere. He listened to the bells and / noted their rhythms. At the beginning of June he travelled, together with Simov, Sanin and a group of actors, to Rostov-Yaroslavskiy and other towns along the Volga river, where they familiarised themselves with various aspects of Russia's medieval past. On 12 June, Stanislavsky observed in his notebooks: 'Nearly all the models for *Tsar Fedor* are ready. I have never seen anything more original or more beautiful. . . . This is the *genuine* past, not something dreamed up by the Malyy Theatre' (Bassekhes 1960: 19). On 5 and 6 August Stanislavsky was in Nizhniy-Novgorod, where he discovered properties and other items discarded by a local monastery, which he picked up at the local market. These he bought in bulk, including oriental couch covers, samples of head-wear, ancient bridal headdresses, footwear, shawls, scarves, belts, brooches, wooden drinking scoops, wooden plates and much else.

The choice of play was intriguing. According to Simov, Stanis-lavsky had shown little interest in Russian history or the Russian past prior to his work on *Tsar Fedor*. He was familiar enough with the world of Spaniards, Moors and Italians but was generally ignorant when it came to the manners and mores of 'aboriginal boyarism' (Guryevich 1948: 283). The play is the second in a trilogy dealing with the final days of the Rurik dynasty. Set in the late sixteenth and early seventeenth centuries, the trilogy chronicles the last days of Ivan the Terrible (Part One); the unstable rule of his successor, Tsar Fedor (Part Two); and the *smutnoye vremya* (troubled time) presided over by the scheming usurper Boris Godunov (Part Three). *Tsar Fedor* was written in 1868 but forbidden performance by the tsarist censorship. Eventually, an amateur production was given in St Petersburg, in 1890, but the first professional pro-duction was at Suvorin's Theatre there, just two days before the Art Theatre's own production.

The three plays span three successive reigns from 1533 to 1604 and dramatise an epoch in Russian history which is roughly parallel to the height of Tudor power in England. The action of *Tsar Fedor* is set during the middle of that pious and weak monarch's reign (1584–98) and, besides being influenced by Shakespeare, contains other interesting historical links and parallels to the Tudor age. The Russia which we see in the drama has been exhausted by the bloody fanaticism of Ivan the Terrible, whose insane temper has done to death Fedor's elder and abler son. Fedor has succeeded prematurely to the throne, real power being exercised during his minority by the Prince Regent, Boris Godunov. The Fedor we meet in the play has grown up and reigns ineffectually over a country torn by factional disputes among the boyars. The two principal opposing groups are led by Fedor's Imperial Chancellor and *éminence grise*, Boris Godunov, and by Prince Ivan Petrovich Shuyskiy. These two represent a struggle between declining and ascending historial epochs, ancient and modern. Shuyskiy is spokesperson for traditional feudalism, whereas Godunov stands for a much more contemporary, Machiavellian sense of political expediency and *realpolitik*. Striving passionately to compose these feuds, but powerless in his vacillation and pious religious confusion to affect their course, Fedor finally and helplessly concedes to the inevitable logic of Godunov's succession.

In Act One, Prince Ivan Petrovich Shuyskiy attempts to rally the clergy and merchants of Moscow in an effort to curb the power of Godunov. The former Prince Regent has reinforced his own power with the tsar's marriage to his sister, Irina. Shuyskiy utilises the childlessness of the marriage as a pretext to get the clergy and merchants to sign a petition for its dissolution and for Fedor's marriage to Princess Mstislavskaya, Shuyskiy's own niece. Not only would this give hope of producing a successor but would also strike directly at Godunov's power. Mstislavskaya is already engaged to Prince Shakhovskoy but this does not trouble the conspirators in the slightest, especially since Shakhovskoy is of the Shuyskiy faction and his compliance is taken for granted. For Tolstoy, this is no simple confrontation between Godunov's 'black' and Shuyskiy's 'white', but both are guilty of comparably devious measures in order to get their own way. However, Godunov's consciousness of his pursuit of power appears preferable to Shuyskiy's self-deceptive conspiratorial strategies; masquerading as altruism and concern for the social good, these render him the more vulnerable because he lacks a clear perception of his own motives. Pathetically devoted to the feudal institution of tsarism and tsarist authority, he is caught in a trap of his own making which is undermining that same institution. Godunov is unsentimental about tradition, being mainly concerned with the *effective* operation of power.

Godunov counters Shuyskiy's conspiratorial move by feigning reconciliation in the presence of Fedor and, immediately afterwards, by causing Shuyskiy's supporters to be arrested. Shakhovskoy also proves less inclined to give up Mstislavskaya than had been assumed. The naive and trusting Fedor, more devoted to the Holy Spirit than to Holy Russia, is pathetically grateful for what appears to be reconciliation between the warring factions, but his joy is short-lived. Hearing that Godunov has arrested his supporters, Shuyskiy resolves to rouse the people against Godunov; he, in turn, demands that Fedor sign a warrant for Shuyskiy's arrest. Fedor refuses. However, when he learns of the Shuyskiy-inspired plan to separate him from his wife and remarry him to Mstislavskaya, the tsar signs a warrant for the arrest of the entire Shuyskiy clan.

The background to these events is a Tartar advance on Moscow and Godunov's scheme to oust a rival claimant to the throne, in the person of Dmitriy, a son of Ivan the Terrible by one of his many 'wives', whom Fedor considers his step-brother and rightful successor. Godunov contrives the appointment of a new nurse for Dmitriy, with less than benevolent intent. In its final dramatic moments, the play brings together the death of Shakhovskoy in a brave attempt to lead the people to free Shuyskiy from prison; report of the 'suicide' of the incarcerated Shuyskiy, and the news that Dmitriy has 'accidentally' met his death through falling on a sharp instrument. Fedor concedes, hopelessly, that Godunov has triumphed and empowers him to defend Moscow against the advancing Tartar hordes; he bewails the fact that God should have decreed that he, Fedor, ever became Tsar of Russia.

According to P. P. Gnedich, who directed the 1898 St Petersburg production, the play (indeed the entire trilogy) was written under the influence of Casimir Delavigne, Shakespeare and Edward Bulwer-Lytton. He also suggested that Godunov combined traits of Macbeth and the then Russian Minister of the Interior, Timashev (Varneke 1971: 408). Others have pointed to resemblances between Fedor and Shakespeare's Henry VI. Another instructive parallel, not previously suggested, is the conflict between the 'ineffectual' and 'helpless' Richard II and the politically skilful usurper, Bolingbroke. There is also an indirect debt to Shakespeare via Pushkin's *Boris Godunov*, as conveyed through Mussorgsky's opera.

Stanislavsky's own view of the historical period was informed by a Russian translation of the writings of Giles Fletcher, who was sent as English ambassador to Russia in 1588 and reported on conditions there.[1] Fletcher's work was translated into Russian during the first half of the nineteenth century and has been plundered consistently by Russian historians. Another source was an account of his journeying in Russia given by Sir Thomas Smith to George Wilkins in 1605, which was published in Russian for the first time in 1893. Smith was a witness to the bloody finale of these events. In 1605, he wrote that the history of Godunov was 'like a theatrical play ending in catastrophe . . . worthy to stand alongside *Hamlet*' (Rostotskiy and Chushkin 1940: 44).

Some critics complained of the historical inaccuracy of the production, arguing that the kaftans worn on stage belonged to the seventeenth and not to the sixteenth century. However, Stanislavsky felt that artistic integrity was more important than complete historical fidelity. As he said to Simov, 'most important is to stage things in such a way that they can be believed in' (Vilenkin and Solov'eva 1980: 22). In fact, the drama itself plays fast and loose with historical accuracy, compressing into a short time-span events which were widely separated. The deaths of Shuyskiy and Dmitriy, which are announced simultaneously at the end of the play, in fact belonged to the years 1589 and 1591 respectively. Shuyskiy's conspiracy took place in 1587 and the gift of monkeys from the Emperor Rudolph referred to occurred in 1597. In the play, Shuyskiy is said to have hanged himself in prison. In fact he died abroad in exile, in 1589, two years after the discovery of the conspiracy.

According to the author, the subject of *Tsar Fedor* was the struggle for power between two political parties – the representatives of reaction and those of reform. Other remarks Tolstoy made help to explain how the Art Theatre interpreted the play. The sense of tyranny (in the first play of the trilogy) was being countered in *Tsar Fedor* by an upsurge of thrusting life like the return of spring to the earth following a welter of repression – a brief flowering of popular passion and energy before the autumnal reign of Boris Godunov (25). This feeling was certainly apparent in the *mise-en-scène* for 'the feast' in Scene One and in the energetic scene on the banks of the Yauza river (Scene 8). It was also visually present in the sumptuous colours of the costumes and in the exotic décor which Simov provided for the interior locations.[2]

A talented theatre designer, Simov was also a genre painter of stature. The exterior scenes and, in particular, the crowd scenes were frequently described as evidencing the influence of nineteenth-century Russian painting.[3] Writing to his wife, Meyerhold described the décor:

> In terms of originality, beauty and truth the décor for the settings can go no further. You can look at them for hours and never tire. . . . Especially beautiful is the décor for Sc. 2 of Act 1, 'A Chamber in the Tsar's Palace'.

He also described the highly original set for Shuyskiy's garden (Scene 4) where 'trees' were placed across the forestage, filling the proscenium opening, creating a trellis-like effect and with action proceeding between and beyond this 'tree-screen', lit by moonlight and with the porch of Shuyskiy's house in the background (Meyerkhol'd 1976: 19).

The heroes of the production, according to Nikolay Efros in a review published in *Novosti dnya* on 20 October 1898, were 'the *mise-en-scène* and Mr Moskvin'. In a performance of originality and power, Moskvin's interpretation lent emotional unity to a production which was, otherwise, in danger of becoming a series of striking scenes. Stanislavsky had imagined the role as that of a folkloric wise saint or an Ivan the Fool. Initially there had been five candidates for the part – Meyerhold, Moskvin, Adashev, Krasovskiy and Lanskoy, who all alternated the role in rehearsal.[4] Stanislavsky favoured Meyerhold. In the event, Moskvin alone played Fedor until Kachalov took over the role, followed by Khmelev.[5] Meyerhold played Prince Vasiliy Shuyskiy, and Knipper played Princess Irina – a role which brought her to Chekhov's notice when he attended a rehearsal in October. He wrote to Suvorin:

> Incidentally, before leaving Moscow I was at a rehearsal of *Fedor Ioannovich*. I was pleasantly moved by the intellectual tone and by the breath of true art which wafted from the stage, although there were no outstanding performers. Irina, in my opinion, is magnificent. Voice, presence, warmth – it was so splendid that it brought a lump to your throat. Fedor seemed to me rather inferior, Godunov [Vishnyevskiy] and Shuiskiy [I. P. Shuyskiy – played by Luzhskiy] good and the old man [Kuryukov played by Artem] marvellous, but best of all was Irina.
>
> (Yarmolinsky 1973: 315)

In his 'Project for a Production of *Tsar Fedor*', Tolstoy noted that the central role demanded subtle and complex work by the interpreter – especially since the tragic element and a touch of the comic 'flow together like rainbow colours in a shell', a foil to set the other off and 'lightly colour the pure soul of Fedor' (Rostotskiy and Chushkin 1940: 46). It was this element which Moskvin managed to convey and which was apparent from the moment he entered, having just been thrown by his horse:

> In he ran, slightly out of breath . . . then threw off his short fur coat, and wiped his broad face and neck with a lilac-coloured silk kerchief. The little peasant-tsar, small, sickly, his hair framing a slightly puffy face of a yellowy-whitish tinge which looked as if he had just been crying, a guilty smile playing about his faintly trembling mouth.
>
> (*Novosti dnya*, 20 October 1898)

Moskvin managed to convey the impression of both spiritual and physical lassitude, as of someone with a weak heart and little time to live. Nemirovich saw parallels between this Fedor and Hamlet – a man incapable of action whilst others (like Fortinbras) pursue their goals singlemindedly over the corpses of the dead (Stroyeva 1973: 25–32). This feeling of mortality in Moskvin's performance was recorded by Stanislavsky when auditioning him: 'Meyerhold produces the feeling that Fedor is Ivan the Terrible's son; Moskvin's Fedor has just a year's more life left to him; Platonov's [Adashev's] is good-natured and fussy' (Vinogradskaya 1976: 236).

Stanislavsky had initially thought everyone, apart from Meyerhold, 'too stupid' for the part. However, at a rehearsal on 18 September he was moved to tears by Moskvin who had been coached in the role by Nemirovich. The other major role, of Prince Ivan Petrovich Shuyskiy, was played by Vasily Luzhskiy as a severe, law-abiding individual, in no sense a fanatic, but with firm ideas born of a sense of duty. Physically, one felt the unbending, stubborn neck of someone who found it easier to prostrate himself at another's feet than to bow or bob the head in acquiescence or servitude (31).

Stanislavsky performed the tiny, but important role of the minstrel on the occasion of the production's fiftieth and one hundredth anniversaries. He also performed some of the minor religious roles during the company's European tour in 1906 when Russian censorship laws could be ignored. He also took over the part of Ivan Petrovich Shuyskiy when reviving the production for the company's American tour in 1923–4. Clad in chain mail, made-up to look like the Lord of Hosts, with a long grey beard and wielding a huge broadsword, Stanislavsky's Shuyskiy seemed more reminiscent of a romantic viking or *bogatyr* of heroic legend than a sixteenth-century Russian prince. It was said at the time that, had Nemirovich been in charge, he would never have allowed it. Others suggested, ironically, that a more self-aware Stanislavsky would not have permitted it either. His Shuyskiy was described as a grown-up child, naive and helpless in the world of political intrigue, who hid a tender heart beneath the severe exterior of a *voyevoda* (Rostotskiy and Chushkin 1940: 149). Stanislavsky's Shuyskiy entered the state apartments clad in armour and carrying his massive sword unsheathed – something which court etiquette did not permit but which was designed to illustrate the character's open spontaneous nature. Stanislavsky also contrived a comic touch when, excitedly anxious to hear the tsar's response to a question, Shuyskiy let fall his sword which struck the floor with a resounding clang (146).

It took Luzhskiy years to discard the more exotic elements of his Shuyskiy interpretation, whereas Vishnyevskiy's Godunov thrived on the picturesque. His performance was characterised by a sculptured expressiveness composed of broad, flowing gestures and static poses combined with an elevated, ceremonially declamatory way with the verse. For the final confrontation between Godunov and Fedor, Vishnyevskiy conveyed an irreproachable, mask-like, coldness which derived less from a sense of innate cruelty than from a gift for abstraction and an unrelenting sense of political necessity. This contrasted with Fedor's lack of will and permanent desire to absent himself from the necessities and decisions of power. Godunov's 'It must be!' (*'Nado!'*) was countered by Fedor's childishly wilful 'I won't have it!' (*'Ne khochu!'*) (Vilenkin and Solov'eva 1980: 43).

Crucial to the depiction of Boris was his environment, which became a projection of some future dream of an earthly paradise founded in reason, the attainment of which necessitated present political expediencies. If Shuyskiy's accompanying imagery consisted of house, feast and orchard, Godunov's persona found its likeness in the murals of his chamber. This was a literal representation of a heavenly city as described by ancient scribes. However, a sense of iron-willed necessity as a prelude to entering the gates of paradise was thematically present in the décor:

The walls of these paradisal chambers were held together by iron clamps – a motif which is a familiar feature of ancient buildings but which, in a décor connected with Godunov, could be perceived metaphorically as well.

(32)

Aleksey Tolstoy characterised Godunov as someone whose actions, 'however cruel, must be seen as less the actions of an ambitious man than those of someone who has a nobler aim at heart – the good of the entire country' (Rostotskiy and Chushkin 1940: 53).

The director's score for *Tsar Fedor Ioannovich* is incomplete, in so far as Stanislavsky planned only six of the ten scenes. It was also composed at intervals and not all the sections are in Stanislavsky's own hand. The first scene of Act One, 'The House of Prince Ivan Shuyskiy', retitled 'The Feast at Shuyskiy's' and moved from an indoor to an outdoor setting, is written by Stanislavsky. The second and third scenes have been written by Sanin, with the exception of the episode involving Kuryukov (an old man of the Shuyskiy faction) which is by Stanislavsky. The fifth scene has been done by Stanislavsky with the exception of a few pages, which are again the work of Sanin. There are no director's comments pertaining to Act Five and two scenes are omitted from Act Four – 'The House of Ivan Petrovich Shuyskiy' and 'Godunov's House'. The seventh scene – the 'Tsarina's Quarters in the Palace', to which Stanislavsky gave the title 'The Saint', contains only a few jotted comments. Scene Eight – 'The Banks of the Yauza' – is worked out in considerable detail in a separate prompt-book, which otherwise contains little apart from details concerning lighting and the following list of scenes: (1) Shuyskiy's Feast (2) —— (3) Reconciliation (4) Garden (5) Boris's Resignation (6) Shuyskiy's Conspiracy (7) At Godunov's (8) The Saint (9) Yauza (10) —— (11) Archangel Cathedral. Scenes Two and Ten were not given titles.

The production subsequently underwent cuts, largely because the crowd scenes proved too costly and complicated to tour – which meant that St Petersburg did not see the production until 1910 when a version excluding the scene on the Yauza toured there. During the first overseas tour in 1906 the production was cut to seven scenes (omitting Scenes One, Six and Eight).

The key to Stanislavsky's conception derived, possibly, from Tolstoy's statement that in a genuine tragedy the dominant feeling is the awakening of the earth to life and the rhythm and movement associated with this. Stanislavsky discovered distinct rhythms for individual characters and scenes. The rhythm of the opening feast merged with that of the conspiracy; the rhythm of state ritual with that of revolt; the rhythm of formal and cultivated etiquette with the flowing rhythm of domestic life. This 'polyrhythm' of life was felt to be like the spirit of the Russian national character itself (Vilenkin and Solov'eva 1980: 33–4). Seeing the first scene less as a conspiracy than as a feast of celebration, Stanislavsky moved it into the open air as if it were happening on a roof overlooking Moscow. To this end, Simov designed a broad, covered gallery supported by thick wooden columns which seemed to be built on an invisible lower storey. Beyond this raised gallery, ringed by a balustrade, the audience was treated to a view of the steep slopes of the house roofs and, receding into the distance, the rooftops of Moscow.

A specially composed overture introduced the play which began with Andrey Shuyskiy's opening words: 'I place great hopes in this affair', which, on opening night, appeared to Stanislavsky to have a double significance. He himself provides an effective description of the opening scene with the covered terrace disappearing round a corner of the house, giving the impression that action continued off-stage. He describes the colourful costumes of the boyars and the procession of servants carrying platters of roast fowl, chines of beef, mountains of fruit and their rolling barrels of wine on stage (Stanislavskiy 1988: 272–3).

The score begins with a list of stage directions to accompany the opening of the curtain, as well as cues for the hubbub to die down so as to permit those speaking to be heard. Two stewards pour mead into wooden jugs, while another rolls in a barrel of wine. Nine others carry in huge dishes piled with meat and fruit. A steward sips the drinks before handing them to the guests, hinting at a way of life in which the fear of poisoning is an everyday concern. The same steward, Starkov, then sets off at the end of the scene to denounce his master with the same sense of mechanical servitude with which he has performed his drink-sampling. As he conveys his intentions to the audience, Stanislavsky has him perform his usual menial tasks, casting the dregs from the cups onto the 'roofs' as he cleans out the goblets. Starkov acts as a foil to Shuyskiy, in whom notions of service and conspiracy are also woven together seamlessly.

At the point where everyone lines up to sign the petition calling on Fedor to divorce Irina and take Mstislavskaya as his wife,

Stanislavsky suggests that they line up in a queue 'like people at a railway station ticket office'. The signing is accompanied by local detail such as Vasiliy Shuyskiy dipping the pen in the ink before handing it to Ivan Petrovich, who 'tucks up his sleeve' before signing and 'having taken the pen in his fist' then 'wipes the nib with his hair'. The signing ceremony proceeds 'in total silence' (Vilenkin and Solov'eva 1980: 83 / Tolstoy 1922: 4).

In the following scene, the production score seeks to evoke the tender relationship between the tsar and the tsarina which the Shuyskiy faction wishes to destroy. The tsarina's pet-name, 'Arinushka', is rendered more intimate by Moskvin's stressing its third syllable. The score emphasises the couple's intimacy by indicating 'tender embraces and kisses' between them. 'An intimate scene . . . the tsaritsa holding a book in one hand embraces Fedor with the other and lovingly adjusts his hair. . . . Fedor kisses her hands and she caresses his head.' Then two jesters bring in Irina's workbox. She playfully ruffles Fedor's hair when he speaks of the attractiveness of Mstislavskaya (101/10–11).

The scene in Act Two where Godunov swears an oath and kisses the cross in witness of his intention henceforth to live in peace and amity with Shuyskiy (133/24–5) was censored. However, Stanislavsky imagines the scene as a 'tableau', a term which he utilises again when the delegates enter and kneel 'in tableau' (135/25) before moving to one side 'like a frightened herd'. The pictorial aspect of the production frequently obtrudes in Stanislavsky's score and is a reminder of the important contribution made by Simov to his imaginative conception of the play.

The scene in Shuyskiy's garden, where the matchmaker Volokhova has arranged a rendezvous between Mstislavskaya and Shakhovskoy, has undoubted comic potential as the lovers eavesdrop on the plan designed to separate them. It concludes with Shakhovskoy seizing the petition with its incriminating signatures from the hands of the conspirators and running off to reveal the plot to Fedor. The score indicates: 'Shakhovskoy runs off. The crowd after him'. For the sake of 'authenticity' Stanislavsky notes: 'Keep running as far as the dressing rooms'. He then adds that the exit of the crowd needs to be heard for between ten to fifteen seconds before the curtain closes (177/42–3).

In the production score for Scene Five (Act Three, Scene Two) it is early morning in Fedor's study. A pale morning light. Godunov has been sitting at a table all night long over a pile of documents.

The flickering candlelight gives a sense of the night's fatigue. His faithful warrior servant, Kleshnin, enters with a bundle of papers, bows three times to Godunov and they exchange embraces. From a distance comes the faint sound of church bells. Irina enters from early morning service, preceded by boyarins in white dresses carrying lighted candles. There follows an exchange of bows and embraces with Boris followed by a slow, ceremonial unrobing during which Irina exchanges her outdoor clothes for a loose dress with wide sleeves, embroidered in silk and decorated with precious stones.

Fedor enters, as if from sleep, although his cold shivers are not simply a physical sensation but an expression of an inner cold which has seized him – a result of a terrifying dream and a premonition of the tragedy to come. In response to low obeisances from Godunov and Kleshnin, he leans against a stove and warms his back and hands. Irina embraces him and tidies his hair. Fedor then sits on the arm of Boris's chair, his hands tucked into his sleeves. The contrast between the naive ineffability of the one and the power-wielding assurance of the other is graphically represented (181/44).

When presented with state papers, Fedor 'begins to read them, then yawns, puts them aside and pushes them towards Godunov' (183/45). The score then describes his 'dangling his legs' like a child. In response to his question about the Tsar of Iver, 'Where lies his country?', Boris makes a sign to the deacon who brings in a globe. Boris points it out. Fedor again yawns and, without listening, revolves the globe like a toy. Then, day-dreaming, with his arms still tucked into his broad sleeves, he puts his feet on the chair and twiddles his thumbs (185/45–6). He later lolls at Irina's feet with his head in her lap, while she strokes his hair (187/46–7).

A slightly melodramatic element begins to obtrude at the point later in the scene where Shuyskiy discovers that Godunov has broken his oath and arrested members of his faction. He now confronts him, 'running up to Boris like a tiger' and, 'face to face, they measure each other with their eyes'. Irina and Fedor seek to part them and the score notes: 'Fedor appears pitiful between two colossi' (193/49).

The *pièce-de-résistance* of the entire production was undoubtedly the scene on the bridge over the river Yauza. A scene which occupies a mere five-and-a-bit pages in the original (Tolstoy 1959: 222–7) occupies ten pages in the score and consists of fifty-one detailed notes accompanied by complicated diagrams indicating stage movement. This is preceded by a number of introductory observations relating to individuals in the crowd who are to form part of what Stanislavsky calls a *narodnaya tsena* or 'folk-scene'. Of the seventy-three who are to take part, detailed descriptions of fourteen are provided. The first is a Jew who, apart from being portrayed rather stereotypically, is referred to as a 'typical yid' (which perhaps helps to explain some of the objections levelled at the interpretation of Shylock in the second production of the first season). The portrait of the German and his 'fat wife' are equally stereotypical and would appear to pander to prejudices against Germans which were rife in nineteenth-century Russian literature:

(1) At the front of the stage, with his back to the audience, sits a Jew on some sort of crate. In front of him is a wooden counter with goods (nuts, spices, old clothes). . . . He is putting the goods on display and counting his money, before hiding it in his stocking. Wipes away sweat, waves his arms about and bows importantly to each passer-by, proffering his wares with a gesture. When the minstrel sings, he walks a little distance from his stall but keeps an eye on it all the while to ensure that nothing is stolen.

(2) From a barge owned by some German or other, two carriers dressed in rags hump sacks of flour across the bridge towards the fortress. As one goes towards the fortress with a sack, so the other returns to the barge empty-handed, and vice-versa. A third carrier brings sacks from the barge up a ramp on to the stage where he deposits each one before returning for another. The other two carriers, mentioned above, bear these same sacks to the fortress. Whilst the minstrel is singing, these labourers, worn out by their heavy work, pay no attention to the singer but get on with their carrying. They have no time for songs! . . . But at the moment of the revolt they seek revenge for their enslavement in more terrible fashion than anybody else. Bear in mind that the three carriers only move six sacks during the course of the entire scene as the first and second, having borne the sacks across the bridge take them off-stage and put them back in the barge (the rear of which disappears off-stage left) whence they return empty-handed.

(3) As the curtain opens, the German (in foreign garb) crosses towards the barge. Meeting a carrier, he asks him something to which the carrier replies unwillingly before moving off, whereupon the German catches him by the sleeve and questions him again. It is evident that neither understands the other (this piece of action should last for fifteen seconds). Having checked the sacks which are lying down, he undoes one of them, takes a handful of flour, examines and tests it. Then he walks up the ramp to the barge and returns only when the trouble starts; then, together with his wife, he attempts to rescue their goods.

(4) The German's wife – self-important, fat, with a headscarf – submissively follows in his wake. She waits patiently until her husband has finished talking with the carrier. As her husband checks the sacks, she notes the number and quantity on a piece of paper. For this purpose she has hanging from her neck an inkwell and, in her hands, a quill pen and paper. When the husband exits into the barge, she sits on a log and waits patiently for his return.

The score then goes on to describe ten other individuals or groups, which include two laundresses wringing out linen in the river, a drunken peasant with a (real) horse and cart, two peasant fishermen with their nets, two crippled beggars and one beggar-woman, two 'well-fed' Mordvinian women and a fat villager leading another horse by the bridle. Precise directions are given as to how each individual or group reacts to the singing of the minstrel. In addition to the above, Stanislavsky lists a further twenty-five groups and single persons including a boy to lead the blind minstrel, two messengers, four *streltsy* (sixteenth-century regular soldiers), an escort group of twenty soldiers, five merchants, ten peasants – a total of seventy-three to be cast from among 'our supernumeraries' or 'students from the Philharmonic School' (210–14).

The scene on the banks of the Yauza begins with the entry of Kuryukov, bearing a massive axe, followed by a boy with a *veshchun* (some kind of warning device?) leading the blind minstrel, 'like the one we saw in Rostov', explains Stanislavsky unhelpfully. The minstrel starts to strum on his *gusli*, which acts as a signal to a group of five peasants with rakes, forks and spades, who appear stage-right and proceed to cross the bridge. The end of the singer's first couplet: 'A king was going to war/To march against the town of

Pskov' is the cue for three merchants to appear at the rear of the stage, then to cross the bridge and take up positions near the singer. This also acts as a cue for a girl with buckets on a yoke to appear stage-left and halt to listen to the song (219/73).

The beginning of the third verse is the cue for three members of the crowd to enter and for a drunken peasant, who has been silent hitherto, suddenly to begin singing a different song to the one being sung by the minstrel, and in a different key. Kuryukov stands near the minstrel observing the faces of the crowd and gauging its mood. The line 'Glory to Prince Ivan Petrovich!' (i.e. Shuyskiy) is taken up by the crowd with much waving of caps. At the end of the fifth verse, the carriers throw down their sacks and begin to pay attention, 'scratching their muscular arms'. At the second 'Glory' of the final three lines of the song,

> Glory be to the sun shining in the Heavens!
> Glory be on earth to Prince Ivan Petrovich!
> Glory to all Christian folk!

Kuryukov falls on his knees and takes up the refrain, whereupon the crowd does the same and the song concludes with everyone singing. There then follows the first of the *narodnyye tseny*, for which Stanislavsky provides almost a page of explanatory direction calling for a great deal of general movement as well as isolated pockets of action, such as the moment where some pranksters make fun of the Jew (shades of a similar scene in *The Merchant of Venice*). This concludes with the overturning of his counter and with the 'horrified Jew' attempting to retrieve his scattered wares. The minstrel takes up a collection; the villager's daughter leads the horse away (223–5/74–5).

When the messenger arrives with the news that the Tartars have crossed the river Oka and are advancing on Moscow, there follows the second *narodnaya tsena*. The crowd falls silent, frozen with fear. Then some old women begin to howl and chant. The howling of the women and the stillness of the crowd are sustained for ten seconds. Then a member of the crowd breaks the silence with his bravura naming of Prince Ivan Petrovich – a cry which is taken up by the crowd. Kuryukov adopts a stance on a fallen log, dons a helmet and addresses the crowd (227/76). At the point where voices shout: 'We shall permit no harm to come to the Shuyskiys! No! No harm shall befall our father, Ivan Petrovich!!', Stanislavsky observes: 'Let everyone on stage learn this line by heart and pronounce it *once only* (not one word more)' (227/76). Then each person on stage says: 'To the rescue!' three times 'and not one word more'. In the distance can be heard the sound of chains, drums and tambourines. (To Fedor's orders, engineered by Godunov, Shuyskiy is being escorted to the tower in chains.) There follows another *narodnaya tsena* consisting of a brawl begun by the three carriers, who each grabs a club and launches himself into the fray 'like lions' (229/76).

During the fight which follows, Stanislavsky notes that one person is wounded in the head and another slightly wounded in the hand. He even goes so far as to advise splattering cranberry juice on the simulated head-wound (231/77). Kuryukov, who is described as 'falling from the bridge' in the text of the play, is here made to die at Shuyskiy's feet. Before the latter delivers his speech in which he confesses his guilt he 'stands on the bridge and silences the crowd with the expression on his face (as his hands are tied)'. Complete silence. The crowd falls to its knees. Towards the end of Shuyskiy's monologue, the weeping of the women intensifies. The crowd then strains towards him but is held back by the soldiers. To the sound of drums and tambourines, the procession makes its way towards the rear of the stage. The crowd follows, weeping (233/77–8).

Shakhovskoy arrives, repentant for having contributed to Shuyskiy's arrest and wishing to make amends. He leads the crowd in an attack on the prison, pursued by the soldiery. After a fight, the stage is left scattered with the dead and wounded. The Russian historian, Vasiliy Klyuchevskiy, declared that, hitherto, he had merely known how the revolt had ended; now he knew how it had begun (*Sovyetskoye iskusstvo* 1938: 24 October).[6]

Single strokes on a bell sound an alarm summoning the people to the defence of Moscow against the advancing Tartar armies. At the point where Godunov says (to Mstislavskiy): 'I am a man of counsel – you a man of war. [. . .] Lead on to battle. I shall follow you like a soldier!'

the bells all ring out with shattering exultant power, as if to express the patriotic excitement which grips the people. Gradually the sound dies away and, from the cathedral comes the sound of hushed ceremonial hymn singing. It was against this background that Tsar Fedor spoke his final words: 'Oh God, oh God! Why did you ever make me Tsar?'

(Izralyevskiy 1965: 51)

The score for Scene Eight then concludes with a very revealing instruction, which suggests that Stanislavsky anticipated just how effective the scene would be: 'As the curtain closes, rehearse with the extras, who have exited running upstage left, their re-entry downstage right for curtain calls'. There follows a sketch indicating where they go off and where they come on, plus an arrow from the opposite side of the stage, to which is appended the confident coda: 'The directors come on stage after the curtain has been opened' (235).

The production posters named Stanislavsky and Sanin as the directors. Nemirovich's name was conspicuously absent, despite the fact that Moskvin's resounding success was largely attributable to him. As Rudnitskiy later expressed it: 'Moskvin's Fedor was, without exaggeration, an entire epoch in the history of the Russian actor's art' (Rudnitskiy 1989: 53).

According to Vishnyevskiy, the success of the production had become apparent as early as Scene Three. By this point it was clear that the directors had 'really said something new'. According to the reviewer in *Moskovskiye vyedomosti*, Stanislavsky was 'a great master of directorial affairs' in whom 'there is some kind of inexhaustible inventiveness to which is added undoubted artistic taste' (Vinogradskaya 1976: 247).

However, as was often the case during the first and subsequent years, public popularity did not always go hand-in-hand with critical acclaim. The director of the Moscow office of the Imperial Theatres noted in his diary: 'They acted badly; the settings are pretentious and the general impression is one of an amateur production by a Russian Meiningen troupe.' Similarly, Sofya Tolstaya noted: 'They acted well, although there was an air of caricature about everything and the desire for realism was overreached; there was also too much noise and bustle on stage' (Tolstaya 1978: 422–3).[7]

Efros was among the critics most impressed, not only with Moskvin's performance, but also with the crowd scenes in which he saw 'genuine life', not the usual theatrical crowd, but a living mass and, 'as in life, differentiated' (*Novosti dnya* 1898: 20 October). The critic in *Russkiye vyedomosti*, on the other hand, was 'unpleasantly struck . . . by the organisation of the crowd . . . there is too much superfluous business, premeditation and correctness, which reaches the point of absurdity' (1898: 16 October). The critic in *Kur'yer* agreed with Tolstaya that there was 'too much movement and bustle', but thought that, 'nevertheless, there passes before the audience a picture which seems precisely to capture the sixteenth century. Not for a moment does this vision of ancient *Rus* disappear from before the audience's eyes' (1898: 19 October). G. Arseniy, in the St Petersburg journal *Teatr i iskusstvo*, wrote ironically of the Moscow critics' reactions:

> Having seen 'real' headdresses, ancient kaftans with swept-back collars and slits in the sleeves, not badly done, although with rather lacklustre sets, and a more or less strictly disciplined crowd, they decide that they have witnessed the eighth wonder of the world.
>
> (1899: no. 22: 230)

The auditorium was not full to capacity on opening night and the mood among the spectators was characterised as one of 'unfriendly curiosity', the opening scenes being received with 'great scepticism', according to Petr Yartsev.[8] However, by the final interval, 'it was already possible to overhear in the foyer and corridors the great words "an event"' (Kholodov 1987: 431).

By January 1899, Nemirovich-Danchenko was writing:

> Material existence, or more truthfully the takings, exceed all expectations. [...] *Fedor* will receive its 41st performance tomorrow and, despite this, the theatre is sold out within a few hours. If Moskvin did not tire, then we could act it five times a week, seventy to eighty times a season, and still be sold out. In actual fact we shall be acting it between 55 and 60 times and, certainly, to full houses.
>
> (Nemirovich-Danchenko 1979: 168)

Had the production not been so successful, the Theatre's losses at the end of the season would probably have been such as to make it doubtful whether, even with Morozov's support, it could have managed to survive. In other words, if the staging of its very first production had proved a flop, there would very likely have been no history of the Moscow Art Theatre to speak of.

Five days after the première of *Tsar Fedor*, the Theatre staged a revival of Stanislavsky's production of Hauptmann's *The Sunken Bell*, the substance of which is recorded in *My Life in Art* (Stanislavskiy 1988: 237–44). Many of the details anticipate the later production of Ostrovsky's *The Snow Maiden*, also described by Stanislavsky in his autobiography (280–6). The staging of the Hauptmann play was in marked contrast to others presented in more naturalistic vein but was, ideologically, of particular interest. A comment by a critic, writing in the newspaper *Kur'yer* on 22 October, lends support to the argument that many of Stanislavsky's productions both at the Society of Art and Literature and at the Art Theatre, reveal an interest in types who stand above the crowd, who are defined by a proud, even tragic, isolation and separateness. The type usually takes the form of the artist, the philosopher, the outcast or, most often a combination of all three, the 'superman'.

> The entire fantastic aspect of the fairy tale, all the scenes with the elves now appearing from nowhere and then disappearing just as mysteriously, all the singing and dancing of mountain fairies, gnomes and water-sprites – . . . take on the forms of some misty dream. . . . The representative of the earth – Stanislavsky/Heinrich – is a powerful figure, half titan, half human.

The line is one which may be said to continue that begun by 'companion' productions, which include *Uriel Acosta, The Polish Jew, Othello, Twelfth Night* (in which Stanislavsky acted Malvolio) and even Dostoyevsky's *Stepanchikovo Village* – a play and a role, that of the 'other-worldly' Colonel Rostanyev, to which Stanislavsky returned in 1917. As for the actual revival of *The Sunken Bell*, the general public tended to regard it as a rather old-fashioned costume play, despite the virtuoso aspects of the production itself.

A similar interest in tragically isolated individuals may be said to have characterised Stanislavsky's staging of *The Merchant of Venice*. The Theatre decided to retitle the play *Shylock* and to focus on the character's Jewishness (repeating aspects of the Gutzkow and Erckmann-Chatrian plays). At the same time, care was taken to ensure that Shylock did not dominate the play. Consequently, attention was lavished on those scenes in which Shylock is absent – the casket scene and Act Five, following the trial scene. The latter had never been staged in Russia before, previous productions having concluded with Shylock's humiliation (Ryndzyunskiy 1899: 64).

A further aspect of Stanislavsky's interest in this play would appear to hark back to impressions of the 1890 Meiningen production and the possibilities it offered to stage spectacular crowd scenes. Meyerhold noted in a letter to his wife:

> *Shylock* will be staged in Meiningen style. Historical and ethnographical accuracy will be observed. Old Venice will be

brought to life before the public's gaze. The old Jewish quarter, dirty, gloomy [. . .] the square in front of Portia's palace full of poetry and beauty. There gloom, here light; there oppression and subjugation – here brightness and joy. The setting alone underlines the meaning of the play.

(Meyerkhol'd 1976: 18)

Taking a leaf out of the Meiningen book, Stanislavsky had gondolas 'floating' in the darkness, with lamps burning at prow and stern. A procession of Portia's suitors took up an entire scene, during which armfuls of flowers were strewn at her feet. However, the most controversial aspect of the production was the interpretation of Shylock, whom Stanislavsky caused Darskiy to act as a vulgar provincial with a strong Jewish accent. Protests broke out in the newspapers. Darskiy was accused of 'perverting and distorting Shylock, turning the terrifying portrait of the Jew of Venice into the comic one of a pitiful Polish Jew' (*Moskovskiye vyedomosti* 1898: 28 October). Stanislavsky was accused of anti-Semitism and even of belonging to the reactionary 'Black Hundreds'. The production was only given ten performances. Later, Stanislavsky confessed that Darskiy had been forced to 'over-do the realism' (Stanislavskiy 1954–61: vol. 7: 131).

The revival, on 4 November, of a production which had caused great excitement on the amateur stage – of Pisemskiy's *Despots* (*Samoupravtsy*) – was greeted coolly by Art Theatre audiences and was taken off after nine performances. Of Stanislavsky's performance as Prince Imshin, *Moskovskiye vyedomosti* noted:

In Stanislavsky's performance, Prince Platon [Imshin] does not appear before the spectator in the customary manner. This is no ferocious wild animal with blood-flecked eyes, mercilessly persecuting all around him and evoking horror with his animal-like roarings. No. Before us stands a person who brooks no obstacles to the expression of his own nature.

(1898: 30 November)

Stanislavsky's philosophy, at this stage of his life, appears to perceive human beings either, ideally, in active combat with the natural world as 'forces of nature' themselves (a romantic view) or, negatively, as passive victims of destructive forces, helplessly crushed by social and natural environments (a naturalistic view).

The première of *Greta's Happiness*, on 2 December 1898, in a double-bill with Goldoni's *The Mistress of the Inn*, was something of a curiosity and the Art Theatre's first contemporary play. As with *The Seagull*, it was the enthusiastic choice of Nemirovich. He had mentioned *Greta's Happiness* to Stanislavsky in a letter of 21 June 1898, in the context of other modern plays which he thought should form part of the Theatre's repertoire. Stanislavsky had believed that such plays might threaten to 'change the physiognomy' of the enterprise. Nemirovich took up the phrase:

> In your letter there is an important passage. A few words almost thrown in as an aside seem to require clarification. If we stage *In the Meantime* [a contemporary play by Girolamo Rovetta] and similar plays, are we not likely to change the physiognomy of a theatre staging *Fedor, Antigone, Merchant, Uriel, Hannele*, etc? As far as I am concerned, this matter was resolved long ago. If a theatre dedicates itself exclusively to the classical repertoire and does not reflect contemporary life at all, then it risks very rapidly becoming deadly academic. The theatre is not a book with illustrations, which can be taken down from the shelf whenever one feels the need. In its essence, the theatre must serve the spiritual demands of the contemporary spectator. [...] If the contemporary repertoire was as rich and varied in colour and form as the classical, then the theatre might only stage contemporary plays and its mission would be broader and more fruitful than with a mixed repertoire. [...] *Greta's Happiness* is a very uncomplicated, but very powerful three-act drama in the vein of so-called 'Norwegian' literature. There is something of both Ibsen and Tolstoy in it. The young girl is given in marriage for material gain and she cannot stand all the horror of belonging to someone alien to her, runs away and nearly goes mad. The play is written with taste and character. Production – three sets. Costumes – contemporary. The play is not a long one.

> (Nemirovich-Danchenko 1979: 128)

The drama, set in Vienna, was by the Austrian playwright Emilia Matthai – the pseudonymous Emil Mariott. Nemirovich not only liked it but saw an acting opportunity for Roksanova, of whom he had high hopes and whom he had cast as Nina in *The Seagull*. Unfortunately, her performance was not much liked by either audiences or critics. N. Efros found character and situation difficult to believe in (*Novosti dnya* 1898: 3 December) and Sergey Glagol' thought the character 'psychotic' from the moment she walked on stage (*Kur'yer* 1898: 4 December).[9] *Russkiy listok* thought the actress exaggerated Greta's physical revulsion in the presence of her husband, shuddering, shaking her head, eyes and mouth wide open, transfixed to the spot and prone to hysterics. The critic concluded: 'Pity the poor actress if such an interpretation has been dictated by the reading of the part and the directions given her by the play's producer, Mr Nemirovich-Danchenko' (1898: 5 December).

The performance of *The Mistress of the Inn* went some way towards redeeming the evening in the opinion of some. A critic in *Russkaya mysl'* commented on Stanislavsky's performance as Ripafratta:

> Stanislavsky was magnificent in the role of the misogynist in love with the mistress of the inn. All the other actors, not excluding Mr Tarasov in the role of the cavalry officer's servant, sustained the ensemble irreproachably and harmoniously, ensuring the total success of the play . . . The public laughed wholeheartedly and called out the actors in the same spirit. The impression from the unsuccessful Viennese play was soothed over and all left the theatre in a good mood; 'All's Well That Ends Well'.
>
> (1898: 5 December)

The production of *The Seagull*, which opened on 17 December, and which proved so epoch-making has, of course, been written about extensively and we are fortunate in having Stanislavsky's complete prompt-book in English translation.[10] Despite the production's success with the public, Chekhov expressed disapproval of both Stanislavsky's performance as Trigorin (he was originally cast as Dorn) and of Roksanova's performance as Nina (Nemirovich blamed Stanislavsky for misleading the actress and forcing her to play some kind of 'little fool') (Nemirovich-Danchenko 1979: 162).[11] Stanislavsky himself later criticised the production for its over-reliance on external detail – something which he found characteristic of his early fondness for a realism achieved at the expense of fidelity to inner feeling. However, despite this predilection, it remained characteristic of Stanislavsky to imagine his roles in terms of a thwarted idealism, especially if the character was 'exceptional', either as artist or 'outsider'. The possibility that 'the great artist' might be a grubby person with an even grubbier soul was something that Stanislavsky was certainly alive to, but seemed loath to incorporate in his own performances. The studio photograph of Roksanova and Stanislavsky, the latter elegantly coiffured, clad in evening dress, mournfully contemplating the middle distance with pencil and notepad, suggests someone more intent on resurrecting the dead seagull in deathless prose than plotting the casual seduction of the ardent female by his side.

The actual production had been prepared by Nemirovich on the basis of Stanislavsky's score, and he chose to ignore many of the suggestions that Stanislavsky made. Other modifications were introduced by Simov, who had to cope with the limited space and equipment of the Ermitazh. Reading the score today, whilst marvelling at its sheer integrity, it is easy to criticise its procedures and to question points of interpretation. The production was criticised at the time. Prince Aleksandr Urusov, in a long article following the second performance on 28 December, suggested that the impression of sunset at the beginning of Acts One and Four was more reminiscent of a conflagration.[12] The actors, who sat with their backs to the audience in Act One, were inaudible. The silhouettes produced by the footlights made an unattractive impression. The action was too slow with too many pauses. The scenes between mother, son and Trigorin in Act Three were too crude. Meyerhold, as Konstantin, was too loud and his tone too querulous. Nina's last-act monologue did not work, although the critic generally approved of Roksanova's performance, as he did of Knipper's (Arkadina) and Stanislavsky's. Luzhskiy (Sorin) he thought less effective than Davydov had been in the 1896 production and Vishnyevskiy (Dorn) was similarly eclipsed by Urusov's memory of Modest Pisaryev's performance (*MKhT 1898–1914*: vol. 1: 52–4).[13]

Stanislavsky was prepared to admit that he did not fully appreciate the quality of Chekhov's play. He had deferred to Nemirovich's enthusiasm, which he did not share, whilst acknowledging his partner's subtler appreciation of contemporary drama. He had experienced great difficulty in coming to terms with his original role as Dorn. As late as September 1898, he was writing to Nemirovich: 'I myself do not know whether the production plan of *The Seagull* is of any use or totally worthless', but the settings, the lighting and the complex sound score doubtless helped to contribute to the play's positive public reception. Criticisms of Stanislavsky's own performance echo the sense of dissatisfaction felt by Chekhov (although the latter expressed differing views of the production at different times to different correspondents):

Before us, with short, slow strides, there moves some sort of paralytic, a person with a soft, sickly voice, talking agonisingly, through set teeth. It is impossible to imagine that such a person could produce a charming impression on a woman.

(*Kur'yer* 1899: 31 January)

Efros thought Stanislavsky's performance was too concerned with the weak-willed aspect of Trigorin and that his depiction appeared to make the character appear psychologically sick: 'This is no longer simply weakness of will, of which we are all guilty, but something pathological' (*Novosti dnya* 1899: 1 January). Prior to the St Petersburg tour, Chekhov wrote feelingly to Nemirovich:

it is necessary to re-fashion Alekseyev-Trigorin a bit. Put some spunk into him or something. . . . playing Trigorin as a help-less impotent will arouse general bewilderment. My memory of Alekseyev's acting is so gloomy that I can't shake it off.

(Chekhov 1974-83: vol. 8: 319)

Some reviews even accused the Theatre of 'slandering life', turning the characters into 'abnormal and psychically sick types' and the stage itself into 'a clinic for the spiritually sick' (*Moskovskiy listok* 1898: 20 December). However, in order to account for the production's phenomenal public success, it is necessary to note that this kind of negative criticism can, at a certain point, easily transform itself into positive appreciation. In this other sense, the sickness was interpreted as 'the sickness of our nervous age' where the 'general mood of disconnectedness, of dissatisfaction, of spir-itual loneliness [reach] extreme limits of suffering', all of which is 'excellently conveyed by the actors of the Art Theatre' (*Russkaya mysl'* 1899: no. 1: 167). As a friend wrote to Chekhov, 'the per-formers do not act a play called *The Seagull*, but life itself'. To quote the otherwise critical Prince Urusov: 'At times, it seemed that what spoke from the stage was life itself and more than that the theatre cannot give' (Kholodov 1987: 108).

When planning Sophocles' *Antigone*, which opened on 12 Janu-ary 1899, Sanin is reported to have told Simov: 'We will create a production which will resurrect the ancient world . . . If my dream is realised, we will put the Meiningen Theatre in the shade'.[14] To achieve ethnographic authenticity, Sanin did away with the curtain and removed two rows of stalls as a concession to a Greek *orkhēstra*. To simulate daylight playing conditions, the entire production was acted with the houselights on. In addition, a Greek *skene* was introduced in the form of a raised stage at the rear of the main one, with Creon's palace painted on a backdrop showing a hilly landscape with classical temples in perspective. The chorus occupied the forestage, grouped around an altar placed up-stage of the prompter's box. Thus, most of the action was confined to the rear *skene*, which stood about twelve feet from the stage floor and was reached by steps. According to one critic, this had the effect of forcing spectators in the front stalls and boxes to observe the action from an angle of about forty-five degrees. The musicians sat on raised side benches playing on instruments designed to look genuinely ancient. Critics then wondered why 'authenticity' had not extended to the wearing of masks and *cothurni* and asked why Creon had been given black instead of white slaves.

Commentators managed to suggest that the production's rather 'studied' earnestness contained unintended elements of self-parody:

The production began [. . .] with pomp and circumstance [its start was heralded by a loud fanfare instead of the theatre's usual quiet gong]. It continued in this spirit to the end of the tragedy. The costumes and the décor undoubtedly cost quite a lot of money. The melodramatic tone of the actress playing Antigone [Savitskaya], the declamatory pathos of King Creon [Luzhskiy], the slow-paced gestures, the artificial plasticity of the poses, the burning torches, the urns, the funeral procession, the litters, the chariot, the grey beards of the elders, the swords and shields of the young warriors – all these, taken together, strengthened still further the purely external and, so to speak, pre-conceived solemnity.

(*Novosti dnya* 1899: 11 January)

A sense of the archaeological was underpinned (possibly undermined) by the physiological. If the score for *The Seagull* called for characters to wipe away dribble, blow their noses, smack their lips, wipe away sweat, or clean their teeth and nails with matchsticks, Meyerhold's Tiresias appeared to transfer some of these characteristics into the remote past, portraying the seer

as some sort of disgusting old man with yellow teeth in an otherwise toothless mouth, with a sagging lip and with a sallow, unpleasant face. He comes on stage bent double over his staff. It is apparent that his spinal column has atrophied completely. Then suddenly, for greater theatrical effect, he begins to climb upwards along his tall staff, extending himself to his full height before the audience.

(*Russkiy listok* 1899: 16 January)

Critics also noted, bemusedly, the inclusion of Mendelssohn's music sung by a choir as having little connection with Ancient Greece. The problem of the Greek chorus was overcome by having collective declamation replaced by a *choregus*, who spoke all the chorus's lines whilst the chorus itself simply listened. In compliance with images derived from ancient pottery friezes, Antigone was obliged to carry a water-pitcher on her shoulder during the whole of her scene with Ismene, which not only interfered with her movements but could be seen to be empty whenever she leant forward. Finally, when Antigone was being led away to punishment, the orchestra for some reason broke into a presto. However, despite these apparent shortcomings, the first-night audience went wild, calling out every member of the cast and presenting Sanin with the victor's laurel wreath (*MKhT 1898–1914*: vol. 1: 57–9). The production proved popular with young people, especially when reduced prices were offered to educational institutions.

The theme of contemporary spiritual malaise presented in *The Seagull* was expressed in the Theatre's final production of the first season, Henrik Ibsen's *Hedda Gabler*. However, in this case, an attempt was made to transcend or overcome spiritual disability. Mariya Andreyeva interpreted Hedda as someone devoid of moral feeling, weighed down by a kind of 'amoral idiocy', perpetually bored and seeking to fill a spiritual vacuum. To this end she created 'an artificial cult of the beautiful' and 'sacrificed herself on the altar of this cult' (*Russkiye vyedomosti* 1899: 21 November). This aspect of her character was conveyed during Hedda's exit at the end of Act One, when Andreyeva crossed to the pistol case, extracted one, then 'pointed it first at her own head and then at Tesman' (Shaykevich 1968: 21). The burden of spiritual transformation was borne by Lovborg. In contrast to Hedda, Stanislavsky (who also directed) interpreted Lovborg as an inspired genius, whose genuine spiritual qualities Hedda was incapable of appreciating and which could only arouse her destructive impulses. Stanislavsky acted the scene over the photograph album in a passionate, low whisper with despair on his face and with much hand-wringing at the memory of how Hedda had rejected him in the past. This intensity contrasted with Hedda's apparent emotional coldness and indifference. The feeling of misplaced talent which Stanislavsky had previously brought to his interpretation of Trigorin metamorphosed, in Lovborg, from anguished passivity into the temperamental passion of unacknowledged genius:

> Over Lovborg there hangs the aureole of genius. This almost invariably fails in the theatre. Genius is spoken of, but never makes itself felt . . . Stanislavsky knew how to communicate this feeling . . . And this was, in my view, the most valuable element in his interpretation of the role. What is more, his Lovborg is a volcano of passion, his whole being is storm and whirlwind, a thunderstorm. And it was this elemental aspect which the performer knew how to convey.
>
> (Efros 1918: 88–9)

Despite the production's popularity, critics were unimpressed. The limited number of performances can be attributed to the fact that it was premièred late in the season. Nevertheless, a decision was taken not to revive it for the next.

8

SECOND SEASON:
1899–1900

The second season began with Aleksey Tolstoy's *The Death of Ivan the Terrible*, the first play of the trilogy in which *Tsar Fedor Ioannovich* forms the second, and *Tsar Boris* the third part.[1] There were opportunities here to capitalise on the huge success of the Art Theatre's première production. Once again, Stanislavsky carefully prepared a director's score stressing the opposition between social levels which were mirror images one of the other. On the 'lower' level was a cowed people; on the 'higher', a sycophantic, hypocritical, self-seeking group of aristocratic boyars, in thrall to the living corpse of a senile and semi-demented ruler. The opportunities for naturalistic over-indulgence which this situation provided were grasped with both hands.

The plot of the historical tragedy concerns the decline of the half-crazed Ivan the Terrible, racked by remorse for the murder of his own son and terrified at the rise to power of Boris Godunov. A boyar faction plots to turn the people against Boris but the latter hoists the plotters with their own petard, assuming tacit power as Prince Regent to the new child ruler, Tsar Fedor. Stanislavsky acted Ivan the Terrible before falling ill and being replaced by Meyerhold.

The production plan was actually prepared by Sanin, based on notes made by Stanislavsky who supervised only thirty-three of the eighty-four rehearsals. *My Life in Art* contains a vivid description of the opening scene in the Council of Boyars and those which follow in the tsar's bedchamber (Stanislavskiy 1988: 276–7). The contrasts between the religious asceticism of the tsar and his sumptuous surroundings were stressed, as was the ironic discrepancy between the enfeebled old man and his tyrannical power. Stanislavsky's interpretation derived, in part, from the style of the Italian actor Ernesto Rossi, who had appeared in St Petersburg in the 1890s, but was at odds with his grandiloquence. Instead, he based it on a sense of ending, less as a tyrant, than as a semi-demented old man – a mere human who had failed in the superhuman task which the feudal system had set him. When death finally overtook Ivan it was in the manner of tragi-farce.

Critics complained that Stanislavsky had reduced a tragic hero to a character-sketch. His Ivan mumbled through toothless jaws, shivered and hobbled on decrepit legs like a victim of senile dementia. There was altogether too much emphasis on the naturalistic. They had a point; for example, the score for Scene Two ('The Tsar's Bedchamber') refers to Ivan's 'convulsions', to his 'hissing' rather than speaking, as well as to his 'staring at one and the same spot', 'wheezing' and 'scratching'. There are also moments of grotesque humour, which some thought were out of keeping with regality, as when the enthroned tsar poked a bare, thin leg out from under a blanket in 'capricious and clown-like' fashion. A similar moment occurred when, predicting the day of Ivan's death, a soothsayer made as if to kiss the tsar's foot, which was retracted with an expression of horror before being used fastidiously to nudge the soothsayer away 'as if he were a kind of toad or something equally loathsome' (Vilenkin and Solov'eva 1980: 44–71).

Critics also accused the production of portraying 'the people' as a mere rabble, whilst the aristocratic boyars 'seemed to spend too much time grovelling on their stomachs' (*Moskovskiye vyedomosti* 1899: 16 October). Strongest criticism was reserved for the scene in which the hungry citizens encounter the corn dealers, concluding with a raid on a bread shop. According to the score the crowd is 'downcast, half-clothed, frozen and hungry'. A skinny little girl 'keeps on raising her legs like a goose, first one then the other'. The episode culminates in the storming of the shop and the looting of flour, followed by the lynching of a provocateur, Kikin, a nobleman disguised as a pilgrim. The episode disturbed audiences and critics alike, to the extent that it was omitted after the first few performances. Its violent naturalism was reminiscent of a moment during the trial scene in *The Merchant of Venice* when Shylock, having been given permission to cut the pound of flesh from Antonio's body, summoned a group of executioners who chained the merchant to a stake the better to facilitate the operation. In this case, Stanislavsky contrived that the tearing to pieces of Kikin should appear absolutely realistic: 'Kikin, brought to bay by the crowd, is torn to pieces by it – handfuls of his clothing go flying into the air and even, God forgive me, bits of his body', wrote a critic in *Kur'yer* (1899: 1 October). St Petersburg critics were even more hostile: 'The crowd literally tears a man to pieces. On to the stage fall torn-off arms, legs and a head. This was something both wild and inartistic' (*Severnyy kur'yer* 1900: 21 January). The moment was reminiscent of the one in Stanislavsky's production of *Uriel Acosta* (1885) when the eponymous hero (played by Stanislavsky) was torn to pieces by an angry mob: 'the fiendish delight of the crowd which cannot endure "exceptional intelligence" grew; passions flared, a single wild emotion seized the crowd ... [which] rushed at the man who had dared oppose it and tore him to pieces ...' (Benedetti 1988: 48–9).

According to Yelena Polyakova, Stanislavsky 'flopped dismally' as Ivan the Terrible. 'It was the first of his many crises' (Polyakova 1982: 115). He seems to have been intent on undermining the conventional image of Ivan, to which end the reductionist perspectives of the naturalist movement served his purposes well. Having undermined a *traditional* notion of 'the great' and 'the terrifying' he sought to re-establish an image of contemporary heroism through his portrayal of a middle-class 'superman', in *Doctor Stockmann* (Ibsen's *An Enemy of the People)*, the following season.

Very little is recorded of *Twelfth Night*, which opened on 12 October 1899, apart from Meyerhold's wonderful performance as Malvolio in which he exploited an element of grotesquerie which had made his interpretation of the Prince of Arragon in *The Merchant of Venice* so memorable. His Malvolio was different from Stanislavsky's 1897 interpretation, which was said to have emphasised the darker sides of the character. Knipper acted Viola and Mariya Andreyeva was a demure Olivia. Luzhskiy played Sir Toby Belch. S. Vasil'yev recalled the version staged at the Society of Art and Literature and thought that the current production 'retained the extraordinary sense of ensemble and infectious gaiety' characteristic of the earlier work (*Moskovskiye vyedomosti* 1899: 3 October).[2] A better-known version of the play was the revival, staged by Stanislavsky at the First Studio during the 1917–18 season, with the mercurial Michael Chekhov as Malvolio.

Twelfth Night was followed by Hauptmann's *Drayman Henschel* on 5 October 1899, a play which had just been produced at both the Korsh and Malyy Theatres. Here again was the sorry tale of a powerful individual brought low by his powerlessness over circumstances. In this case the freight-hauler Henschel's vitality and good nature are destroyed by a combination of misgivings and guilt over the death of his first wife and his second marriage to an ambitious maidservant, their former housekeeper, whose cruelty drives him to suicide. Stanislavsky again prepared a detailed production score in which a scene in a tavern was choreographed with special care and into which he introduced a host of extras to add authenticity to this low-life scene. The sound-score included the constant striking of billiard balls (something he was to exploit again in *The Cherry Orchard*), the chink of coins, and the strains of an orchestra playing a banal waltz.

V. L. Yuren'yeva recalled the special 'timbre' of the production, in which the intimacy of the acting strengthened the feeling of theatrical illusion:

> The people are really alive . . . There is very little make-up and no 'theatricality' whatsoever. They eat real sausage for breakfast, slice cheese with holes in it from a square block. The housemaids smell of freshly starched aprons and the rustle of their skirts can be heard about the stage. The actors literally ignore the audience, acting for and between themselves. They are swallowed up by their own feelings, weigh and absorb the eye contact of their fellow actors.[3]
>
> (Yuren'yeva 1946: 100–1)

'The authentic heroes of the production', wrote the critic Nikolay Efros, 'are Messrs the directors; the designers and the actors are merely their assistants'. However, the directing, in his view, often lacked a sense of proportion in being over-inventive and in incorporating superfluous detail (*Novosti dnya* 1899: 8 October).

In 1901, great interest was aroused by a series of articles in the journal *Mir bozhiy* under the general heading 'A Doctor's Notes'. These reported that, between 1889 and 1892, of any ten doctors who died, at least one turned out to be a case of suicide. Chekhov was, of course, a doctor, as is Astrov in *Uncle Vanya*, premièred on 26 October 1899. This melancholy reflection (or something like it) might well have been uppermost in Stanislavsky's thoughts when he came to prepare the production, in which he himself acted Astrov. The spiritual vacuum at the heart of Russian provincial life seemed to affect the person of Astrov most intensely, whether sitting in the garden tormentedly brushing away mosquitoes or wandering about the soulless house amidst the furniture arrayed in dust covers, listening to the ticking of the clock or to the sound of a cricket; or else simply contemplating a large horse-collar hung above the dining-table. 'It's a fine day to hang oneself', as Vanya comments in Act One. 'We hung the horse collar on a nail, like a noose', explained Simov, who saw his designer's task in conveying the prosaically factual, the coldly correct, the complacently smug – in fact, the spirit of 'Serebryakovism' which reigned on the estate (*Sovyetskoye iskusstvo* 1934: no. 21). Often Astrov/Stanislavsky would sit, slumped in thought, with his forehead pressed against the darkened windowpane or staring intently and seemingly endlessly into space. His inconseqential lines addressed to the map of Africa in Act Four seemed to express, finally, the tragedy of a spent life and wasted potential.

The famous scene of attempted murder at the end of Act Three appears to have brought out the agony and the futility, rather than the comedy, of the situation:

> Act finale: Crowd scene. General noise. Voynitskiy shrieks, leaps at Serebryakov – Yelena screams, grasping Voynitskiy by the arm. Telyegin runs backwards, waving his arms and moaning. Serebryakov has run in and presses himself against the wall; Sonya tries to stop him ... Marina has hurled herself into a corner, afraid of the shooting. Mariya Vasil'yevna is on the divan. *A dog jumps off her lap and runs about the stage. A shot. General scream; everyone trembling ... Voynitskiy puts the revolver to his own head*; the women grab him and pull his hand away. [...] *Yelena begins to cry convulsively* ... clutching at her heart and sides – falls on her knees, her face in the piano stool. Voynitskiy rubs hard at his forehead and sits by the stove. Sonya embraces Marina in the corner. Telyegin, from behind a column, clutches a handkerchief and breathes heavily, without daring to approach. Serebryakov flattens himself against a wall and doesn't dare move. Ten second pause. All frozen in helplessness.
>
> (Stroyeva 1955: 76; *emphases in original*)

The last phrase seems peculiarly apt and might be said to have characterised the mood of the production as a whole. At the final curtain, when Lilina's magnificent performance as Sonya reached its apogee, Vanya wept 'helplessly' until the final 'quiet, slow curtain'.

The critic Aleksandr Kugel', who was generally hostile to the Art

Theatre and especially critical of its over-dependence on naturalistic effects, was appreciative:

> All the acts begin with a pause. The pauses act like an
> introduction to the inner world of this stagnant life. The
> pause is a special characteristic of Act 2. The professor sits at
> a table near his wife with his legs extended. The window is
> open onto the garden. The curtains flutter in the wind like
> sails. Then a soft rain begins to fall, then harder – a storm is
> brewing. A sound rings out on its own, incidentally, of a
> breaking pane. The window is fastened and once again the
> measured sound of falling drops can be heard.[4]

He gave a similarly appreciative evocation of the play's final
moments:

> A few moments of silence, and then the chirp of a cricket
> starts up. This is a musical symphony of slumbering life. . . .
> Sonya speaks her monologue, Telyegin plays softly on his
> guitar, Nanny darns a stocking – each on his own, each in his
> own shell, isolated – all incidental episodes gathered up in a
> single room.
>
> (*Teatr i iskusstvo* 1899: no. 8: 169–70)

A few took up the critical refrain of *The Seagull*, accusing both
Chekhov and the Theatre of being 'unchristian', pessimistic, and
of 'slandering life'. Nemirovich was exercised by some of the
naturalistic excesses and tried to tone these down in rehearsal. He
thought there was 'superfluous exaltation' in the scene where
Sonya and Yelena vow eternal friendship and that Astrov's 'out-
burst', during his thwarted love scene with Yelena, needed modi-
fication. As he wrote to Chekhov on 27 October:

> Unfortunately, I have to admit that most of these blemishes
> belong, not to the actors, but to Alekseyev as director. I did
> everything I could to eradicate from the production his love
> of emphases, shrieking, external effects. But something of this
> remained.
>
> (Nemirovich-Danchenko 1979: 203)

Sensing that Chekhov would have disapproved, Nemirovich protested against the handkerchief which Stanislavsky insisted on
wearing in Act One to protect his head against 'mosquitoes'. The
director's score indicates that everyone appears troubled by

mosquitoes during the act, either wafting them away with their arms or puffing cigarettes to keep them at bay. By 1909, when Kugel"s ire was at its most intense, Stanislavsky wrote resignedly to the cast: 'All right, let's stop annoying Kugel' and refrain from swatting mosquitoes. It's autumn, the leaves are yellowing and there aren't any' (Stroyeva 1973: 98).

One of the most heartfelt responses to the production was that of Maxim Gorky, who wrote to Chekhov in November 1899, approximately one month after the opening:

> A few days ago I saw *Uncle Vanya*. I watched it and wept like an old woman. [...] as I observed the actors I felt I was being sawn through with a blunt saw. Its teeth penetrated straight to the heart. [...] Your *Uncle Vanya* is a completely new type of dramatic art, a hammer with which you strike the empty heads of the public. [...] In the last act ... when, after a long pause, the doctor speaks of the heat in Africa, I was thrilled with admiration for your talent and trembled with fear for the people of our colourless, wretched life.
>
> (Gorky 1966: 15–16)

The St Petersburg critics, as usual, tended to be more hostile than their Muscovite counterparts, describing Knipper's Yelena as 'simply a very phlegmatic lady' instead of Chekhov's 'frozen water-nymph waiting to be thawed into life' (*Peterburgskaya gazyeta* 1901: no. 49). Knipper herself described the critical mauling she and other members of the company received in a letter to Chekhov of 21 February 1901:

> We have acted *Uncle Vanya* twice. Audiences take to it but the newspapers curse shamefully. Oh, how they curse! ... The reviewers are illiterate, stupid and hiss like snakes. But we act on and don't let them get us down. ... They have eaten me and Meyerhold alive, as well as Andreyeva and Moskvin.
>
> (Knipper-Chekhova 1934: 323)

The season concluded with a production of Hauptmann's *Lonely Lives* (*Einsame Menschen*) premièred on 16 December 1899. In the role of Johannes Vockerat – a free-thinking biologist whose simpleminded wife is not interested in his philosophical and scientific speculation – Meyerhold was given the opportunity to repeat aspects of his role as the doomed writer in *The Seagull.*

Johannes finds solace in a platonic relationship with one Anna Mahr, who becomes his intellectual companion, before friendship becomes contaminated by feelings of physical desire. Unable to resolve the dilemma, Anna goes away and Johannes drowns himself. Like *The Seagull*, the play deals with a destructive conflict betwen 'spirit' and 'matter' (the subject of the play-within-the-play in Chekhov's drama), presented here as the irreconcilable opposition between bourgeois materialism and the life of the spirit. The play contains a criticism of a philistine, bourgeois ethos which suffocates any manifestation of intellectual life, any attempt to go beyond its mundane limits.

The evidence of Stanislavsky's production score suggests that he judged Johannes more harshly than did his author. Rather than admit Johannes's rights as an individual, Stanislavsky stressed the egotism of his claim to intellectual freedom and self-expression. Having struggled to free himself from the toils of middle-class dogma (the score of the first act stresses the pedanticism and routine nature of German bourgeois existence), Johannes is shown to fall, with Anna's help, into the trap of an even more inhuman dogma – a parody of the genuine ideal which Chekhov, for example, saw Johannes as representing (Stroyeva 1973: 53–8).

Chekhov warned Meyerhold, who had solicited interpretative assistance, against emphasising the role's neurotic characteristics 'to the point of allowing his [Johannes's] neuropathological nature to obstruct, or subjugate, that which is more important: his loneliness' (Surkov 1961: 109). Meyerhold failed to avoid this danger, with the result that audiences tended to be unsympathetic towards Johannes's irritability and depression. Only after Meyerhold's departure, and Kachalov's assumption of the role, did it acquire a degree of calm and the production a greater sense of harmony. In this instance, as in earlier productions of plays by Hauptmann, Stanislavsky appeared interested in the theme of the artist, or individual, incapable of resolving the demands placed upon him by the opposed worlds of creativity and domesticity, who is caught in an eternal tug-of-war between the lower and the higher passions.

Yuriy Belyayev described his reponse to both the Chekhov and Hauptmann productions during the company's St Petersburg tour: 'All the principals act somehow "to themselves", at half-pitch, without the least expression, and without the least desire to interest the audience.[5] The minor players act slightly better'. Of *Uncle Vanya*, the same critic wrote:

> The troupe does not contain a single talented actor apart from Mr Stanislavsky who is, at one and the same time, director and head of the business. Here is a magician and conjuror, who can produce something out of nothing. One cannot remain indifferent to him. There are no actors, and yet a sense of ensemble is apparent, a general tone, a mood. All this is the handiwork of Mr Stanislavsky ... Because the actors are devoid of talent and personal initiative, obliged to see only what appears in the eyes of the director, obey his orders, count the beats and sustain the pauses, they are instructed, for the sake of greater liveliness, to yawn as realistically as possible, cough when others are talking and blow their noses ... This, naturally, has an effect with audiences.
>
> (*Novoye vremya* 1901: 21 February)

9

THIRD SEASON:
1900–1901

The Art Theatre's production of Ostrovsky's *The Snow Maiden* (*Snegurochka*) – a poetic fantasy on traditional Russian folk themes set in a mythical land ruled by Tsar Berendey – embodied in more exotic form some of the antinomies of the Theatre's previous work. Snegurochka, the personification of purity and chastity (as well as iciness) begs for the warmth of love and, as a consequence, is melted by the sun. In response, her potential lover drowns himself. Oppositions here find expression in Spring versus Winter (who are personified in the play), Heat versus Cold, Youth versus Age, and the world of poetic imagination opposed to that of 'reality'. The line initiated by this production, whose staging forms commenced from the point where fantastic elements in *The Sunken Bell* had left off, was continued in Maeterlinck's *The Blue Bird*, in 1908.

Of the forty-seven original plays which Ostrovsky wrote, the one chosen was among his least typical. It was also a risky choice, in that four versions of the play were currently running in Moscow, including one at Lenskiy's New Theatre. The dangers of 'over-kill' were obvious and a potential threat to receipts. Like *The Blue Bird* later, the play appears to have appealed to Stanislavsky precisely because it represented an alternative to the grim realism of contemporary plays in the repertoire, whilst reflecting some of their themes in a more idealised form.

The trips to regional Russia which had characterised preparations for *Tsar Fedor* were repeated by journeys to the north in search of authentic objects of folk art. In addition to these, the production contained a whole arsenal of effects, ranging from avalanches to snowstorms and transformation scenes. Gorky was delighted:

> *The Snow Maiden* is an event! A colossal event, believe me!!
> ... The Art Theatre workers stage the play magnificently,

extremely well! I was at a rehearsal without décor or costume but left the Romanov Hall [a theatre on Malaya Bronnaya where some Art Theatre rehearsals took place] enchanted and rejoicing to the point of tears. How they act – Moskvin, Kachalov, Gribunin, Olga Leonardovna [Knipper], Savit-skaya! They are all good, each better than the other, and, My God . . . they are like angels sent from heaven to tell people the depths of beauty and poetry.

(Gor'kiy 1949-56: vol. 28: 130)

This rather exalted view was not corroborated by L. Sobinov who, whilst admiring Munt's performance as the Snow Maiden and Kachalov's Berendey, disliked Roksanova, Knipper, Moskvin and Vishnyevskiy. He thought the costumes marvellous but the char-acters lost beneath the painstaking attention to detail. It had been staged 'intricately but uninterestingly' with a great deal of inventiveness but little poetry. 'Everything is somehow obscured by Meiningenitis' (Sobinov 1970: 86–7). This view was supported by another critic: 'The play is staged too heavily, too realistically, with an overload of detail. At times it has an almost operatically banal artificiality and lacks the appropriate simplicity' (*Teatr i iskusstvo* 1900: no. 441: 722). Chekhov thought the theatre would be better off staging Hauptmann (Chekhov 1974–83: vol. 9: 125) and Meyer-hold, who during rehearsals thought there were enough beauties in it for ten productions, was forced to concede that it had not been a success (Meyerkhol'd 1976: 27–8).

The production of Ibsen's *An Enemy of the People*, which opened on 24 October 1900, caused a sensation – not so much on the occasion of its Moscow première, but when it toured St Petersburg in February 1901. As was the case with *The Merchant of Venice*, the production sought to refocus attention on the central character, renaming the play *Dr Stockmann*, and excising or rewriting those elements which did not accord with the view which the production wished to propagate. Stanislavsky sought to tone down the 'un-democratic' side to Stockmann whilst (especially during Act Four) playing up his role as an exceptional, albeit unconventional, leader of men.

Critics considered that Stanislavsky had portrayed Stockmann, neither as conventional heroic figure, nor even as reformer, but as a naive and trusting idealist, a 'beautiful-souled Don Quixote'. In fact, they thought he had deliberately set out to 'lower' Ibsen's hero to the level of ordinary humanity, with the suggestion that 'the heroic and suprahuman are discoverable in the everyday, and accessible to Everyman' (Stroyeva 1973: 72). According to Yelena Polyakova, Nietzscheanism and hard-nosed positivism had become obsolete by the close of the century and, in this context, Stockmann's social Darwinism sounded not only naive but reactionary (Polyakova 1982: 137). This justified, in her view, Stanislavsky's abridgement and revision of the text. At the same time she sees him as having reverted to the role of Uriel Acosta – a crusader for truth who suffered for his convictions:

> Stanislavsky was not merely defending his hero – he was exalting this man who stands in his defiled home . . . and who declares pensively, 'You should never wear your best trousers when you go out to fight for freedom and truth.
>
> (137)

The humour which this line might have been calculated to elicit was certainly not a feature of Stanislavsky's interpretation and became the occasion for shouts of enthusiastic approval when uttered in St Petersburg.

The St Petersburg première took place the day after a three-day conference of the Holy Synod which had resulted in a decision to expel Leo Tolstoy from the Orthodox Church and, in a sense, declare him to be 'an enemy of the people'. The following day Gorky reported: 'Stockmann went with thunder and lightning. What a to-do after Act 4! . . . numerous ovations by the mass of the public. An extraordinarily grandiose spectacle' (Gor'kiy 1949–56: vol. 28: 154). According to the St Petersburg press, the second performance 'brought an even noisier and warmer ovation than the first. Stockmann's speech in Act 4 was interrupted by applause several times . . . At the end of the play, the excited audience gathered at the footlights with cries of "Thank you, Stanislavsky!" (Rossiya 1901: 28 February). For the moment, anyway, Stanislavsky/Stockmann had clearly become synonymous with Leo Tolstoy. However, whilst apparently seeking to 'democratise' the central character by tampering with the text, Stanislavsky achieved, by sleight of hand, what he apparently set out to do – namely, to convert the 'average' into the 'exceptional', the human into the superhuman – a design better illustrated by more sinister examples than Tolstoy.

Some considered Stanislavsky to have done precisely the opposite. In a piece entitled 'Woe to Heroes!', Ivan Ivanov argued that, although Stanislavsky's interpretation was impeccable as theatre, it did not accord with Ibsen's intentions.[1] Stanislavsky had, in fact, turned Ibsen's 'hero' into a myopic dreamer, a Stock-man had been turned into a Stock-child, a babe in arms, pathetically helpless in the face of life. If, Ivanov concluded, audiences believed this character to be a hero of modern times, then 'woe to heroes, who have degenerated into puling infants' (*Russkaya mysl'* 1900: 30 December).

In concentrating on the role of Stockmann, commentators overlooked the important role of the community. The view of the 'compact majority' inscribed in the production score certainly appears to underwrite what, in the play, can be construed as Ibsen's contempt for the crowd. In fact, the view of the crowd in Stanislavsky's production score is not unlike the one in *Uriel Acosta*. The mass is an irrational entity requiring leadership whilst bent on destroying the figure of truth who constitutes that leadership potential. The enthusiastic St Petersburg audience's reaction to Stockmann's speech at the meeting in Horster's house was, ironically, the opposite of the one which the score anticipates and which Stanislavsky emphasises is a *hostile* one, designed to spill over into involving the *real* audience in the actual theatre.

The score for the meeting has Stockmann standing like a 'majestic statue'. He addresses the on-stage crowd as 'mad things' in a whisper of 'terrible contempt', before raising his voice at the line: 'I say *to you* . . .', whereupon 'the whole crowd, as one man, leaps up as if to rush at him and tear him to pieces' (shades of the fates of both Uriel and Kikin). Further on, Stanislavsky indicates: 'Mass scene. Riot. Repeat the assault with doubled force'. At the end of the act, as the curtain falls, Stanislavsky gives the direction: 'Shouts of the crowd beyond the curtain. Certain voices can clearly be heard crying "Enemy of the people, enemy of the people!" Whistles in the (theatre) auditorium' (MKhAT museum, Stanislavsky archive no. 18887, Rudnitskiy 1989: 140). These are not the whistles of 'claquers'. Stanislavsky clearly imagined, and wished to stimulate, hostility among the 'compact majority' who constituted the actual audience for the play.

The Act Four meeting acted as a kind of 'transformation scene', during which the 'low' became the 'high', the 'ordinary' transfigured into the 'extraordinary' and, more disturbingly, the 'democratic' became the 'élitist' as Stock-mann was transformed into Stock-superman, a force of nature, which the metaphors of storm and tempest (in Stroyeva's account of the scene) served to underpin. Stockmann, hitherto the 'absent-minded professor', metamorphosed into the lone captain on the bridge, heroically riding out a storm which, like the image of the swimmer over the theatre's portal, was being offered as the condition of life itself – a truth from which the 'compact majority' (whether conceived as 'bourgeois' or 'working class') shied away in intimidated and hostile terror. Stanislavsky seems to have failed to see the dangers of which Ibsen was surely aware.

> Act 4 was a mammoth crowd scene with each individual given his own characteristics. The room is as if turned into a battlefield, or the deck of a ship (the sea and the swaying masts can be seen through the window and the room is full of model boats and steamers – the captain [Horster] uses this room as his own domestic museum). In this naval battle, Stockmann is raised above the crowd, as if on the bridge, to rail against the compact majority. In this scene the modest 'slippered' Stockmann turns into the grand old professorial Stockmann. The satirical key opens the door onto the heroic. The force of negation gives birth to the fighter. Formerly the eccentric, short-sighted Stockmann nibbled sweet cakes, stroked a new lampshade with pleasure, practised physical exercises, played the fool, acted the part of a player taking a curtain call and clumsily danced a sad polka. . . . Now, faced with the fact that nobody seems interested in the truth he turns into a 'terrifying tribune'. The hostile, stormy sea of faces does not trouble him. He speaks with 'terrible heroic strength' . . . he is 'full of majestic grandeur amidst the threatening throng'.
>
> (Stroyeva 1973: 70)

Whether certain St Petersburg critics were protesting against the production's naturalism or its reactionary emphasis is not clear from Stanislavsky's own account, which records that Kugel' and Belyayev 'stood up demonstratively in the front row whilst the actors were being called out, turned their backs to the stage, pulled faces, and lambasted us with swear words' (Stanislavskiy 1954–61: vol. 7: 205–6).

Nemirovich's production of *When We Dead Awaken*, which followed on 28 November 1900, afforded an interesting contrast. Unfortunately, the director seems not to have appreciated the extent to which Ibsen's last work dealt with symbolic abstractions.

The play was imagined to be as 'realistic' as *Hedda Gabler* or *An Enemy of the People*. As a consequence, Nemirovich decided to work in a number of crowd scenes and a host of extras to represent the population of a typical mountain spa-town. In this he was aided by Stanislavsky, who dreamed up multi-coloured marquees in bright sunlight, café tables in front of a hotel, people dressed for climbing, or clad in national costume. He suggested introducing contrasts between a tedious group of invalids who have come to 'take the waters' and an animated group of French cyclists. He also proposed introducing sounds of a game of tennis taking place off-stage as well as the noise of croquet mallets. As with the production of *Ghosts* later, Stanislavsky thought the masts of a steamer might be visible as it passed along a distant fjord, with steam coming from its funnel for good measure (186–7). Nemirovich listened politely but chose to ignore most of these suggestions, with the exception of the croquet mallets. He did, however, introduce a scene with hunting dogs, which noisily accompanied Ulfheims's exit, creating havoc amongst the invalids: 'noise, shrieks – a whole scene' (Nemirovich-Danchenko 1979: 220–1).

The production foundered beneath the weight of this naturalistic detail, faults compounded by Simov's settings which introduced 'a genuine mountain stream' cutting across the stage, 'winding between rocks, gurgling and foaming'. In order to set the scene for 'a ravine' in the final act, as many as twenty-eight stage-hands were needed (*MKhT* 1955: 68). The final moments were accompanied by a whole avalanche of 'snow' which broke off from the 'mountain peaks' but, despite these effects, or maybe because of them, audiences remained as unenthusiastic about this as they were about most of the Art Theatre's attempts to stage Ibsen.

Neither were audiences wildly enthusiastic, at first, about Chekhov's *Three Sisters*, which was the final première of the season on 31 January 1901, and which is now recognised as one of the Theatre's finest productions.[2] However, by the end of the season, Knipper was reporting to Chekhov: 'The audience went wild and we hurled flowers at *them*. Our ears rang from the shouts and the applause'. Gorky saw the production in St Petersburg on 28 February and wrote to Chekhov in glowing terms: '*Three Sisters* is going marvellously! Better than *Uncle Vanya*. Music, not acting' (Gor'kiy 1949–56: vol. 28: 157).

Again, despite the play's focus on a communal situation, Stanislavsky would appear to have isolated and, to a certain extent, idealised his own role as Vershinin the visionary – the man who can see beyond the present to what life will be like in a thousand years' time. Admittedly, the production score does indicate an attempt to undercut his 'philosophising' in Act Two, but a St Petersburg critic probably grasped the essential point:

> In Stanislavsky's portrayal of Colonel Vershinin, there is manifested the one fresh, healthy, and completely moral force and therefore the strongest and most seductive individual among the remaining 'tedious' persons. He holds sway over the remainder – all the various Prozorovs and Kulygins, causing the spectator to understand full well why it is that Masha is completely swept off her feet by him.

The critic also considered that Stanislavsky's performance went a long way towards mitigating the oppressive feeling which the play produced in a reading (*Peterburgskaya gazyeta* 1901: 19 March).

Resuming the onslaught on previous Chekhov productions, some critics accused it of being 'heavily oppressive', or 'hopelessly pessimistic'. N. Yezhov described the characters as 'nonentities' and 'eternally dissatisfied people' and suggested Chekhov was encouraging 'reactionary tendencies' (*Vostochnoye obozreniye* 1901: 29 July). The critic in *Russkoye bogatstvo* called the characters 'sea polyps' rooted to their vegetative existence, passing their lives in empty dreams whilst spouting phrases about 'work' (1901: no. 55: 175–6). On the positive side, Leonid Andreyev thought those who accused the play (and the production) of being pessimistic were mistaken.[3] It was, in his opinion, about a longing for life:

> Don't believe that *Three Sisters* is a pessimistic thing, giving rise to despair and pointless pining. It is a light, lovely play. Go and see it, sympathise with the sisters, weep with them for their bitter lot and catch their invocatory cry on the wing: 'To Moscow! To Moscow! Towards the light! Towards life, freedom and happiness!'
>
> (*Kur'yer* 1901: 21 October)

It proved to be the Art Theatre's most popular Chekhov production and remained in the repertoire until 4 May 1919. In 1940, it was successfully revived by Nemirovich-Danchenko in a completely new version.

10

FOURTH SEASON:
1901–1902

The critical reception of Ibsen's *The Wild Duck*, directed by Stanis-lavsky and Sanin, premièred on 19 September 1901, was harsh. Even an enthusiastic supporter like Nikolay Efros thought the Theatre was 'chasing after chimeras' in a 'mist of hidden symbols' (*Novosti dnya* 1901: 26 September). Petr Yartsev, on the other hand, was critical of its chimerical blank spots.[1] The production had been unfaithful to the play; it was 'coldly deterministic' and weighed down with a superabundance of external detail and, consequently, ignored the 'highest notion' of the work. Its 'soul' had been killed off through the clarity of the realism. The audience was bored or, worse still, 'left without waiting for the last act' (*Teatr i iskusstvo* 1901: no. 40: 712–13). Chekhov attended a rehearsal on 14 May and was also at the première. He described it as 'pale, uninteresting and weak' (Chekhov 1974–83: vol. 19: 139). Thus can a poor production by a first-rate company mar the reputation of a great play.

The production of Hauptmann's *Michael Kramer*, premièred on 27 October, continued to explore the theme of the failed artist and the conflict between aspiration towards the creative heights and the countervailing pull of the banal, the habitual and the sensual. The hero, a teacher of painting whose talents have never attained their hoped-for ends, dreams of inspiring his son, Arnold, to become the artist he himself would have wished to be. However, being weak and spiritually ineffectual, as well as physically deformed, Arnold is incapable of scaling the heights. He gets involved with a worthless woman and ends his miserable life by committing suicide. The production was, once again, built on a series of contrasts – between the grotesque, animal-like Arnold and the world of a low-life tavern, set against the monkish cloister of the higher spirit, represented by the professorial study of Michael Kramer, with its unfinished painting of the crucifixion, books and beautiful fabrics.

There was a touch of Pagliacci about Moskvin's portrayal of Arnold, with his white, clown's face and intelligent, tragic eyes. If the son wore the mask of a clown, the father (Stanislavsky, who acted the role) demanded the loftiest standards in the realm of artistic ethics. Only when dead could the spiritually and physically deformed son achieve his apotheosis through the transforming power of a higher art. The moment where Michael Kramer, to the sound of church bells, stood over his son's coffin and began to complete the canvas of the crucifixion by adding the likeness of Arnold's face to the portrait of Christ was prefaced by the artist 'reaching his arms ecstatically to the skies' (Stroyeva 1973: 83).

In the Act Three scene set in a tavern (not the 'old-style restaurant' which Hauptmann calls for) the crowd was depicted as a group of performing circus animals (complementing the clown-like Arnold) in what was, allegorically, a kind of living hell, the 'lower depths' of life. The scene was set below ground level, the 'upper' world being visible only through high windows which revealed (typically) only the lower halves of humanity, its mud-splattered feet and mud-bespattered clothing. The scene in the tavern-cellar became an exercise in the public humiliation of Arnold as the vulgar, coquettish Liese Bänsch sang sentimental songs in which Arnold's genuine pain and anguish were mocked. Her admirers stuffed their faces, danced the can-can in a grotesque human chain, grimacing and imitating the sounds of an orchestra. One or two took to the tavern stage and began to mimic Arnold's affliction, whilst others tipped a basket of bread over his head (84–6).

The punctilious professor and the vital but vulgar Liese could be seen as two sides of the same bourgeois coin. However, Stanislavsky attempted to suggest that the father's ethical principles and his uncompromising absolutism represented the 'lofty' and the 'beautiful'. Much emphasis was placed on the humiliation of Arnold; he was made to 'grunt like a pig', 'smack his lips like a horse', and squeeze his spots in front of a mirror. Stanislavsky appears to have found nothing objectionable in Michael Kramer, offering him as an example of 'the scrupulous certainty of high morality' in opposition to that to be found 'at the level of the tavern' (Rudnitskiy 1989: 153). In the opinion of I. Ignatov, the play fell into two sections: 'into the drama, which could be called *Arnold Kramer* and into the conference lectured by Michael Kramer' (*Russkiye vyedomosti* 1901: 29 October).[2] According to Petr Yartsev, Stanislavsky's Michael Kramer resembled a prophet, 'with an inspired countenance, confident movements and measured, flowing, modulated speech. He cut a figure striking in its power and inherent beauty' (*Teatr i iskusstvo* 1901: no. 45: 814). Knipper reported to Chekhov that 'there was little sense of success in the auditorium' (Knipper-Chekhova 1936: 151).

The next production – of Nemirovich-Danchenko's own drama of high society, *In Dreams* (*V mechtakh*) – in which fashionable, Schopenhauer-influenced notions predominated, was premièred on 21 December 1901, and precipitated the Theatre's first major backstage crisis. Stanislavsky had laboured over the production score for nearly four months. The result was that a stage which had hitherto played host to Ivan the Terrible and Nina Zarechnaya appeared to have been taken over by a group of fashion-conscious socialites in a play which seemed to consist of an extended meal, during the course of which pretentiously and expensively clad ladies and gentlemen gave vent, in elaborate speeches punctuated by toasts, to a celebration of the good life. Critics were bemused:

> We observed the jubilee in Act One; the entire act is devoted to it. It emerges, however, that the second act is devoted to the jubilee as well; and also in its entirety. In Act One the jubilee is held at home – in the second it is held in a restaurant. The décor is luxurious and quite exclusive.
>
> (*O teatre* 1909: 95–7)

There were backstage mutterings. Meyerhold and Knipper agreed with Boborykin (whose play the theatre had turned down) that it was improper to stage one's own play in one's own theatre, especially if the play in question was an inferior one. Boborykin's play (*Ladies*) may have been just as bad, but Sergey Naydenov's *Vanyushin's Children* certainly was not, and that, also, had been turned down by Nemirovich in favour of his own work.[3] Nevertheless, Stanislavsky had been talked into accepting it and Morozov, hitherto the object of Nemirovich's hostility, gave generously out of his own pocket, over and above the production budget, to provide elaborate costumes for Andreyeva in the leading role, as well as for the other actresses. There is little doubt that what drawing-power the production possessed lay in the costumes and accessories. This 'shallow play', which was 'a very good forgery of a profound one' (*Novosti dnya* 1901: 23 December) and which caused Knipper 'confusion in the head and haze in the soul' (Knipper-Chekhova 1972: 435), was the last to be staged in the modest environment of the Ermitazh Theatre.

The next production – of Gorky's *The Merchant Class* (*Meshchane*) – was premièred in St Petersburg on 26 March 1902 whilst the Lianozov Theatre was being converted into the Art Theatre's new home. The production was something of a landmark, in that it heralded the advent of Gorky the playwright, hitherto known only as a writer of short stories. The play also introduced a 'positive hero' onto the Russian stage in the shape of Bessemenov's foster-son, Nil, a young worker with a lust for life who lodges with this family of *meshchane* ('petty bourgeoisie', or 'philistines'). When Nil decides to marry someone else, the schoolteacher daughter, Tat'yana, whose philosophy of life runs: 'Life is just a huge muddy river which you get so bored with, you don't even bother to wonder why it flows', tries to poison herself.

When referring to the play in *My Life in Art*, Stanislavsky makes no mention of Nil (Stanislavskiy 1988: 324–8). If this production had a hero then it was Teteryev, a drunken choir-singer and armchair-philosopher. Nil was the *raisonneur* of the play, as Gorky admitted to Chekhov, but censor's cuts led to a significant reduction in the character's radical potential. In any case, Stanislavsky does not seem to have been interested in the play's politics. In fact, the majority of reviewers suggested that the production's centre of gravity shifted from the political to the diurnal. It was full of life-like detail characteristic of the daily tedium of a Russian provincial town at the turn of the century. There was a great deal of eating and sleeping; much carrying of a weighty samovar; laborious heating of its coals with a bellows; much washing of clothes, house-cleaning, correcting of exercise books, etc. Pauses were filled with 'typical' everyday activity – the coming and going of painters with buckets and brushes, the hanging-out of washing, the eating of soup, even the regular striking of a large clock, the hammer of which had been muffled with an old rag. At one point in the score Stanislavsky noted: 'It would be good to train a cat to come on at this point' (Stroyeva 1973: 90).

11

FIFTH SEASON:
1902–1903

The new building opened in October 1902 with Gorky's *The Merchant Class*. However, the first play to receive its première in the Art Theatre's refurbished, 'art nouveau' surroundings, on 5 November 1902, was Tolstoy's play about peasant life, *The Power of Darkness*. This involved another naturalistic descent into the lower depths – this time into the primitive morass of the Russian countryside – an excursion through the mystical and the violent which culminates in the murder of an infant who is crushed to death. Stanislavsky defended his choice of play. People wished to see 'truth' on stage; they were tired of the artistic lie. It was possible to discover poetry in mud and in the peasant's sheepskin coat (98). In fact, the setting was imagined as a sea of mud, with carefully sculpted ridges containing puddles of water and even, in Act Two, a muddy pond. The score calls for a horse and cart to appear and for a cat to wander about a barn in which there were also to be pigeons, calves and hens. Ethnographic attention was paid to the way in which peasants ate, hung footcloths to dry, scratched their backs (on the corner of the stove, like cattle), blew their noses (on a shirt corner) or washed themselves by first taking water into the mouth and then spitting it into their hands (98–9). Tolstoy may have believed, as suggested by the title of another of his plays, that light shone in darkness; there was little evidence in this production to suggest that Stanislavsky agreed with him.

The scene following the murder, when Nikita buries the child, was staged melodramatically. The gaps and holes in the walls and roof of the barn were pierced by shafts of moonlight, lending an atmosphere of mystery. Birds could be heard fluttering in the darkness, having been disturbed by the sound of running feet. Those on stage were invisible, their voices emerging from the

132

darkness, the light from a flaming torch casting their huge shadows onto the barn walls. The tragic scene of the burial was followed by a semi-comic one as Nikita remorsefully tried to hang himself and, in the process, accidentally trod on a fellow-peasant who emerged, drunk and half-asleep from beneath a pile of straw. 'Don't be afraid of laughter at this point', urged Stanislavsky. 'The tragic suicide has changed into a *balagan* [clown-show]. Such is the fate of everything in life, which does not have logical meaning. [...] This scene needs to be acted as a vaudeville' (102–3). The remark is worth noting, as it can be seen to have affected the staging of *The Lower Depths*.

The production was up against stiff competition. The play had already been staged, with strong casts, in St Petersburg and Moscow. Stanislavsky clearly wanted to go one better and really make the public sit up. Even before the opening, the papers were full of sensational news about the unusual preparations being made – concentrating, in particular, on the mud and the puddles which could be mistaken for the real thing, 'even with the aid of binoculars. [...] Special electric lights cause the puddles to glint as they do in sunlight' (*Novosti dnya* 1902: 11 October). Audiences remained resolutely unimpressed by these 'effects' and critics, generally, felt that the play had been sacrificed on the altar of naturalism. Efros noted that external detail took away the play's 'spirit and reason', which not even the presence of no less than three different horses at three different times, 'munching oats, snorting quietly and moving their ears', could compensate for. There is no record of Tolstoy himself having attended either the rehearsals or any of the performances (Rudnitskiy 1989: 173).

THE LOWER DEPTHS

At the beginning of January 1902, Gorky wrote to Chekhov announcing that he had begun writing a second play, with twenty characters, about people who went 'barefoot'. He was, he said, 'curious to see what would come of it' (Gor'kiy 1949–56: vol. 28: 21). On 25 July, he sent both Chekhov and Olga Knipper a copy of the finished work called, at this stage, *Na dne zhizni* (meaning 'the lower depths of life', or more literally, 'at the bottom of life'). The following day, Knipper wrote to Stanislavsky:

I read the play through avidly and will send it off tomorrow. In my opinion it shouldn't be staged so soon after *The*

Merchant Class as the public will flee from our theatre: *The Merchant Class, The Power of Darkness* and the new play – all grubby people; they'll say the stage smells. . . . Interesting to hear what you think of it.

(Vinogradskaya 1976: 389–90)

A meeting of the governing body took place on 21 August, following which Luzhskiy recorded a feeling, similar to Knipper's, that the Theatre's repertoire was threatened with monotony (391). On the evening of the following day, Stanislavsky, together with a group of actors and the designer Simov, were taken on a tour of Khitrov Market – a haunt of Moscow down-and-outs. This episode, which Stanislavsky recounts in *My Life in Art* (Stanislavskiy 1988: 328–33), led to their gaining an unexpected insight into the violence which lay just below the skin of the 'insulted and injured'. An unconsidered remark by Simov nearly led to one, if not more, of the party being killed. As a result of the visit Stanislavsky thought he sensed the characteristic spirit of this underworld which became the main theme of the production: 'Freedom at any price! . . . That freedom for the sake of which people will lower themselves into the depths of life, without realising that there they become slaves' (331–2).

Rehearsals began in August 1902 whilst work was still continuing on the conversion of the new premises. Stanislavsky commenced work on the score on the 28th whilst still rehearsing *The Power of Darkness*. Having overcome censorship problems and obtained permission to live in Moscow to attend rehearsals, Gorky gave a reading to the company on 6 September, fleshing out the background to some of the characters. He had brought with him photographs of dosshouses and their typical inmates. Gorky's reading was expressive and moving. His interpretation of Luka was said to have been very sympathetic, despite the fact that the play itself makes him seem more of a cynical consoler of others' misery. Gorky even wept during the scene between Luka and the dying Anna. According to Luzhskiy, he appeared to sympathise with Luka more than with anyone else – a fact which may well have affected Moskvin's interpretation.

The score for Acts One, Two and Four was completed during September. For some reason, the sheets pasted into the prompt-book relating to Act Three remain blank, apart from a few notes. To that extent, the score remains frustratingly incomplete. Rehearsals began almost immediately. V. P. Verigina recalls attending rehearsals at the end of September at which Stanislavsky gave brilliant, if slightly intimidating, demonstrations of most of the parts, young and old, men and women.[1] She also noted that it was Nemirovich who talked to the actors and offered verbal explanations, where Stanislavsky tended to offer a physical demonstration designed to inspire rather than serve simply as a model for imitation (Verigina 1974: 33–4). N. N. Litovtseva also recorded how:

> At one of the rehearsals, Stanislavsky demonstrated to I. A. Tikhomirov, who at that time was cast in the role of 'the Actor', how to make an exit – this was so extraordinary, so tragic and, at the same time, so infinitely simple that, when he had finished the demonstration, there was a moment of dead silence and, after a long pause, the helpless voice of Tikhomirov could be heard saying: 'Yes, but I certainly couldn't follow that!'[2]
>
> (Litovtseva 1949: 390)

As well as rehearsing the play, Stanislavsky was also preparing the part of Satin and, typically, was agonising over its difficulties. At some point between September and December, Nemirovich wrote offering advice. He suggested that Stanislavsky's dissatisfaction with himself proceeded less from the fact that he needed to create a fresh image for Satin and more from a lack of new acting methods. His approach, based on a combination of emotional flair and nervous energy, was becoming too familiar. He needed to 're-generate himself a little'. In the first place, he needed to be as familiar with his lines as he was with the Lord's Prayer and work up a rapid and light delivery unencumbered by significant pauses so that the words flowed effortlessly and without tension. Something of this then needed to be applied to his movements. One of Stanislavsky's problems lay in his lack of faith in the audience's intelligence and his apparent need to 'hit it over the head' with every single phrase. The result was an excessive 'pointing' of each line and 'explanatory' gesture which made it difficult for an audience to listen to him, especially since it could anticipate what he was going to say because of all the preparatory signalling.

What Nemirovich wanted to produce in this tragedy (and it *was* a tragedy, he insisted) was precisely the opposite of a tragic tone – something lighter and more cheerful. For example, the first act needed to be played like the first act of Chekhov's *Three Sisters* (which was light in mood, celebratory and spring-like, as inter-preted in 1901) but in such a way that not a single tragic detail was lost. It was precisely the absence of this cheerful lightness of tone which was weighing down Stanislavsky's acting. The only successful moment to date, as far as Nemirovich could see, had been Satin's Act Four disquisition on 'Man', precisely because the lines had been delivered rapidly, heatedly, by rote, as if they were second nature.

He next listed a number of points which he felt Stanislavsky ought to bear in mind. The role did not cease to exist at those points when a great deal of acting was not called for and when the situation did not warrant it. If there was nothing *to* act then it was a mistake to act anything at all. Moreover, too much 'acting' led to the audience's premature boredom. He needed to learn the lines by heart, avoid excessive movement and, above all, keep the tone vigorous and carefree, with plenty of 'nerve'. Even Satin's opening line: 'Who was it beat me up last night?' needed to be spoken rapidly, not-withstanding the pains in his head and body. 'Like in a vaudeville', concluded Nemirovich (Nemirovich-Danchenko 1979: 305–8).

The tormented Stanislavsky did not argue and rehearsals im-mediately went with more of a swing. Soon Nemirovich was inform-ing Chekhov that they had worked out a new tone for the play which was firm, rapid and cheerful and did not encumber it with superfluous pauses and uninteresting detail (310). Knipper and Moskvin were giving outstanding performances, he said. Stanis-lavsky, Vishnyevskiy, Luzhskiy and Kharlamov[3] were doing pretty well, and there were 'flashes' of ability from Muratova and Gribunin. On the other hand, Burdzhalov, Zagarov and Andreyeva were fairly dire.

Shortly after the première, Stanislavsky wrote to Chekhov pro-claiming that 'victory was on our side', stating, not without irony, that Nemirovich had discovered 'the right way' to act Gorky: 'It seems all we have to do is to "report" the role simply and lightly. It is difficult to be in character in such circumstances.' Only Knipper, he felt, had incorporated her own self in the part. The others had delivered bits of the role to the audience successfully but had left their own selves behind somewhere. He concluded: 'I am not pleased with myself, despite being praised' (Stanislavskiy 1954–61: vol. 7: 252). After only five performances he asked his understudy, Sud'binin, to take over. It was with Sud'binin as Satin that Gorky saw the production a year later, on 5 October 1903, following which Knipper wrote to Chekhov on 9 October: '*The Lower Depths* is going appallingly. It's come apart at the seams. Gorky swore.'

The dress rehearsal took place on 12 December 1902, in the presence of the head of the Imperial Theatre offices, P. M. Pchel'nikov, who, with an eye to potential subversiveness, reported his findings to his superiors: 'The general impression is extremely heavy; the mass of comic moments with which the play is over-laden are performed in such a way that the tragic ones stand out even more sharply.' Fortunately, he did not suggest that the production should be banned and the official feeling was that it did not need banning as it was likely to prove unpopular. The production opened on 18 December with the following cast:

KOSTYLEV, *landlord of a dosshouse*	G. S. Burdzhalov
VASILISA, *his wife*	E. P. Muratova[4]
NATASHA, *her sister*	M. F. Andreyeva
MEDVEDYEV, *their uncle, a policeman*	V. F. Gribunin
VASKA PEPEL, *a thief*	A. P. Kharlamov
KLESHCH, *a locksmith*	A. L. Zagarov
ANNA, *his wife*	M. G. Savitskaya
NASTYA, *a streetwalker*	O. L. Knipper
KVASHNYA, *a dumpling-seller*	M. A. Samarova
BUBNOV, *a cap-maker*	V. V. Luzhskiy
SATIN	K. S. Stanislavsky
THE BARON	V. I. Kachalov
THE ACTOR	M. A. Gromov[5]
LUKA, *a wanderer*	I. M. Moskvin
ALESHKA, *a cobbler*	A. I. Adashev
KRIVOY ZOB, *a porter*	N. A. Baranov[6]
THE TARTAR	A. L. Vishnyevskiy

A curious point about the posters and programmes for this production is that neither included the names of the directors. In fact, the names of Nemirovich and Stanislavsky did not appear on any posters until the 1930s – a sign, possibly, of their disagreements and a matter which creates problems when it comes to relating Stanislavsky's score to the production itself. However, important elements of the score seem all of a piece with Nemirovich's sense of the play as a kind of tragic vaudeville based on generic and thematic contradictions and contrasts. These appear as contrasts between the world of the cellar and the world outside – the world of indifferent nature and that of suffering humanity; between the romantic and the naturalistic; between freedom and imprisonment; between the 'reality' of life and its simultaneously 'illusory', theatrical aspects where shadow and substance intertwine and human beings can seem as 'real' or as 'unreal' as marionettes in a puppet show. The suffering and degradation are 'real' enough, as is the 'suicide' of the actor, the 'death' of Anna and the 'murder' of Kostylev but, in the score, it is their *theatrical* nature which seems to be insisted upon. Even suffering and death involve an attitude, a pose, in a situation which is both the bottom of the barrel among the dregs but where the planks which form an uncomfortable bed also serve as a platform, or miniature stage. The 'lower depths' in this sense appear to have been conceived as both a theatrical space and a naturalistic habitat. At any moment in the score one half expects a character from *Waiting for Godot* (composed less than fifty years later) to appear and enquire whether, by any chance, this place is known as 'The Board'. There is a dimly imagined sense throughout of life which consists of mutually self-cancelling opposites – of sleeping and waking, sunrise and sunset, eating and going hungry, being drunk or sober, being bored or entertained. The imaginative intuitions of the production score seem to belong to the realm of the Russian Symbolist movement rather than to that of the naturalists. An analogy suggests itself between the shadow play in the cellar and Plato's cave, or the world as represented in Aleksandr Blok's *The Fairground Booth*, directed by Meyerhold in 1906, as a *balagan* or clown-show.[7] The imaginative insights which the score appears to evince are on a par with something as abstract as the Blok work. However, the actual production – largely the work of Nemirovich – seems never fully to have appreciated this fact. Despite being successful in its own terms, it would seem to have been weighed down, finally, by an excess of naturalistic detail.

Stanislavsky opens the score by introducing a host of characters who do not feature in Gorky's text but who, far from seeming arbitrary, would appear to have been chosen specifically to amplify mood and bring out underlying themes. The first additional character is, significantly, a 'copier-out of theatrical parts' – a youthful member of the intelligentsia dressed in a shabby suit. He has arrived in the dosshouse fairly recently and hopes to leave soon. He copies zealously, hurrying to complete and hand in the work; comes and goes frequently, does not talk to anybody and often lapses into thought.

The second newcomer is an organ-grinder, or Punch and Judy man, 'a foreigner, possibly a Jew'. When repairing the instrument he turns its handle 'which causes it to emit a strange sound'. The third invented character is another Punch and Judy man (referred to as 'a Petrushka') of unknown nationality – 'a suspicious-looking individual, thin, pock-marked and with a very large nose'. His hair, moustache and goatee beard are very black, possibly dyed. He is the father of a multifarious, black-haired, dark-complexioned family. Returning from the outside world with his children 'he carefully sets to rights the canvas screens and the puppets of the Punch-and-Judy show'.

The other additional characters introduced by Stanislavsky are as follows:

(1) A young girl with a bird-cage, small, dark, with short hair and dark eyes. Almost certainly a Jewess. Returning from work she occupies herself with the cage and the birds.

(2) Three boys, one of whom is smaller than the others. One is a hunchback, another has a bad case of whooping cough. The third is a bright lad who runs about all the time dragging behind him a rope with a piece of paper tied to it. They are all very dark-skinned and tousle-haired.

(3) A red-haired drayman, who is large and stockily built; permanently gloomy because permanently drunk.

(4) A woman with a crying infant at her breast. She is pale and thin and the child causes her a lot of trouble. She is constantly drying nappies and the child disturbs everyone with its crying (done with a gramophone, says Stanislavsky). She spends a great deal of time combing her greasy hair.

(5) A prostitute. Very fat. Heavily made-up. Sleeps almost all day. Snores heavily. When everyone else gets ready for bed she gets ready to go out.

(6) An idle youth with an accordion from which he is inseparable; always drunk.

(7) A melancholic with an intelligent face. Stands for hours on the same spot and stares at a single point. Then, suddenly, will take his cap and leave. Returns lifelessly and adopts his former pose in his previous place.

(8) An old man.

(9) An old woman.

(Vilenkin 1986: 308–9)

Stanislavsky's sketch for the ground plan of the dosshouse is complicated as it needs to accommodate not only those whom Gorky imagined inhabiting the place but the additional characters as well. Consequently, there is an entire area towards the back of the stage, set at an angle, sections of which would not have been visible from certain parts of the auditorium but where many of the inmates have their own, or share, a plank bed. It is therefore possible to imagine that, when a note in the score indicates that the sound of 'snoring' accompanies three or four pages of dialogue, a sizeable din is the result, as at least twelve plank beds are shown to occupy the space towards the rear of the stage. Downstage right is Anna's bunk, rather like a child's cot and with a curtain. Behind it is the stove on which the Actor sleeps and behind that a door leading to the kitchen where the Baron and Nastya are housed. Centre stage are four plank beds, slightly raised from the floor and looking like a small stage within the larger one, which accommodate the copying clerk, Krivoy Zob, Bubnov and Satin. Downstage left, is a self-contained 'cell' which has a partition wall and its own door. This is Vaska Pepel's 'private' room and serves as an indication of his special relationship with the dosshouse owner, who acts as receiver of his stolen goods. A door and stairs in the back wall lead to the Kostylev quarters and another exit leads to the outside yard and the street. The place is dimly lit by oil lamps and has three small windows.

As the play opens it is a sunny morning and there is a continuous sound of chirruping sparrows, especially apparent whenever the outside door is opened. The Tartar is on his knees saying his morning prayers; Bubnov is on his bunk, sewing. Others are preparing to go out or are getting washed and dressed. The children of the Punch and Judy man are about to go out to play in the street, where Stanislavsky imagines them sailing paper boats in a puddle in the melted snow. The mother breast-feeds the child throughout the act. The first prominent on-stage sound is the Baron's laughter at something Kvashnya has said. The other, permanent sound is that of Kleshch filing metal. There is also repeated 'business' with Kleshch pouring water into a metal container and mixing glue with a sliver of wood. The static figure of Satin, who has just woken up, contrasts with the to-ing and fro-ing of the Tartar, Kvashnya's crossing to talk to Anna, and the Baron's teasing of Nastya, who is trying to read her escapist romance. His tormenting forces her to read whilst walking about the stage until she settles near a window, where she can take advantage of the light.

The organ grinder, the Punch and Judy man and his children go out, taking with them the screens for the show booth, the barrel organ and a metal triangle to summon a crowd. Stanislavsky writes a note to himself to 'ensure that the door and stairs are wide enough' for the screens and the barrel organ to pass through. He also reminds himself to ask Burdzhalov to record on a phonograph the distant noises of an organ grinder and a puppet show. The 'Punch and Judy' element is apparent on stage as the Baron pokes, pinches and torments Nastya, snatching her book and hitting her over the head with it. Satin suddenly sits up from under the blanket and the Actor's head 'suddenly pops up on the stove' like a jack-in-the-box. Satin is more like Pierrot than Punch – 'sleepy, pale with a beautiful, not very old, intelligent face and beautiful, thoughtfully-sad eyes' (Vilenkin 1986: 313–21)/Gorky 1973: 1–4). Whilst the Baron exits with baskets on a yoke hurriedly pursued by Kvashnya with her basket of dumplings, Satin lies motionless on his stomach, his back to the audience, waving his legs in the air.

The end of this 'scene' is followed by the opening of another as Anna draws the curtain of her own stage/bed and leans out wanly. The Actor suddenly speaks in a burst of nervous energy but then 'as with alcoholics, his nerves subside and he freezes in a pose' (325/5–6). In addition to a world on-stage, an entire off-stage world is evoked through the sound score, whether it be bird-song or the sound of wind and rain, drunken singing, the noise of a distant quarrel, a police whistle, or the distant sounds of a crowd being entertained by the puppet show.

There follows a theatrical 'turn' involving Kostylev, who, suspecting his wife is sleeping with Vaska, has come looking for her. He is carrying two salted herrings wrapped in paper 'with their heads and tails showing'. He puts them down and starts fiddling with one of Kleshch's locks 'with a key sticking in it' (Stanislavsky's underlining), shaking it, abstractedly, a few times. There are sounds of Kleshch's filing, the rocking of the baby, the distant noise of the organ grinder and a girl's song (335/8–9). Vaska, 'bored with the scene', bursts from his 'cell', grabs Kostylev by the shoulder who screams ('together with the cloth he has fastened on flesh') and shoves the frightened dosshouse proprietor out. The Actor mutters the words 'a comedy' and curls up with laughter like a child. Satin has also got up 'to admire the scene'. Vaska and Satin then eat the

141

abandoned herrings between them. When Satin leaves, he dons his coat like a cloak in the manner of a Spanish grandee (349/13).

Luka's entry is itself a piece of self-conscious theatrical presentation, as he appears in the doorway accoutred with the accessories of a 'holy wanderer'. Having disappeared to the kitchen he then reappears in the doorway, barefoot, holding a pair of bast shoes and foot cloths which he places to dry on the stove. As the Baron talks about his past, Stanislavsky describes his 'slightly foppish walk and manner' and the way he lingers significantly over certain words. The red-haired drayman enters 'dead drunk' and a lively scene ensues as the drunken Aleshka arrives with his accordion. When referring to Medyakin, Aleshka swats the bunks with his cap as if he were swatting his enemy. Like a mechanical toy he 'suddenly lies down flat on the floor; then 'gets up frantically', before falling over again. 'Everything is done rapidly and lightly' (367/119–20). There is more farcical by-play as Aleshka hides from Vasilisa under the bunks whilst she attempts to grab him and haul him out. All this lively action in the foreground is accompanied by constant snoring in the background. Bubnov takes up a position by the stove and rests his hand against it 'and, for some inexplicable reason, stands like a lazybones in this idle posture for a whole half-hour' (377/23).

The six lines of dialogue during which Medvedyev quizzes Bubnov (383/25) are interspersed in the score by a sequence of ten pauses. Later, Gorky's own stage direction: 'Noise and footsteps from the hall, muffled shouts' (389/26) is worked out in the score as a precise off-stage scenario:

A public brawl. Begins in Kostylev's quarters. A noise of medium strength. (a) Vasilisa's shouting and a sustained pause. Natasha's replies are inaudible (b) Short pause (Vasilisa has thrown something at Natasha) (c) Sudden shriek from Natasha (d) Vasilisa has Natasha by the hair and vice-versa. Shrieks of both women. (e) Sounds of running steps down a stone stairway and gasping breath. Sounds of running past the door (rear) voice and shriek of Natasha becomes louder for a second, then more muffled, because she's run behind the door. Then she runs and cries 'Help, rescue!' (e) Vasilisa running after her. Crude swearing and gasps for breath. (f) Pause, voices more distant (g) Medvedyev: 'A row?' Bubnov: 'Sounds like it'. Kvashnya: 'I'll go and see'. (runs out) (h) Belated passage of Kostylev past the door. Gasps for breath, exclamations: 'My God! What's going on!? Vasilisa!!' . . . runs past and voice fades away (i) Distant shrieks of the women who have, once again, got hold of each other. Five seconds. (j) Kostylev and Kvashnya join in (shouts, attempts to part them) (k) other voices.

The final direction for the first act, which has included thirty-eight detailed sketches of stage movement as well as a ground plan, is the 408th (391/27).

At the beginning of Act Two, it is after dark and there is the sound of howling wind in the stove and of rattling glass in the window frames. Light emanates from lamps above the bunks and from the reflected glow of a fire in the kitchen. The copyist has wrapped some newspaper round his lamp to protect his eyes and this lends 'a rather secretive air' to the surroundings. The opening 'prisoners' song' which accompanies the card and draughts games is 'sung in several octaves' and seems 'to travel from bunk to bunk'. It is accompanied by the gurgling of water in the drainpipes, the sound of falling rain, the scratching of pen-nibs and the turning of pages (395/28). The draught-players (Stanislavsky notes later) are using make-shift counters – knuckle bones, buttons, bits of string, cotton reels.

As the Actor prepares to leave, he oscillates rapidly between moods. Luka's talk of a cure for alcoholism (409/32) is spoken in a 'kind and gentle' voice 'as if addressing a child'. It is apparent that 'he is telling lies'. As if enlivened by the promise of a cure, the Actor's exit becomes a grotesque vaudeville 'turn'. As he says, 'Goodbye, old one!' he whistles 'some kind of complicated roulade', leaps nimbly off his bunk, hurriedly dons his coat, jumps about and uses his voice in a peculiar way ('a complete turn on its own'), Stanislavsky adds in brackets. As the Actor exits, Stanislavsky notes:

I should like to try something awful: a comic exit after a piquant love scene by some banal operetta actor. He smiles obscenely, emits some exclamation or other, dances on the spot. Pokes his neighbour insidiously in the stomach, does a little dance again, pokes again and runs off almost dancing a waltz. His audience would undoubtedly have given him a curtain-call.

(411/32–3)

There follows the dramatic scene between Vasilisa and Vaska during which she attempts to persuade him to do away with her husband.[8] In Gorky's text, Luka pretends to exit to the kitchen at the beginning of the scene but then, in full view of the audience, sneaks back and hides above the stove to eavesdrop. This enables him to intervene at the crucial moment when Vaska threatens to throttle Kostylev. Stanislavsky took a different course. In order to make the scene more melodramatic, he precedes it with Luka's exit and conducts it in almost total darkness so that, as far as the audience is aware, apart from the other sleepers on stage, Vaska and Vasilisa are alone. 'Mysteriously she nods to Pepel and pulls him in behind the partition. In the darkness of the partitioned-off corner their figures are invisible and only their voices can be heard. It is essential to speak very distinctly and to give the voices a tinge of mystery' (431/40). To add to this mood, when Kostylev enters, 'The audience must not notice' where he has come from. 'It seems as if he has materialised out of thin air.' The reason for his arrival is not because he is on the prowl, suspicious of his wife's infidelity. According to Stanislavsky, he has come to re-fill the oil lamps and has discovered the rendezvous by accident. He is 'carrying a dirty bottle with oil and a battered box which contains wicks and other items for lighting icon lamps' (437/41–2).

The confrontation between Kostylev and Pepel is elaborated melodramatically. 'They face each other. The atmosphere is pregnant with murder. Kostylev suddenly screams. Pepel grabs him by the throat. Bearing down with his whole weight, he presses Kostylev's face against the floor.' At this point the sounds of Luka yawning cause Pepel to release his victim and back away, frightened. Stanislavsky's explanation for Luka's presence is that he has climbed back onto the stove from the kitchen 'unobserved by the audience'. Then, intentionally or otherwise, Stanislavsky points up a connection between the near-demise of Kostylev and Anna's final moments by describing the noise they both make as a 'croak', a word he later uses to describe the Actor's voice immediately prior to the latter's suicide (437/42).

Whilst Pepel questions Luka as to how much he has overheard, Luka insouciantly sucks tea from a saucer through a lump of sugar held in his mouth. Another 'croaking sound' signals Anna's death rattle, following which Luka arranges a *mise-en-scène*, placing the hands of the corpse together, then quietly closing her bunk curtains. The death scene is accompanied by the snores of the inmates.

Then the prostitute makes her exit 'unpleasantly prinked out, berouged, wearing a frightful hat' (445/44). This moment is immediately succeeded by the entrance of the drunken Actor, declaiming Béranger 'with banality and warmth'. Natasha then hurries in with medicine for the deceased Anna. The grotesquerie is underscored by Stanislavsky's having the actor walk about the stage 'happily'. 'Perhaps he takes to the plank beds and walks about them as if on a stage' (447/45). The act ends with its 384th direction and with the twenty-third of its accompanying sketches, together with a note from Stanislavsky addressed to himself: 'Think about the ending. As it is, it's a bit of a mess. For the moment I can't come up with anything.'

As mentioned earlier, there is no accompanying commentary to Act Three, which takes place on a piece of waste ground outside the dosshouse (the scene of the Actor's suicide in Act Four) and which concludes with the murder of Kostylev, Vaska's arrest, and Luka's sudden and unexplained disappearance. In a few pencilled notes on the first page of an otherwise blank score, Stanislavsky has noted: 'A ladder. A floorcloth of green grass. Kostylev looking out of Vasilisa's window'. He has then added a few directions for moments later in the act, one of which includes Satin and the Actor climbing through gaps in the surrounding, dilapidated fence.

Stanislavsky sets the scene for Act Four in the usual way by establishing its 'mood'. It is a warm, spring moonlit night. Silence reigns apart from a howling dog. Distant sounds of a passing carriage and the whistle of a shunting engine. He anticipates the act's conclusion by noting:

> This is the Actor's last night. At dawn, just as the light of the moon is struggling with the light of morning, he will have hung himself in the shadow of the evil-smelling courtyard. His swaying corpse, lit by the dying green light of the moon and the first new-born rays of the sun, appears as a monstrous and sinister apparition. The dogs, on seeing it, howl even louder.
> (456–7)

The cellar is lit by a single lamp which gives it 'a sinister air'. Satin is inspirationally drunk (459/74). The Actor is described as looking like a pathetic puppy dog begging bits from his master's table as he watches the vodka container being passed from hand to hand (461/75–6). Satin's speech beginning 'What is truth? A human being! – that's the truth', is delivered, according to the score, 'with his back to the other characters, facing the stove, so as not to have to look at their ugly mugs' (467/77). However, in the letter from Nemirovich cited earlier, he suggested that Stanislavsky deliver this, and his later speech on 'Man', not as suggested in the score but with his hands behind his head looking directly into the auditorium towards the circle:

> Thus he sits for a long time, without moving, and delivers all his lines without ever once looking at those who also have lines to speak. He contemplates one and the same spot throughout, stubbornly thinking about something, whilst listening to everything that's going on around him and responding rapidly to all that is said.
>
> (Nemirovich-Danchenko 1979: 306)

The production photographs would seem to indicate that this course was adopted. Stanislavsky's score then continues:

> Sitting thus he delivers his speech drunkenly and with increasing inspiration. There is the feeling of a kind of bitterness and something confessional. In him there sound strings which have long been silent but which are not quite broken, the best in his soul. . . . Satin is drunkenly inspired . . . You can sense the person of talent – the drunken pub orator.

The Actor leans out and 'croaks' something. The Baron applauds 'as if he were sitting in the front row of the stalls' (467/77).

Satin's speech in which he describes the corrosively beneficial effect of Luka's presence runs the gamut of extreme and often contradictory emotions and is the most turbulent in the entire score. Satin 'beats his head with his fist, as if trying to beat out a tormenting idea which has taken possession of him', then speaks with 'tormenting pain and bitterness', striking his knee with his hand 'so as to have somewhere to direct his bile and pain'. He speaks 'drunkenly, angrily, entreatingly, questioningly . . . shakes his head with a terrible, wild expression on his face and with powerful temperament' (481/81).

Compared to the amount of comment on the speech above, Satin's famous soliloquy on 'Man' receives very little attention.[9] The score merely states: 'Satin speaks his speech on Man with excellent feeling. He is a sincere and good debauchee. Much love and feeling of beauty in Man. One senses the artist in him' (485/82–3). Stanislavsky also notes that the speech is accompanied by snoring, the noise from the accordion and the Tartar's praying. One of its consequences is the Actor's suicide:

The shuddering actor climbs down from the stove. Nervous, unable to find the footholds . . . Legs, arms, everything shaking. His pale face has taken on a greenish hue. Under his jacket he inexpertly hides a dirty rope, the end of which hangs out from beneath his jacket. Before his death he has combed his hair and has become somehow sleeker and still more vile-looking.

(489/83–4)

His exit to death in the 'wasteland' is immediately followed by a scene from a pantomime as Kvashnya chases Aleshka about the cellar. He scrambles under the bunks while she tries to hit him and he grabs her leg (499/88). The mood changes abruptly as the frightened Baron enters, out of breath, to announce that the Actor has hanged himself. The others hurry outside. 'In the distance a dog howls, or perhaps again the cry of the awakened child, or the bell for matins.' And as if to suggest the indifference of the world of nature, Stanislavsky concludes his score 'and in the room the light of a new day begins to extend itself'. This is the 272nd direction for Act Four which has also been accompanied by seventeen sketches indicating stage movement.

Olga Knipper recorded the phenomenal success of the first night in a letter to Chekhov dated 20 December 1902:

And so, *The Lower Depths* has been acted. With huge success for both Gorky and the theatre. The whole auditorium was one agonised groan. It was almost exactly like the first night of *The Seagull*. A similar triumph. Gorky appeared on stage several times at the end of each act. The audience went wild, climbed onto the stage, blew whistles. Everything was acted evenly and well, a production without the least element of caricature or exaggeration. I acted intensely; with nerve, and almost overdid the crudity of the character as a result. . . . The newspapers damn it but that's nothing. Moskvin has had a tremendous success. He plays Luka so well and with extra-ordinary gentleness so that everyone wants to listen to him. Kachalov is outstanding. K. S. [Stanislavsky] is very good in places, although he isn't happy with himself despite the fact that they praise him. . . . The most important thing is that the colours weren't laid on too thickly, everything was simple, lifelike, without any striving after tragic effect. The settings are magnificent. Our theatre has experienced a rebirth. If *The*

Lower Depths had been pallid it would have taken us another two years to regain our former artistic level.

(Knipper-Chekhova 1972: 155–6)

According to Stanislavsky, the first performance was torture for the actors and 'had it not been for the noisy reception accorded the first act, I doubt whether our nerves would have held out to the end' (Stanislavskiy 1954–61: vol. 7: 252). In a letter to the work's dedicatee, Konstantin Pyatnitskiy, Gorky declared:

The play's success is exceptional – such as I'd never expected. And, do you know, in anywhere other than this remarkable theatre the play would not have had the same success. Vladimir Ivanovich Nemirovich has made sense of the play, has worked it out in such a way that not a single word is lost. The acting is staggering! Moskvin, Luzhskiy, Kachalov, Stanislavsky, Knipper, Gribunin – have accomplished something amazing. It was only at the first performance that I saw and realised what an extraordinary leap these people have made, who are accustomed to performing the types of Chekhov and Ibsen. . . . The audience roars with laughter. Can you imagine? Despite the number of corpses in the play laughter fills the theatre throughout all four acts . . . Satin in Act 4 is magnificent – like the devil himself. Luzhskiy as well . . . wonderful artists.[10]

(Gor'kiy 1949–56: vol. 28: 277)

The *Kur'yer* critic echoed Gorky's sense of what the theatre had managed to achieve:

To be capable of infecting with the mood of the dosshouse an auditorium full of well-fed souls glittering with diamonds, and dripping with silk and lace; to be able to bring tears to the eyes of people sated with all kinds of arts festivals, is an enormous task of almost heroic proportions. We can declare with complete justification that the Art Theatre company has accomplished this task brilliantly. The whole theatre was awash with sighs and tears.

(*Kur'yer* 1902: 20 December)

Writing to Efros in 1922, Nemirovich declared the production to have been:

one of my most splendid triumphs in the theatre. Especially when you consider that, in constructing the new venue,

Morozov wanted to place me in the second, third or even the tenth rank, without ever going so far, however, as to manage matters without me. And the theatre – for the umpteenth time is it? – was saved by me.

(Nemirovich-Danchenko 1979: vol. 2: 261–2)

Nemirovich's 'triumph' it may have been, but Stanislavsky was not very happy with the success and insisted on asking Nemirovich whether he was really satisfied with a production which he, Stanislavsky, considered 'inartistic'. Nemirovich's response was swift:

An extraordinary thing has occurred. Prior to *Depths* the theatre had been going to the dogs. *The Power of Darkness*, for all its brilliant directorial talent, was staged in such a way that, had I not taken a hand – the same story would have repeated itself as with *The Snow Maiden*, which is to say that Stanislavsky is hailed as a great man and the production falls flat on its face. I handled *Depths* almost single-handedly from the first rehearsals, that is to say I laid down the throughline of the main idea of the production; a play needs *first and foremost* to be a *harmonious whole*, a creation of spiritual unity, and only then will it exercise power over people, the separate manifestations of talent always remaining precisely that – manifestations of talent. *Depths* had an enormous success. The theatre was immediately raised to a distinguished level. And what have I deserved from you? An incessant reminder that the production of *Depths* is not artistic and that this way leads us closer to the Malyy, which coming from your lips is the greatest form of abuse.

(Nemirovich-Danchenko 1979: 347)

As someone critical of the production, Stanislavsky found himself in unwelcome company, chief amongst whom were the snobbish and reactionary St Petersburg critics who had their knives out for the Theatre's spring tour in 1903: 'The sensation was like being thrown with violence onto a rubbish heap! Gorky harps on the lowest and vilest strings of the human soul' (*Sankt Peterburgskiye vyedomosti* 1903: 9 April). 'There is too much cruelty, inhumanity, groaning, swearing . . . too many bestialised people. Can life really be like this?' asked another critic, who described the prison-camp song which the dosshouse inmates sing as 'recurring like a doleful hymn' (*Birzhevyye vyedomosti* 1903: 6 April). Another noted that the

Moscow Melpomene has appeared to us in a guise which is scarcely festive. She is clothed in rags and tatters, barefoot and sporting a black eye. A deity from a dosshouse. The stage is full of worn-out rags, galoshes on bare feet, quarrelling, fighting and face-smashing.

(*Peterburgskiy listok* 1903: 10 April)

During the Theatre's American tour, Stark Young, in a generally critical review in which he was especially severe on Stanislavsky's Satin, nevertheless noted some elements which concur with the production's 'theatrical' emphases:

Alyosha's entrance, for one example, where he danced into the room so delightfully in his rose-colored togs, was quite as much a 'number' as anything ever seen in vaudeville. All this spotting and separate rhythm and glare would be well enough so far as I am concerned; I like the effect of pure theatre frankly played as such; and I like the presentation of Gorki's play as high theatricality, which it essentially is rather than naturalism; [...] On the whole I came away, when the performance was over, stirred and swept and shaken in my memory as after certain great numbers on a concert program, but with no sense of any deep mood or of one single, profound experience, either of art or of poignant life.

(Young 1948: 16–17)

It is notable that a production considered to represent the apotheosis of naturalist staging was performed at a time when European theatre was turning away from naturalism towards more 'modernist' trends. Meyerhold had left the Art Theatre in 1902 to begin his experiments in Symbolist staging. Strindberg had begun to experiment with new dramatic forms and the Expressionist movement was already beginning to emerge. These trends would be taken up more consciously by the Theatre in its seventh season, the fifth concluding with Nemirovich's production of Ibsen's *The Pillars of Society*, in which Stanislavsky played Consul Bernick.

Why Nemirovich chose this play is something of a mystery as he appears to have considered it weak: 'What a torture it is not to believe in the beauty of a play and to have to inspire the actors' faith in it', he complained to Chekhov (Nemirovich-Danchenko 1979: 318). Stanislavsky grumbled about having to act in such 'a disgusting play' (Stanislavskiy 1954–61: vol. 7: 254). Lilina echoed his sentiments: 'That cursed play; we rehearse it endlessly, now in the French manner, now in the Norwegian, and make no sense of it' (Lilina 1960: 191). Meyerhold thought the production attempted to enliven what it took to be 'boring' material by introducing extraneous activity – eating, tidying the room, packing, making and wrapping sandwiches, etc. (*Kniga o novom teatre* 1908: 145). Reviewers made uncomplimentary comparisons betwen Ibsen and Gorky, to the detriment of the former – something which seems scarcely credible today.

12

SIXTH SEASON:
1903–1904

The season contained only two premières – of *Julius Caesar* on 2 October 1903, and *The Cherry Orchard* on 17 January 1904. Stanislavsky retired into his shell somewhat after *The Lower Depths*, although much time and effort were spent in mastering the role of Brutus. He was also preoccupied with reorganising the Theatre and with disagreements which were a consequence of this and which had led to the departure of Meyerhold, Sanin and others. He also began work on the director's score of a Turgenev play, *The Parasite*, although he did not stage it until 1912.

As Joyce Vining Morgan has pointed out in her reconstruction of the production (Morgan 1984), Nemirovich was well aware that the Elizabethan theatre was a 'theatre of convention' but chose to stage *Julius Caesar* in the archaeological style of the Meininger, despite having disagreed with that company's interpretation of the play in 1885. The principal character in his production was to be Rome itself. Endless research went into reconstructing a vision of the city in Caesar's day, from the Capitol to market-stalls and from hairstyles to footwear. As Joyce Morgan has indicated, some details seemed unconsciously satirical of Stanislavskyan naturalism, such as the scene with scattered toys supposedly left behind by his children, in Brutus's orchard, and with a background of night birds, croaking frogs, howling dogs, and the roar of wild beasts from circus cages (44).

There were many disagreements, especially over Brutus, whom Nemirovich saw as a flawed human being and Stanislavsky as a tragic 'superman'. The production was expensive, but no more so than *The Cherry Orchard*, despite the employment of 200 extras, including 'Jewish booksellers', 'Roman armourers', 'street urchins', 'senators', 'legionnaires', and the contents of an entire barber-shop.

What might be described as a 'typical' direction ran: 'The Numidian is busy trying to catch his donkey' (66).

Despite this, Sergey Diaghilev admired the production, and both Leopold Sulerzhitskiy and Yermolova were full of praise for Stanislavsky's Brutus.[1,2] He, nevertheless, remained in despair for most of the run. The production, which had been given one hundred rehearsals, was staged eighty-four times and as often as five times a week during the first month, and always to full houses. Despite this, it was taken off after the 1903/4 season as it became increasingly encumbered with the weight of the armour, the animal skins, the shields, the weapons, the togas, and the 200 extras. It must have been something of a relief when the sets and costumes were sold off to the Solovtsov Theatre in Kiev.

Leonidov, who played Cassius, complained that he could not hear himself speak during the storm scene with its 'real rain and genuine thunder', but the new stage came into its own with its revolve, trap doors, recesses and sections which could be raised or lowered. Moreover, the new lighting equipment permitted wonders. Gorky praised the 'amazing production', the Roman crowd and Kachalov's Caesar but, generally, found it 'long and tedious' (Gor'kiy 1949–56: vol. 28: 289). Lenskiy wrote to his wife:

> The production is excellent but, in my view, it is acted very badly. There's a lot of shouting, much of it completely senseless. There is no nobility of tone. One frequently hears 'neow' [*tiper'*] instead of 'now' [*teper'*] and 'awfter' [*posli*] instead of 'after' [*posle*] as well as similar things. [...] Apart from monumentality, I see nothing in Alekseyev, who is more the merchant than the noble Brutus. I refer, essentially, to his voice and facial expression. Leonidov's Cassius is shout, shout, and more shout [a scarcely surprising comment in view of Leonidov's remarks above]. Vishnyevskiy's Antony is a fool from the moment he enters, smiles and opens his mouth. Some people like him; I don't.
>
> (Rudnitskiy 1989: 180)

The exception was Kachalov's Caesar, whom Lenskiy thought was truly Caesar-like, attaining 'the heights of Shakespeare's meaning' (180).

Nemirovich was bitterly resentful of the fact that both Stanislavsky and Morozov had a low opinion of the production, considering it 'unnecessary' and little better than anything staged at vy. 'So I have to take your word for it and Morozov's', he Stanislavsky, 'that five months' uninterrupted work in ...ich I have placed *all* my spiritual energy, all I know, all my experience, all my fantasy does not amount to anything artistic?' (Nemirovich-Danchenko 1979: 347–8). There was talk of each abandoning the Art Theatre and going his separate way.

The production of *The Cherry Orchard*, which opened in January 1904, marked the end of an era for the Moscow Art Theatre in many respects, although this was only their sixth season. Not only was this the last major production of a Chekhov play until the revival of *Three Sisters* in 1940 (the production of *Ivanov* later the same year was not especially significant) but the première was soon followed by Chekhov's death – a real body-blow to the Theatre whose reputation was almost synonymous with Chekhov's. The 1904–5 season was also a political and artistic watershed. Not only was Russian society beset by revolutionary rumblings, but the season saw the Theatre's first experiments in Symbolist stage forms. These events, together with attempts to establish an experimental studio on Povarskaya Street, plus the death of Morozov, marked the sixth and seventh seasons (1904–6) as critical in the Art Theatre's history.

THE CHERRY ORCHARD

In many ways, the Art Theatre's production of Chekhov's *The Cherry Orchard* was the most problematic and contentious of all its efforts to stage his plays. Events surrounding the composition of the play and its staging were not propitious. Chekhov wrote it over a prolonged period during which he was an increasingly sick man. The première, in January 1904, was closely followed by the dramatist's death in July. What is more, Chekhov's dissatisfaction with the production was couched in terms of frustration and anger unlike anything to be found anywhere else in his correspondence. To what extent these sentiments can be attributed to his illness, rather than to real inadequacies in the interpretation, compounds the difficulties which the play and the production jointly present.

Another problem relates to the nature of the play itself. There had been earlier disagreements between the Theatre and the dramatist as to the generic nature of his drama. This had been the case especially during rehearsals of *Three Sisters*, which Chekhov insisted was 'a comedy' but which Stanislavsky conceived as a serious play. The problem with *The Cherry Orchard* was even more acute. In this case, Chekhov insisted that he had written not simply a comedy, but something more like a farce or a vaudeville. Stanislavsky felt Chekhov did not understand what he had written. If the play belonged to any particular genre, he said, it was sooner that of tragedy.

Disagreement about the nature of the play continued to haunt the Theatre long after Chekhov's death. Some twenty-five years later, when Nemirovich admitted that they had not understood how Chekhov's refined realism hovered on the borders of symbolism, he still insisted that any suggestion that the play owed a debt to Russian vaudeville could not be entertained seriously: 'Just read the play and you will see that here someone weeps or speaks through tears, which is not done in a vaudeville' (Stroyeva 1955: 183). Nevertheless, it should never be forgotten that Chekhov's first dramatic efforts took the form of theatrical 'jokes' (*shutki*), and that he was the author of a one-act play, *The Wedding*, which demonstrates a masterly handling of the comic-grotesque. These elements are detectable both in his underrated tragi-comic masterpiece, *Platonov*, and in the depiction of the soirée scenes on Lebedyev's estate in *Ivanov*, not to mention the tragi-comic attempted murder episode in *Uncle Vanya*. The characters who inhabit *The Cherry Orchard* estate appear to have been conceived more in the one-dimensional spirit of Chekhov's earlier work than in the more 'realistic' manner of *The Seagull* or *Three Sisters*.

Moreover, Chekhov had become increasingly interested in the Symbolist movement towards the end of his life – a fact already apparent in the writing of *The Seagull* – and had encouraged the Art Theatre to look at the work of the Belgian Symbolist dramatist Maurice Maeterlinck. Within a year of staging *The Cherry Orchard*, Stanislavsky established the experimental theatre on Povarskaya Street where he invited Meyerhold to stage experimental productions of Symbolist drama, including plays by Maeterlinck. Increasingly dissatisfied with naturalistic theatrical methods, he himself was soon to engage in Symbolist experimentation in productions of work by Maeterlinck, Knut Hamsun and Leonid Andreyev. What seems surprising, in the circumstances, is that the production of *The Cherry Orchard* appears, according to many critics, to have avoided any manifestation of these developing influences and to have remained firmly rooted in the Art Theatre's mainstream realist tradition. This was certainly the burden of Meyerhold's critique of the production of a play which he read in an overtly Symbolist, even mystical fashion, as did leading members of the Russian Symbolist movement, Andrey Bely and Leonid Andreyev.[3]

Equally surprising, given the evidence of the production score, is that criticisms of naturalistic excess are on record at all, let alone Stanislavsky's view of the play as tragedy. What would seem to emerge from the score with even greater clarity than that for *The Lower Depths*, is an intuitive sense of the play's problematic nature, hovering between realism and symbolism. An intensely felt opposition between the natural and human worlds would appear to have exercised itself so powerfully on Stanislavsky's imagination that the fully human, three-dimensional, flesh and blood solidity of human character seems held in a state of suspended animation. If a naturalistic conception of a fully rounded, self-sufficient human reality could, *in extremis*, reduce it to mere reflex actions (a world of Pavlovian dogs), a Symbolist version of that same world could conceive it as equally reducible to a series of vague and meaningless (puppet-like) gestures. In these latter circumstances, the ordinary and everyday could legitimately be said to take on the characteristics of an inanimate shadow play or puppet show. If Meyerhold and others are right, then what was acted out on the stage of the Moscow Art Theatre in 1904 was an *inaccurate* reflection of the more abstract intuitions contained in the production score.

The bulk of the play was written during 1903, although ideas for *The Cherry Orchard* had occurred to Chekhov as early as 1900–1. In letters to Olga Knipper of 7 March and 22 April 1901, Chekhov spoke of his intention to write a 'happy' play for the Theatre. By January 1903, he was writing to Knipper as if the play was more or less written, debating with himself whether to divide it into three or four acts (Chekhov 1926: 251). However, in a letter to Stanislavsky written two days earlier, the impression is that he had not even begun writing it. On 27 January 1903, he informed Komissarzhevskaya that the central character of his new play was to be 'an old woman' and, on 11 February, told Lilina that the play would be ready in the spring and that it contained a part for her. The same day he repeated to Knipper his promise to Stanislavsky and said he would begin writing on 21 February. He added: 'You will play the part of a foolish girl' (presumably he meant Varya) and asked 'who is going to play the old mother [Ranyevskaya], who? We shall have to ask Mariya Fedorovna' (Andreyeva, who was in her early thirties) (275).

Chekhov must have drafted whole sections, or at least have had a very clear idea of how it was going to be written if, in February, he was confident of completing the play by the spring.

> I reckon on getting down to writing the play and finishing it by 20 March. It's finished in my head. It's called *The Cherry Orchard*; four acts. In the first act flowering cherry trees are visible through windows, the orchard a solid mass of white. And ladies in white dresses.
>
> (Surkov 1961: 141)

Also increasingly clear is the extent to which Chekhov had particular members of the company in mind when creating the characters. Part of his subsequent irritation is understandable when, with one or two exceptions, his creative conception of the casting which was bound up with the writing was largely ignored, or ridden over roughshod, once the Theatre had got its hands on the play. In March, Chekhov reported that he had 'laid out the paper for the play on the table and written the title' (Chekhov 1926: 285). At this stage he imagined Knipper as Varya and Stanislavsky as Lopakhin, describing them both as 'comic parts' (288).

In a letter to an acquaintance on 13 September he declared: 'I've almost finished the play, which it will be necessary to rewrite; my ailment interferes but I don't want to dictate it.' Letters dated 3, 7, 9 and 12 October suggest that he was having to rewrite sections of the play several times and on 10 October, Chekhov stated that he was rewriting the complete play 'for the second time', promising delivery in three days (Surkov 1961: 149–52). On 17 October, he informed Knipper of some finishing touches which were needed to Act Four and Act Two and 'perhaps two or three words at the end of Act Three should be changed or it may be too much like the end of *Uncle Vanya*' (Chekhov 1926: 324). He was also phlegmatic about the possibility that, as it stood, the play might not be suitable; if so it could be redrafted in a month (!). He had, he said, 'been wearisomely long over it, writing it at long intervals with diarrhoea and a cough' (324–5). In November 1903, the play was submitted to the censor, who demanded two changes in Trofimov's Act Two monologue where he speaks of the appalling condition of the peasantry and refers to the ownership of 'living souls'.

On 18 October 1903 (about twelve weeks before opening night), the play was complete and in the hands of the Theatre. On the 20th, Stanislavsky wrote Chekhov an enthusiastic letter which, regrettably, can be seen to have contained the seeds of all the problems and disputes to come. In the first place, he declared:

> It is not a comedy, not a farce . . . it is a tragedy, no matter if you do indicate a way out into a better world in the last act. [. . .] It is so completely a whole one cannot delete a single word from it. [Stanislavsky was to request the deletion of a whole section at the end of Act 2]. [. . .] I am accustomed to a rather vague impression from a first reading of your plays. . . . I read it for a second time . . . I wept like a woman, I tried to control myself, but could not. I can hear you say: 'But please, this is a farce . . .' No, for the ordinary person this is a tragedy.
>
> (Stanislavski 1958: 123–4)

Nemirovich read the play very rapidly and sent off a 180-word telegram on the day he received the text which, given the labours Chekhov had expended, must have had the author fuming at its rather patronising tone:

> My personal impression is that, as a work for the stage it is perhaps more of a play than your previous efforts. The subject is clear and firm. The play is generally a harmonious whole. This harmony is slightly disturbed by the heaviness of the second act. The characters are new, extraordinarily interesting and present the actors with a difficult task but one which is rich in content. The mother is magnificent. Anya is close to Irina [in *Three Sisters*] but newer. Varya has developed from Masha [presumably he means in *The Seagull* rather than in *Three Sisters*] but has left her far behind. In Gayev I have a sense of outstanding material, but fail to grasp his image in the way I do that of the count [Shabelskiy] in *Ivanov*. Lopakhin is excellent and freshly grasped. All the secondary characters, in particular Sharlotta, are especially successful. Trofimov is weaker than the others so far . . . The most remarkable act in terms of mood, dramatic heightening and cruel daring is the last; in terms of its grace and lightness – the first. That which is new in your work is the clear, sappy and simple dramatic effect. [. . .] It does not disturb me greatly but I don't care for some of the cruder details, such as the superfluous quantity of tears. From a social viewpoint the basic theme is not new, but takes a different tack, is both

poetic and original. I will write to you in more detail, after a second reading.

(Nemirovich-Danchenko 1979: 343–4)

At the end of October Nemirovich wrote apologising for comparing Anya with Irina and ran through the proposed casting. He followed this up with a telegram on 5 November in which he listed the eventual cast, with the exception of Anya, for whom there were four possible candidates, including Lilina who was in her late thirties; there were also four candidates for Varya, including Andreyeva, and three for Sharlotta, including Muratova. Everyone was anxious to be in the play, no one more so than Muratova who said, if she wasn't cast as Sharlotta, she was desperate enough to play Yasha's mother (a character who does not appear). A. Pomyalova, another candidate for Sharlotta, said she would be happy to play a scarecrow in the orchard (Solov'eva 1983: 64).[4] Stanislavsky was so delighted with the play, he wanted to act all the parts.

The first rehearsal was held on 9 November (roughly nine weeks before the opening) and Stanislavsky wrote the production plan of the first act on 12 November. Despite being very ill, Chekhov was so concerned about the fate of his play that he made the journey to Moscow, arriving on 4 December, and began to attend rehearsals. Stanislavsky remembered how Chekhov always sat somewhere in the back rows, resisting invitations to sit in the director's chair. He also remembered Chekhov's response to a request to cut a whole scene involving Sharlotta and Firs at the end of Act Two.[5] He turned pale with anguish, thought for a moment and then said, abruptly, 'Cut it!' Chekhov, in turn, asked for changes in the casting and expressed strong displeasure with the settings, especially for Act Two. He was also depressed by the Theatre's apparent inability to come up with an appropriate sound for the 'breaking string' in Acts Two and Four. Eventually, when he realised that little notice was being taken of his suggestions and that his criticisms were generating antagonism, he simply stopped attending. Stanislavsky even went so far as to blame Chekhov for the fact that, by the end of December, the work had not borne fruit. Chekhov's next appearance at the Theatre was to be his last – on the day of the production's première on 17 January 1904, which also happened to be his name-day. He arrived at the Theatre during the performance and came on stage at the end of Act Three to listen to speeches in his honour, through which he was barely able to stand. He then stayed on and saw Act Four through to the end.

The cast for the first night was as follows:

RANYEVSKAYA, *a landowner*	O. L. Knipper
ANYA, *her daughter*	M. P. Lilina
VARYA, *her adopted daughter*	M. F. Andreyeva
GAYEV, *Ranyevskaya's brother*	K. S. Stanislavsky
LOPAKHIN, *a businessman*	L. M. Leonidov
TROFIMOV, *a student*	V. F. Kachalov
SHARLOTTA IVANOVNA, *a governess*	M. V. Muratova
YEPIKHODOV, *the estate clerk*	I. M. Moskvin
DUNYASHA, *the chambermaid*	S. V. Khalyutina[6]
FIRS, *a footman, an old man of 87*	A. A. Artem
YASHA	N. G. Aleksandrov
A PASSER-BY	M. A. Gromov
THE STATIONMASTER	A. L. Zagarov

The production ran for four hours with three intervals, starting at 8.00 p.m. and ending at around midnight. Settings were by Simov. Music, which included two popular waltz tunes in Act Three 'Dunayskiye volny' ('The Waves of the Danube') and 'Nad volnami' ('Above the Waves'), was selected by N. A. Manykin-Nevstruyev, and played by a group of five musicians who included Ilya Sats. Neither director's name appeared on the posters or in the programmes.

Four days before the première, Chekhov had informed a correspondent: 'It seems my play goes on on 17 January; I don't anticipate any particular success, things have gone pretty sluggishly' (Surkov 1961: 161). On the day following the première, he wrote: 'My play went on yesterday, for which reason I'm in a bad mood' (161). Writing to Fedor Batyushkov on 19 January, he spoke of the acting as being 'confused and unclear' (161).[7] The first night audience had not been especially enthusiastic either and it was some time before the public, generally, began to take to it. Critical opinion differed widely, although there was nothing quite so hostile as some of the earlier responses to Chekhov's plays had been. The unusual characteristics of the merchant type in Lopakhin were not understood, or were assumed to be part of the author's attempt to justify elements of the 'bourgeois' strata of society (*Rus* 1904: no. 110). Lyubov Guryevich thought that Anya and Trofimov represented the typical heartless egotism of the younger generation. (*Obrazovaniye* 1904: no. 4).[8] Gorky expressed ideological objections, which he would probably have kept to himself had Chekhov still been alive:

Here are the tearful Ranyevskaya and other former owners
... egotistical like children, and as flaccid as old folks. They
have failed to die promptly and so pine, seeing nothing
around themselves, understanding nothing – parasites, devoid
of the strength even to batten on life. The rubbishy student
Trofimov talks beautifully about the need to work and does
nothing, entertaining himself out of boredom with stupid
mockery of Varya, who works unstintingly for the benefit of
these idlers.

(*Nizhegorodskiy sbornik* 1905: 15)

The poet Konstantin Bal'mont, who was to translate the three
Maeterlinck plays for the Art Theatre productions of 1906, was said
by Knipper to be wild about the production.[9] She also reported that
Yermolova, who was in the audience on 15 March had been moved
to tears and 'had applauded it warmly' (Surkov 1961: 344). The
performances given in St Petersburg less than a month later were,
unusually, greeted with greater enthusiasm than in Moscow:

It is necessary to go and see the production because the
interpretation is of equal value to the play – immaculate,
artistic, incomparable. Here the Art Theatre is in its element.
Only the actors of this theatre with their tender, sensitive
responsiveness could understand and transmit Chekhov *in
this way* ... There is just a slight note of sadly-goodnatured
laughter in the interpretations and this lends the acting
certain new tones. All the performers have excelled themselves, embodying Chekhov's characters in extraordinary
fashion.

(*Novosti i birzhevaya gazyeta* 1904: 3 April)

According to Aleksandr Amfiteatrov, Stanislavsky had succeeded in
creating

a figure whose humour causes the heart to contract, like the
humour in Gogol's *Overcoat*. There are unforgettable stage
performances, however many years pass since their appearance. I am certain that I shall never forget Stanislavsky-Gayev
– how, when the cherry orchard having been sold at auction,
he enters bearing two small packages [of anchovies] in his
hand.[10]

(*Rus* 1904: 4 April)

Kugel' thought the 'essence of Chekhov's hopelessness, despondency and the meaninglessness of life', its 'elemental cruelty and aimlessness', had been communicated by the Art Theatre 'with great clarity and specificity, if not with great talent'. For Kugel', Chekhov was a 'sad pessimist', hence his astonishment

> when *The Cherry Orchard* appeared in the guise of a light, funny, cheerful interpretation on the Art Theatre stage ... The comic angle on the play was followed through with wonderful subtlety and with great skill.... Certainly it is difficult for me to explain this 're-creation' of the Art Theatre to readers who have not read the play. Well, perhaps the author has to some extent 're-created' himself in pursuing a theatrical course laid down by Mr Stanislavsky ... who depicts Gayev as the most pleasant of 'bon viveurs', an epicurean, a well-groomed landowner for whom everything in life is so much wild grass. Gayev-Stanislavsky is ironic about himself and his surroundings. From his faintly screwed-up, lively eyes there streams a gentle mockery. Undoubtedly, he has been devastated but accepts his circumstances lightly without a groan or a whimper.
>
> (*Teatr i iskusstvo* 1904: 11 April)

Kugel' also declared that the play had been presented in a 'light lively comic vein' betokening 'the resurrection of Antosha Chekhonte' (one of the pseudonyms used by Chekhov in his literary youth when writing short pieces for humorous magazines). In an apparent attempt to cheer Chekhov up and convince him that what they were acting was the farce which the dramatist insisted he had written, Knipper reported Kugel''s comments to Chekhov: 'He thinks that we are playing vaudeville where we should be acting a tragedy and that we haven't understood Chekhov. There, you see ...' (Knipper-Chekhova 1972: 365).

However, in December 1908, remembering these first performances, Nemirovich wrote to Efros: 'Go and see *The Cherry Orchard* and you simply won't recognise in this lacy, graceful picture that heavy, mournful drama which *Orchard* was in its first year' (Nemirovich-Danchenko 1979: 470), a comment which hardly seems true to the production score or to bear out Kugel''s impression. The latter is also on record as describing the play, rather than the production, in the following quasi-symbolic terms:

The speeches of the characters in Chekhov's plays – and in *The Cherry Orchard* in particular – approximate to the form of a monologue, to the Maeterlinckian 'conversation with Fate' ... They live, the denizens of *The Cherry Orchard*, as if half-asleep, transparently, on the borders between the real and the mystical. Life is being buried.

(A. Kugel', 'The Melancholy of *The Cherry Orchard*', in Stroyeva 1955: 199)

A view couched in something of the same spirit and undoubtedly one of the most interesting assessments of both the play and the production was that of Meyerhold, who wrote to Chekhov on 8 May 1904:

Your play is abstract, like a Tchaikovsky symphony. Before all else, the director must get the 'sound' of it. In the third act, against a background of the stupid stamping feet – this 'stamping' is what he must hear – enters Horror, completely unnoticed by the guests.

(Braun 1969: 33)

He felt that the 'overall harmony' necessary for the interpretation of this act was disturbed in the Art Theatre's production:

The author intended the act's leitmotiv to be Ranevskaya's premonition of the approaching storm (the sale of the cherry orchard). Everybody else is behaving as if stupefied: they are dancing happily to the monotonous tinkling of the Jewish band, whirling round as in the vortex of a nightmare, in a tedious modern dance devoid of enthusiasm, passion, grace, even lasciviousness. They do not realise that the ground on which they are dancing is subsiding under their feet. Ranevskaya alone foresees the disaster; she rushes back and forth, then briefly halts the revolving wheel, the nightmare dance of the puppet show. [...] The following harmony is established in the act: on the one hand, the lamentations of Ranevskaya ... on the other hand, the puppet show (not for nothing does Chekhov make Charlotte dance amongst the 'philistines' in a costume familiar in the puppet theatre – a black tail-coat and check trousers). [...] This is the musical harmony of the act, and the conjuring scene is only one of the harsh sounds which together comprise the dissonant tune of the stupid dance. [...] Similar instances of dissonant notes emerging fleetingly from the background and encroaching on the act's leitmotiv are: the station-master reading poetry; Yepikhodov breaking his billiard cue; Trofimov falling downstairs.

At this point, Meyerhold goes on to make his major criticism of the production:

> The director of the Art Theatre has shown how the harmony of the act can be destroyed. With various bits and pieces of equipment, he makes an entire scene of the conjuring, so that it is long and complicated. The spectator concentrates his attention on it for so long that he loses the act's leitmotiv. When the act ends the memory retains the background melody, but the leitmotiv is lost.
>
> (28-9)

Some of his criticism may be justified but, had Meyerhold had an opportunity to study Stanislavsky's production score, he might have felt obliged to modify his viewpoint.

13

SEASON SEVEN TO
SEASON TEN: 1904–1908

In 1893, Stanislavsky had attended the première, at Aurélien Lugné-Poë's Théâtre de l'Oeuvre in Paris, of Maeterlinck's *Pelléas et Mélisande*. Inspired by Chekhov's interest in the work of the Belgian dramatist and by his own increasing dissatisfaction with naturalist stage forms, he turned to drama of an overtly 'symbolist' character. For the opening of the Theatre's seventh season on 2 October 1904, he chose to stage three plays by Maeterlinck. Employing the services of a designer other than Simov for the first time, he turned to a young St Petersburg artist, V. Suren'yants, who made models of settings for all three plays.

The plays themselves are fairly static. *The Intruder* shows a family sitting around a table, at night, waiting for the 'Intruder', Death, to visit the dying mother. In *The Interior*, a death has already taken place with the drowning of a young girl. The action then deals with the anticipation of the effect of the tragedy on the girl's family, who appear as shadows. In *The Blind*, a group of sightless people, abandoned to their fate, stumble through a forest in the direction of an approaching storm when the priest, who has been acting as their guide, falls dead. These highly allegorical works were, rather incongruously, provided with extremely realistic settings by Suren'yants.

The most successful production of the three was held to be of *The Interior*, which critics described as a 'tragic pantomime'. However, the general feeling was that the mystical and the apocalyptic 'had been reduced to the level of a fairy tale to frighten children'. According to S. Glagol':

> I do not recall another instance where such complete mis-understanding reigned in a theatre ... where there was

such evident disharmony between stage and auditorium. The former seemed convinced that it was playing a terrifying symphony and revealing horrible truths to the audience in images of complete and glorious beauty, but all this seemed to the spectators like mere scrapings on an untuned violin, the sound of cork being sliced, or finger nails scratching on glass.

(Russkoye slovo 1904: 18 October)

Some critics berated the theatre for its pessimism: 'Where are the ideals in these plays? Where are the dreams of a better future?' asked a theatre-going medical student, who accused the Theatre of losing sight of its role as a moral educator (Vinogradskaya 1976: 479). Efros, on the other hand, thought *The Blind* had been staged too *optimistically*:

The play has been written by a gloomy mystic-fatalist. In life there is only one truth – Death. In the Art Theatre... the play sounds almost like a hymn to light, a bold thrust forward towards a proud future, towards triumph over any kind of darkness.

(Novosti dnya 1904: 3 October)

Efros was alone in construing the production in this fashion. Lenin's friend, Inessa Armand, thought the effects 'shattering' but the acting 'weak'.[1] In *The Blind*, the 'down-to-earth' acting of Moskvin and Burdzhalov clashed with Savitskaya's performance. In *The Intruder*, Kachalov's acting had been in a 'mystical' key, where that of Luzhskiy and Leonidov had been more realistic (Stroyeva 1973: 150). On the other hand, one or two powerful voices were raised in favour. Diaghilev thought the 'form' unfinished, but then nobody had yet managed to hit on the right form for Maeterlinck. The Art Theatre's experimental example needed to be taken up by others (*Mir iskusstva* 1904: nos 8/9: 161–4). According to Andrey Bely, the Theatre 'had no equal' when it came to matters of staging the relationship between the real and the fantastic. He was especially impressed with their next production, of Chekhov's *Ivanov*, in which he thought they succeeded in expressing 'the fantastic nightmare of life', the 'symbolic essence' of an otherwise weak play (*Vyesy* 1904: no. 11: 30–1).

Bely's assertion appears surprising enough as a statement about a Chekhov play dating from the 1880s, especially since the director, Nemirovich, saw *Ivanov* as a play of the 1870s based on the ruins of the progressive ideas of the 1860s. In fact, he imagined the protagonists as 'Turgenevan heroes in changing historical conditions' (Stroyeva 1955: 206–7). Those capable of heroism – Ivanov, Lebedyev, Sara, Sasha – he saw being dragged down by the surrounding *poshlost'* [banality]. The 'King of the Banal' in this world was the bailiff, Borkin, with Babakina, Kozykh and others in close attendance.[2] According to one critic, the milieu was given an especially grotesque emphasis: 'The Moscow troupe transforms the whole gallery of Chekhovian types into some sort of chamber of rare exhibits, eccentrics and monsters' (*Birzhevyye vyedomosti* 1905: 20 April). This accorded with the Symbolist/Expressionist spirit of the times and, doubtless, appealed to Andrey Bely.

Stanislavsky, who played the part of Shabelskiy (considered then to be one of his finest performances), thought Ivanov ought to be 'a strong man, a fighter . . . and not a sick neurasthenic'. However, in Kachalov's performance under Nemirovich's direction, the traits which predominated were those of 'over-exhaustion' and 'wanness', leading reviewers to detect a distinct absence of the 'heroic'. In conservative quarters, the production was even accused of 'slandering' the character of Ivanov and of turning him into 'an isolated psychopath, a dish-rag and a useless individual' (Stroyeva 1955: 211). By contrast, Efros felt that Kachalov's interpretation constantly hinted at the possibility 'of turning the wheel the other way . . . the lesson is a reverse one: to break out of the shell, albeit at the risk of breaking one's neck' (*Teatr i iskusstvo* 1904: 31 October). Kugel' unkindly expressed a preference for the first production of the play, at the Korsh Theatre, which Chekhov's own account suggests was fairly incompetent (Yarmolinsky 1973: 63–4).

Stanislavsky worked on the score for Ibsen's *Ghosts* between 5 February and 11 March 1905, exploring contrasts between mist and sunlight as opposing symbols of falsehood and truth. The fate of a doomed artist and the inhibiting or destructive effects of environment – as in *The Seagull* and *Michael Kramer* – were once again a major theme. In this instance, however, Stanislavsky seemed anxious to play down the naturalistic aspects of fateful inheritance. For example, Osvald was not to be interpreted as a victim of an incurable disease; there was to be 'no pathology whatsoever' (Stanislavskiy 1954–61: vol. 5: 266–8). Instead, he was to appear 'a being of crystalline purity' imbued with a love of life – someone whose death was a beautiful, 'premature conclusion' to it. As Osvald spoke his famous final line, a ray of sunlight was to illuminate Mrs Alving, encircling her head with 'the halo of a suffering martyr'. Anticipating the criticism which this interpretation was likely to elicit, Stanislavsky jokingly concluded his score for Act Three:

> The rays of the foreign sun [foreign, because produced by new lanterns purchased from abroad] will strike blind the Efroses of this world in the third row and, fortunately, this will mean that the production won't get reviewed and, because the audience is stupid [presumably Stanislavsky is being ironic] it will be a great success.
>
> (Stroyeva 1973: 154)

Stanislavsky spent a great deal of time trying to get Moskvin (Osvald) and Savitskaya (Mrs Alving) to act in what he called 'the French style', relying on facial expression and voice intonation, with a minimum of gesture. He sought the 'virtuosic handling of strong temperament', the actor needing to move rapidly and lightly from one extreme to another, both in terms of mood and in the degree of intensely 'lived emotion' (*perezhivaniye*). Such remarks anticipate the score of *A Month in the Country* and the first full-blown attempt to put the Stanislavsky 'system' to the test.[3]

On the naturalistic/ethnographic side, there was much concern to achieve a degree of national and geographical authenticity. There were to be Norwegian rugs and tables, portraits on the walls, and floors painted white. Stanislavsky was also troubled about verisimilitude in another sense. What was the rationale for Engstrand's entering the house at the beginning of Act One? Apparently missing Ibsen's symbolic point, the production had Engstrand arrive to mend a door which, at curtain rise, he was discovered planing. This involved changing words and transposing phrases. 'What else can one do?' Stanislavsky asked himself, as if dealing with intractable material 'I think it would be pedantic not to make such modifications' (Munk 1966/7: 30–44).

During rehearsal, he warned Savitskaya against adopting too tragic a tone. She needed to perform in the style of French comedy, at least until the end of Act Two. As Osvald had recently returned from Paris, Stanislavsky considered dressing him in a beret, loose-fitting velvet suit and raincoat, 'as clear as crystal. No pathology'. Kachalov was required to act Manders 'with the subtlety, polish and sincerity of a real Frenchman' as 'a sincere, good, naive, but credulous child' (38–42). Not surprisingly, critics missed the 'limitlessly pessimistic mood' of the play (*Russkoye slovo* 1905: 1 April) and, in something of an understatement, the critic in *Russkiy listok* suggested that: 'The leitmotiv of the play – the horror of deterministic inheritance – was insufficiently felt' (1905: 3 April).

Because of the insurrectionary events of 1905 in Russia and the European tour the following year, the 1905–6 season saw only one première – of Gorky's *Children of the Sun* – on 24 October 1905. In this, as in the productions of Ibsen's *Brand* and Hamsun's *The Drama of Life* which followed, the Theatre pursued its exploration of the conflict between the intellectual heights and the lower depths of life, between the world of the stars and the mountain peaks, as opposed to life lived at more mundane levels. Gorky's play actually began life as a joint collaboration with Leonid Andreyev entitled *The Astronomer*. In *Children of the Sun* (Andreyev's contribution became his own play *To The Stars*), the 'heights' are represented by the Russian intelligenstia, the 'children' of the title. Opposed to them are the 'children of darkness', or the Russian masses. The play also deals with the conflict between the life of the spirit and that of the senses. The former is represented by Protasov, a scientist who immerses himself in intellectual pursuits and who professes to belong to a spiritual aristocracy; the latter are represented by his wife, Yelena, who seeks physical love outside marriage, and by his sister Lisa, who feels drawn towards 'the people'. The tension produced by the pull of opposites leads to a death, a suicide, insanity, an insurrection and, finally, a melancholy reconciliation, once a popular revolt has been suppressed. The events of 1905 were a fitting background to the production.

Stanislavsky worked on the score in tandem with that for *The Drama of Life*, as the plays seemed to him to be linked both thematically and ideologically. Gorky's Protasov and Hamsun's Kareno were variations on a theme devoted to noble, intelligent, inspired people – in fact those with characteristics like Stanislavsky himself. The latter's view of the 'exceptional' nature of the artist (the fact that Protasov is a scientist seems irrelevant) had been expressed as early as 1889: 'The artist is a prophet who appears on earth to bear witness to purity and truth . . . He must be an ideal man' (Benedetti 1988: 37). Stanislavsky did not, therefore, share Gorky's view of the inherent limitations of an attitude which blinds itself to the state of the world in turning its attention to the stars. In this case, Protasov was presented as prophet-like – a characterisation which ran counter to Gorky's. Protasov's monologue about the power of science was given special prominence. His remark to the effect that the 'children of the sun' would 'conquer the dark fear of death' was designed to elicit an 'ecstatic response', according to the production score (Stroyeva 1973: 158). Life outside the domestic/scientific bell-jar was conceived in crude and bestial terms to further the contrast with the refined purity inside it. The workaday world was depicted with customary flair. Metalworkers and carpenters demonstrated their professional expertise, cutlets were prepared for breakfast, carriages cleaned, carpets beaten and jam made. There were also real live dogs (159).

Thematically, the crucial line became Lisa's hysterical declaration that, 'Life is full of wild animals!', following the episode when crude sexual overtures are made to her by a Ukrainian vet and after a drunken blacksmith has entered in murderous pursuit of his wife. The final 'revolt of the masses' revealed the crowd, once again, as a brutalised mob. The storming of the house was reminiscent of *An Enemy of the People* but here the audience saw the crowd actually break down a door with battering rams whilst 'stones and pieces of wood' flew through the air (160). At the première, because of the tense political situation outside, the scene produced panic in the Theatre when those who stormed the stage were taken to be representatives of the reactionary 'Black Hundreds', so realistically was the assault performed (Nemirovich-Danchenko 1968: 263).

The first production after the company's return from abroad was of Aleksandr Griboyedov's early nineteenth-century comedy *'Tis Folly to be Wise* (*Gore ot uma*) or *Woe From Wit*, as it is more usually translated), which opened on 26 September 1906.[4] This was the first of four productions of the play which the Theatre would stage during the next thirty years or so, the others being the revivals in 1914 and 1925, and a new production by Nemirovich in 1938. Stanislavsky acted Famusov, the 'Director of a Government Department', in a way which went against the nineteenth-century tradition established by Mikhail Shchepkin, interpreting him as a middle-aged dandy rather than a paternalistic aristocrat.[5] 'The destructive power of slander' seemed to be the production's keynote, culminating in the Act Three soirée, staged as an allegorical whirlpool of lies, animated by the rhythms of a mad world. Kachalov played the betrayed and slandered intellectual 'outsider', Chatskiy. The scene succeeded in merging the real with the fantastic, 'like a feverish nightmare', according to some critics.

Most of the work was done by Nemirovich, Stanislavsky merely introducing minor corrections and additions to Act Three. Stanislavsky's 'Brutus-like' sufferings continued during rehearsals when, apparently, he was not offered a single direction by Nemirovich. Reviewers noted a myriad details which brought the past to life, such as Famusov's coloured waistcoats, the top hats of the guests, the candelabras, three-leaved mirrors, clavichords, clocks with mechanical figurines under glass domes, tinkling coffee spoons and jingling spurs (Koonen 1985: 38). For some reason, Nemirovich opted for a text which had turned Griboyedov's sparkling verse into prose. Meyerhold, whose association with the Theatre had been renewed through his productions at the Studio Theatre on Povarskaya Street and whose first-ever stage appearance had been in this Russian classic, noted sardonically: 'it became necessary to speak the verse like prose in order to inspire the production with authenticity' (Rudnitskiy 1969: 169).[6]

Nemirovich's production of Ibsen's *Brand*, on 20 December 1906, focused on contrasts between domestic and natural worlds – storms at sea, avalanches and landslides, set against domestic interiors and family intimacies. It was closely followed by Stanislavsky's production of Hamsun's *The Drama of Life*, on 8 February 1907, staged in collaboration with Sulerzhitskiy. Georgiy Plekhanov described Kareno, the central character of Hamsun's play, as 'a son of Dr Stockmann', and accused both of talking 'reactionary nonsense' (Stroyeva 1973: 66).[7] Nemirovich appears to have been anxious to 'humanise' the role of Brand in a manner which contrasted with Stanislavsky's attempt to stress Kareno's suprahumanity. The qualitative contrasts between the two dramatists also proved a contentious issue for both directors.

The following notes, taken from Nemirovich's prompt-copy for Act Three of *Brand*, give an indication of his attempt to suggest the human side of a potentially 'inhuman' character. They relate to a moment, following the death of the child and the moment of Brand's demand, consonant with his 'all or nothing' philosophy, that his wife part with everything which reminds her of their dead son:

> In much of what we do, we need to go against the grain of Ibsen's presentation. Carried away by the grandeur of his ideas to the detriment of formal originality . . . Ibsen tends to push his actors in the direction of banal heroic devices. It rests with us to avoid this and bring the tragedy close to the

soul of the spectator by means of modest, lifelike images. For example, in the scene with the gypsy [to whom the dead child's clothes are given], if Brand stands with his hands behind his back and imposes his serious demands on Agnes [Brand's wife] in this attitude, this will be unpleasant. It will be touching if he is near Agnes, embraces and caresses her, even if resting on his haunches (if she is kneeling at the lower drawers of the chest) as if whispering to her what she ought to do. Or he could sit near her on a bench or stool, without any self-pride.

(MAT Museum: Nemirovich-Danchenko archive no. 10317)

Once again, it was felt that excessive realism – the mountain scenery and the scenes by the fjord with large boats in the foreground – swamped the 'spiritual' message of the play (Yablonskiy 1909: 165–72).[8] According to Koonen, who played two minor roles, Kachalov made a fine Brand and the première was well received (Koonen 1985: 41).

It was doubtless the extension of the Stockmann-Protasov theme – the clash between idealism and materialism – which attracted Stanislavsky to *The Drama of Life*. The production was conceived as the tragedy of an idealist who chooses to descend, Christ-like, into a fallen world. The drama of life became the conflict between the elevated and the base, with the 'sinful temptations' of the flesh personified in the snake-like Terezita, combining the attractions of both Eve and the Serpent.

The play is the second part of Hamsun's trilogy about Kareno, a Nietzschean dreamer and philosopher, who inhabits a glass tower constructed for him by Oterman, a rich man who becomes possessed by the demon of avarice. Oterman's daughter, Terezita, is a symbolic incarnation of lust who vainly tempts Kareno to abandon the world of meditation and inspiration to fall in love with her. In the background is a beggar who, like Andreyev's 'Being in Grey' in *The Life of Man*, serves as a silent personification of Fate. Stanislavsky's director's score for the production is one of his most interesting, as well as one of his last (he was soon to abandon the practice) and the imaginative settings by V. Yegorov and Nikolay Ul'yanov made an important contribution to the production's success.[9,10]

The third act, especially, was staged in a highly imaginative manner. The scientist with his head in the clouds falls to earth and is .treated to a vision of Armageddon. The world is seen as a marketplace inhabited by a grey mass (portrayed as shadows) whose silhouettes flicker inside lighted booths which combine a sense of market and fairground. A love scene between Kareno and Terezita, described as a 'mime drama with a boa', takes place following Terezita's snake-like entry from a tunnel, trailing a black scarf behind her, and with a white feather boa entwined about her neck. This scene is followed by one of general orgy, before the participants are overtaken by a cholera epidemic – a sign of God's judgement.

During rehearsals there arose what Stanislavsky described as 'a cult of inner feeling'. In order that nothing should distract the actors from their task he

> took away . . . all external means of personification – both gesture and movement . . . because this all seemed to me to have too much to do with the body, the realistic and the material, and I needed bodiless passion in its pure, naked form, both naturally and emanating directly from the soul of the actor. For the transmission of this, as it seemed to me then, the artist needed only eyes, face and mime. So let him, in immobility, live through the emotion he has to transmit with the help of feeling and temperament.
>
> (Stanislavskiy 1988: 386)

This is very like the method he was to employ on a quite different type of play, A Month in the Country, during which he made almost impossible, not to say torturous, demands of his actors.

Yegorov's designs corresponded to the director's idea that each character personify a human passion which persisted, unchanging, throughout the play. The visual effect was striking, each scene seemingly composed of longitudinal strips of green, yellow and red cloth and with rocks, winding paths, houses, fences, even the sea, sky and clouds apparently woven out of these long, coloured strips. For Act Three, Stanislavsky adopted Ul'yanov's designs – with a towering 'rock' in the middle of the stage and a mass of canvas screens representing booths through which the silhouettes of the actors were visible and which permitted a great deal of 'shadow-play'.

The Symbolists took Stanislavsky to their hearts after this, whilst the Realists walked out in disgust. 'I am happy with the results', he noted. 'The decadents are pleased, the realists are indignant and the bourgeoisie feels insulted' (Stanislavskiy 1954–61: vol. 7: 364). Nemirovich considered the production a mistake as was, in his opinion, the creation of the Povarskaya Studio. According to Stanislavsky, however,

> we did not stage the play in a symbolist style. I don't even know what a symbolist play is. [...] The symbol of *The Drama of Life* is in this grey, boring sense of fate. The audience was determined to see a separate symbol in every stroke of detail.
>
> (*Segodnya* 1907: 4 May)

The conflicts between the directors of *Brand* and *The Drama of Life* became clear in a letter from Nemirovich to Stanislavsky on 11 November 1906, in which he compared the respective merits of the plays:

> I considered that, when the question arose of which was more important, Kachalov in *Brand* or in *The Drama of Life*, then there could be no two opinions on that score. There is nothing to talk about [Nemirovich's underlining]. *Brand* is one of the century's works of genius, whereas *The Drama of Life* is a talented question mark. And when I see that the actors are all for *The Drama of Life*, because there's a part in it for them and because of you – because it's you who are concerning yourself with the play – and that nobody has a good word to say for the outpourings of Ibsen's genius – including Moskvin, whom I suspect of not telling the truth – then the whole bunch of shareholders becomes antipathetic to me, disgustingly so.
>
> (Vinogradskaya 1971: vol. 2: 46)

Nemirovich's production of Pushkin's *Boris Godunov* opened the tenth season, on 10 October 1907. The more logical choice might have been Aleksey Tolstoy's *Tsar Boris*, so as to complete the trilogy, albeit with a much weaker play than Pushkin's. Nemirovich imagined it less as a historical and philosophical drama than as a *narodnaya pesnya* or folk-song – a combination of poem and historical legend. Gradually, however, the production took on a symbolic and mystical cast, with the False Dmitriy portrayed as a manifestation of the popular poetic imagination. Nemirovich's approach became increasingly influenced by Symbolist ideas concerning the social function of theatre. The conversion of the Pretender into a 'fiery seraph' at the head of the people's struggle began to seem like an attempt to create a new historical myth and place the theatre at the centre of a myth-making process. The production score was prepared, in the main, by Luzhskiy. Preparatory notes contained snippets of recondite historical information, such as reference to the fact that the Austrian Emperor Rudolph made Tsar Boris a gift of six parrots. From some other source, Nemirovich had noted the horrific particulars of the fate of the young boy-tsar Mikhail, whose wild screaming whilst being put to death was 'because they were crushing his testicles'. The production did not prove an outstanding success with audiences (Fel'dman 1967: 131–43).

Stanislavsky's production of Andreyev's *The Life of Man*, which followed on 12 December 1907, has been described in some quarters as 'a conception of genius' and one of the most wonderful productions in the entire history of the Art Theatre (Rudnitskiy 1989: 353). Stanislavsky recounts the background in *My Life in Art*, including his famous discovery of the dramatic effects achievable with black velvet against a black background (Stanislavskiy 1988: 398–401). The decision to stage the play in the first place arose out of work in progress on Maeterlinck's *The Blue Bird*. Stanislavsky wished to try out his experiments on the Andreyev play so as not to fail again with a Maeterlinck production.

The drama is a Russian Symbolist *Everyman* and portrays the five stages of life – from birth (in Scene One) to marriage (in Scene Two) to the achievement of wealth and grandeur in Scene Three (a sumptuous but lifeless ball scene), to Man's fall from grace into tragic loss, with the death of his son (in Scene Four) and, finally, to his own death in Scene Five amidst a bacchanal of misshapen drunkards, telescoping memories of the past in ironic and horrific fashion. With Man's death, a progressively dwindling candle held by a 'Being in Grey', whose permanent presence has accompanied the action, gutters and goes out.

'These both are and are not people as if, as in the work of Hogarth, they might sprout the heads of birds, of fish or wild animals at any moment', wrote Sergey Glagol'. The 'toy-like, passionless' musicians (in Scene Three) appeared to be shaped like their own instruments in a ballroom reminiscent of a 'colossal catafalque'. The dead 'Beardsleyish' world appeared to encompass the living Man and crush him to death. The planes of the real and the unreal, the living and the dead, 'interchanged as in a nightmare'. The production was a mélange of the grotesque and the

175

realistic – stylised caricature on the one hand and sincere lived emotion on the other 'but with the latter rendered "algebraic" and "purified", with no trace of the everyday, the temporal, or the purely individualistic'.

> And when in the fourth act a totally 'unghostly' divan appeared within the ghostly contours of a room outlined in space, with a real toy clown over which the Man wept real, bitter tears, then the spectator forgot all about 'ghostliness' and responded to him with a storm of applause.
>
> (*Chasy* 1907: 14 December)

This was the first production for which Stanislavsky had not prepared a production score in advance. Andreyev praised it and declared that the director had 'created wonders'. Stanislavsky himself was disappointed and attributed what he considered his meretricious success to the public's superficial response to the 'magical' effects achievable with white outlines on black velvet against a black background. At the dress rehearsal he was depressed almost to the point of fainting. The première was greeted with acclaim but, despite frequent curtain calls, Stanislavsky declined to appear.

The final production of the season on 5 March 1908 was of Ibsen's *Rosmersholm*, directed by Nemirovich and with settings by Yegorov. Despite his hostility to some of the theatrical manifestations of the Symbolist movement, Nemirovich was nevertheless interested in exploring new ideas and, notwithstanding his initial reservations, considered that Stanislavsky had made positive discoveries in his work on *The Life of Man*. Working with Yegorov, who had designed the settings for the Andreyev production, Nemirovich embarked on his first attempt to stage a manifestly symbolic work in a style which acknowledged the nature of the material – something which could not have been said of his earlier attempt to stage *When We Dead Awaken*.

Perhaps aware of Efros's feeling that the symbolic white horses of Rosmersholm 'had been shod with real hooves by a real blacksmith' (Efros 1924: 276), Nemirovich and his designer did their best to get away from the very solid settings prescribed by Ibsen. To this end, a strong element of stylisation was introduced. The drawing room with its ancestral portraits was discarded and substituted by a single interior wall and a huge *style moderne* divan placed parallel to the front of the stage. The remainder of the stage was hung with plain, grey-green drapes. In this manner, an attempt was made to merge the setting with the auditorium and to establish analogues between the two. Following in Stanislavsky's footsteps, Nemirovich strove to encourage the cast – Kachalov, Knipper, Luzhskiy, Vishnyevskiy, Leonidov – to act with a minimum of gesture and movement. Most of the conversations were conducted in statuesque poses, seated on the long divan. Unsurprisingly, the attempt to bring about a convergence between the scale of Scandinavian saga and the 'nerve thoughts' of the characters proved to be beyond the powers of even this very strong cast who found it 'too difficult to breathe in the purity of this over-rarified atmosphere and too cold to survive on these "glaciers" of dramatic poetry' (278). The play was given only twenty performances.

14

SEASONS ELEVEN AND TWELVE: 1908–1909

During the second half of 1907, Stanislavsky began making notes for a book he was planning on the actor's creativity in which he stressed the importance of 'the will' (*volya*). His notebooks contain attempts to formulate the various sections of a chapter on the will under four headings:

(1) The nature of the will.
(2) The inextricable connection between the will and the other creative faculties. The natural connection between them.
(3) The power of the will.
(4) The properties [characteristics (*svoystva*)] of the will.

(Vinogradskaya 1971: vol. 2: 101)

At the same time he was making notes on the ethics and talents of the actor. In 1908, whilst taking the waters in Homburg, he

> got to know a highly educated and very well-read person, who happened to let fall the following phrase in casual conversation: 'Do you know', he said to me, 'that the emotional feeling and creativity of the artist is based on the recall of affective feelings and memories? . . .' I said nothing, but immediately asked for literature to be sent me touching this question. Soon I was to receive the brochures of Ribot.[1]

(128)

He immediately read (in Russian translations published in St Petersburg in 1900) two works by Théodule Ribot: 'Memory in its Normal and Abnormal [Sick] States' and 'The Will in its Normal and Abnormal [Sick] States'. Henceforth, Stanislavsky was to become increasingly preoccupied with questions of the actor's art.

178

On 6 September 1908, a meeting of all the younger actors in the company was called in the upper foyer of the Theâtre, to hear Stanislavsky announce his intention to found what was to become the First Studio.[2] Luzhskiy recorded first hearing the terms which became the basis of the 'system' at this meeting. Meanwhile, Stanislavsky had been preparing a production of Maeterlinck's *The Blue Bird*, which opened the Theatre's eleventh season on 30 September 1908.

Work on the play had been proceeding for more than a year-and-a-half, during which Stanislavsky's interest in the ethics of acting and dramatic performance had been influenced by his increasingly close collaboration with Leopold Sulerzhitskiy – a disciple of the religious teachings of Leo Tolstoy. Like the 'green stick of happiness' which the young Tolstoy buried in the woods at Yasnaya Polyana, the search for the 'blue bird' of happiness became closely connected with the pursuit of a theatrical ideal. Stanislavsky noted in his diaries that the search for the blue bird of happiness, away from the 'crudity and dirt' of life, was directly connected with the idea of a theatre studio – a place where one could, temporarily, cut oneself off from the world and live with the very best thoughts and feelings.

In his production of *The Blue Bird*, the relationship between Man and a fallen world was explored through the naive simplicity of a child-like vision which perhaps alone could comprehend the secret beauty of nature hidden from an inhuman civilisation. Designs for the play were based on children's drawings so that elements hitherto conceived as discordant could be made to merge in naive and universal harmony. It was in this spirit that the brother and sister set out on Christmas Eve to look for the blue bird of happiness accompanied by the souls of the creatures, objects, phenomena which were inseparable from their lives – Light, Water, Bread, Fire, Sugar, Milk and also their Cat and their Dog.

Critics from the Symbolist camp felt that, in toning down the mysticism and sense of the power of death, the production had been unfaithful to the essential spirit of Maeterlinck. Others were struck by the 'child's fairy-tale' aspect of the drama, its 'beauty', 'magical fantasy' and 'dream-like' nature (*Slovo* 1908: no. 3 November). Efros recommended his readers to 'surrender' to its power and 'fly to its kingdom of enchanted secrets' (*Rech*' 1908: 3 October). Even Nemirovich was prepared to give the production its due. Having initially failed to see anything in the play other than 'a French operetta with pleasant sentiments', where Stanislavsky appeared to see 'some unusual profundity or other' (Vinogradskaya 1971: vol. 2: 132), he later issued a remarkably loyal statement of faith, both in the production and in Stanislavsky:

> The production represented an enormous amount of work for the Art Theatre. It isn't a question of acquiring some machine or other for 20,000 roubles – as someone reported in the newspapers. There is nothing of the kind. The difficulty for Stanislavsky consisted, first and foremost, in the search for the essential principles of the production, and then in gradually, stubbornly, overcoming the technical limitations of the contemporary stage. Rehearsals, both full and in part, normal and dress rehearsals, numbered around 150. [...] The play is presented in bright and joyful tones. The main principles of the production are humour and a touching lyricism. Comic and dramatic elements are intertwined with the fantastic. . . . The completeness of stage technique which Stanislavsky has arrived at, seems to me to have attained forms hitherto unrealised.
>
> (*Rannyeye utro* 1908: 1 October)

The production of Gogol's *The Government Inspector* which followed, on 18 December 1908, was in an altogether different key. Conceived more in the grotesque spirit of *The Life of Man*, or *Ivanov*, it was the first of Stanislavsky's two attempts to stage the play (the second being in 1921 with Michael Chekhov as Khlestakov). In a pre-production press statement, Nemirovich warned people not to expect an original approach along the lines of *The Blue Bird*. In fact, every attempt was made to resurrect the realism of earlier productions but, at the same time, to animate this through a form of poetic hyperbole. Critics noted both how all the details of everyday life in Simov's settings appeared to have taken on an aura of phantasmagoria, and how the characters were transmogrified into a collection of malignant grotesques.

The principle of exaggeration dominated throughout, as though a gigantic magnifying glass had been inserted between the stage and the auditorium, suggesting a kind of Swiftian horror at the detail of everyday life. Every hint in the text was worked up into a whole series of minor episodes. In the scene at the inn, Khlestakov squashed bugs on the wall with his feet, hauled the inn-servant about by the hair, and hurled boots at his own servant, Osip. In the scene at the mayor's house, serving girls dragged in a filthy feather bed for the comfort of the 'distinguished guest from the capital', and an entire scene involved the mayor's prolonged and revolting consumption of a fig. His reprimand to the merchants, once convinced that his daughter is to marry 'a person of consequence', was delivered semi-naked, lounging on a huge, vulgar pink divan. The arrival of the real government inspector was preceded by the off-stage clanking of spurs, reminiscent of the arrival of the statue in Pushkin's *Don Juan*, before an evil-looking, marionette-like gendarme appeared in the rear doors, stunning the whole entourage into a silence lasting a full minute-and-a-half and generating 'a numbed sense of horror in which there sounded a genuine note of tragedy' (Stroyeva 1973: 239–40).

A few extraneous items, consisting mainly of portraits, were discarded during rehearsal. One, on the mayor's drawing-room wall, depicted Napoleon; another, on the wall of Khlestakov's room at the inn, depicted a caricatured general twirling his moustaches and gazing with bulging eyes at another portrait, of a nude, on the opposite wall. A third was a portrait of a priest, around the frame of which had been hung a string of dried mushrooms. Getting rid of these excrescences did little to appease Pavel Markov, who still thought all this was 'naturalistic hyperbole' and 'devoid of humour'.[3] Kugel', inevitably, was not amused:

> One's soul feels insulted and embittered by this sort of Gogol: so crude, so zoological, so clumsy, so arbitrary, so helpless and so vile is Russian life made to appear . . . It makes you want to spit – literally spit on these types.
>
> (*Russkiye dramaturgi*, 1937: 39)

Others detected the influence of Andreyev, seeing this production as simply

> a continuation of *The Life of Man*. Monstrous figures, similar to those we saw at the ball-scene in the other play, moving in a stylised and slow manner, with scarcely any change in the expression of their bulging eyes, pronouncing their words with some sort of strange hissing and whistling effect.
>
> (*Russkiye vyedomosti* 1908: 20 December)

The outstanding production of the twelfth season was, unquestionably, that of Turgenev's *A Month in the Country*, which proved a watershed in Stanislavsky's development, both as actor and director. After this production – the first to put the 'system' into serious operation – Stanislavsky became increasingly pre-occupied with theories of performance. As far as his choice of repertoire was concerned, a note of 'retrospectivism' made itself felt increasingly – the casting of a dewy, nostalgic glance towards the past. If there was a criticism to be made of his production of *A Month in the Country*, it lay precisely in a tendency to aestheticise and idealise a past, now seen through the roseate glow of a 'World of Art' cult of 'the beautiful' – a marked change from the view of the past which characterised the production of *The Government Inspector* only the previous season.

A MONTH IN THE COUNTRY

In *My Life in Art*, Stanislavsky explains that the attempt to stage Turgenev's play arose partly as a result of his failure to achieve the desired results with his production of Hamsun's *The Drama of Life*:

> Notwithstanding the failure of an analogous experiment in *The Drama of Life*, I decided to repeat it again. . . . The powerful passions of the Hamsun play seemed to me more difficult to portray without gestures than the intricate spiritual picture of the Turgenev comedy.
>
> (Stanislavskiy 1988: 406)

The Drama of Life had taken a tentative first step along the path towards introducing the 'system' into the work of the Art Theatre as a whole. Its failure, according to Stanislavsky, had largely been because 'the inner picture' had not been 'painted in detail' with too much emphasis on 'generalisation' which had led to 'vague spiritual contours', unsettling the actors and affecting their self-confidence. Like Hamsun's, the Turgenev play also demanded 'a special kind of acting'. It was 'the inner content' which required emphasis. If it had been difficult to portray powerful passions without gestures in Hamsun, 'the lacework of the psychology of love' in Turgenev could be conveyed by means of an almost static *mise-en-scène*: 'Let there be only a bench or a sofa . . . and let the characters sit on it so as to display . . . the intricate pattern of Turgenev's spiritual lacework' (405–12).

A Month in the Country was seen to provide an opportunity for a full-blooded incorporation of the 'system' into the Theatre's work, thereby establishing it at the heart of future activities. The play itself, in its complete form, Stanislavsky regarded as boring and unstageable (Stanislavsky 1954–61: vol. 8: 103), and he had no qualms about editing what he considered over-long speeches, altering and cutting scenes and generally treating the play in a less than sacrosanct manner. The only roles which really mattered to him were Rakitin (played by himself) and Natalya Petrovna (played by Knipper). Of secondary interest were the roles of the young tutor, Belyayev, and Natalya Petrovna's ward, Verochka. The score barely hints at the existence of Shpigelskiy, Bolshintsov, Islayev, Lizaveta Bogdanovna or Katya and hardly a word is devoted to Schaaf, Kolya, Anna Semyonovna or the servant Matvey. In other words, the form which the production score took was quite unlike any others which preceded it and proved, effectively, to be Stanislavsky's last (if one excludes the 1930 score for *Othello*).

The production may be seen to occupy a significant place in Stanislavsky's ideological development. It was programmatic in so far as work on his 'system' was concerned. However, the production can also be seen to develop ideas from earlier work, arising from the exploration of the clash between life and art, between the contingencies of naturalistic existence and the possibilities of idealistic transcendence and between nature in both its wild and domesticated (human) forms. Stanislavsky appears to have used the play to exemplify an eternal struggle between nature and nurture, between culture and those forces which threaten to overwhelm and destroy it. As expressed in *My Life in Art*, Natalya Petrovna's life in a luxurious sitting-room has been spent 'far from nature'. The artificiality of this protected existence is kin to that of 'hothouse plants'. The introduction of Belyayev into this environment is then seen as equivalent to a force of nature. Natalya Petrovna responds to its call and this 'leads to general catastrophe' (Stanislavskiy 1988: 405–12).

The basic ideological theme of the production became the need to transform 'life' into 'art' in order to transcend 'nature'. This accounts for the decision to concentrate on the relationship between Rakitin and Natalya Petrovna. They both represented a cultured, civilised way of life, a Westernised aristocratic tradition transplanted into a countrified wilderness which threatened to engulf it. In this conflict, Natalya Petrovna and everything she represented was threatened with destruction through her succumbing to the overwhelming power of instinctual passion. Rakitin, as interpreted by Stanislavsky, achieved an exemplary form of aesthetic triumph over the exigencies of both nature and passion. Whilst the husband in the background is building an actual (and presumably ineffectual) dam against the 'flow' of nature, his wife is being overwhelmed by an inner passion which corresponds to those external, natural forces. In these circumstances, Stanislavsky/Rakitin made of himself a transcendental artistic construct, impervious to the exigencies of the moment, a work of art in himself and part of 'the artifice of eternity'.

The ideology of the production makes for interesting comparisons with the apparently very different worlds of Oscar Wilde and Luigi Pirandello. Wilde's 'construction' of an aesthetically self-conscious persona was wittily and knowingly assembled over the abyss into which he knew it could be precipitated at any moment. It was based on a knowing pretence which rendered the 'pretentiousness' of others ridiculous. Pirandello, on the other hand, suggested that any human construct, such as a personality or a philosophical system, was an inherently self-deceiving device developed in order to shield ourselves from the terrors which life itself constitutes as a destructive force on a par with the forces of nature. The only permanent reality that can constitute a form of transcendence is the work of art itself, which survives 'the torrent of life' that sweeps everything else before it.

Stanislavsky may have been conscious, indirectly, of both the 'Wildean' and the 'Pirandellian' outlooks but seems seriously to have considered it possible to convert Life permanently into Art – a difficult, even punishing process (like mastering the art of his 'system') but which had to be gone through if theatre (analogous with life itself) was to be meaningful. As most people are 'ordinary' or only average 'actors' on the stage of life, they need to be disciplined in the art of living (acting) to the fullest extent. There is a natural tendency to avoid this imperative on the grounds that the process is too difficult and involves too much effort and pain. Therefore, the absolute necessity to convert life into art needs to be *imposed*, just as Brand needed to impose the need to ascend the mountain on those who were otherwise seemingly content to grovel in the valley contemplating the mud rather than the empyrean. A consequence of not recognising the absolute demands of an 'All' would be a resultant 'Nothing'. Hence the need arose for a working method, a 'system' which could attempt to convert (in an almost religious sense) raw human nature, inert matter and consciousness, into another superior form of existence – a Life as (or in) Art.

Rehearsals began in August 1909 and had collapsed in disarray by November, largely due to Knipper's breakdown under the strain imposed on her. Having left a rehearsal in tears, she received a letter from Stanislavsky and some flowers. The letter, it has to be said, is extremely revealing. It speaks of the necessity of 'suffering' born of 'torture', of the need to win the 'artistic struggle'. 'Suffering is inescapable' in order to 'attain the true joys of art' and that 'torment will bear magnificent fruit'. He also speaks of having 'frightened' her with 'scientific words' and of being 'brutal' out of 'fondness' for her because he fears the 'pollution' of 'the beauty nature has conferred' on her. The 'battle' has to be won, both for the sake of her talent, but also for the sake of 'the whole of our theatre, which is the meaning of my whole life'. The terms of this letter are extremely disturbing, not just because they refer in terms reminiscent of Stockmann to notions of human 'pollution' conflated, almost mystically, with a human nature which can also 'bear fruit' in a spiritual sense. The tone seems totally unmitigated, even compounded, by the expression of 'heartfelt love from a worshipper of your great talent' with which it concludes (Melik-Zakharov and Bogatyrev 1963: 82–92).

If this were not depressing enough, the letter with which Knipper answered is painful in its spirit of contriteness and self-castigation. It was she who was 'guilty', had 'wept more tears' on receiving Stanislavsky's letter by which she had been 'deeply moved'. She even adds to the sense of wilful self-abasement, by expressing a wish to 'go down on her knees' and 'beg forgiveness' for the painful moments which she has caused Stanislavsky (!) in rehearsals. Only he, with his 'pure, limitless and sincere devotion to art', was capable of forgiving her. The spectacle is unedifying and one wonders what Chekhov would have made of it. Harvey Pitcher interprets the episode more magnanimously, but concludes:

> Stanislavsky was quite ready to overthrow everything in which he had believed previously and to be fanatical in the promulgation of the new truth. Olga Knipper was not the only one to be scared by Stanislavsky's technical terms. He himself describes how the older members of the company protested that they were being treated as guinea pigs and that rehearsals were being turned into an experimental laboratory.
>
> (Pitcher 1979: 185–8)

In fact, the quasi-mystical methods which Stanislavsky employed in rehearsing *A Month in the Country* seem more like spiritualist seances than scientific research. The terms employed were thoroughly unscientific, such as 'ray-emission' and 'ray-absorption', and employed hieroglyphic notation which the actors were required to master. Recollecting all this with a degree of emotional tranquillity some years later, Knipper described herself as 'fearing' and 'hating' Stanislavsky as well as 'revering' him and being 'captivated' by him. 'He was a very strict man, and very exacting. It was at once a torture and a joy to work with him, but torture more often than joy . . . He was a fanatic in art' (Melik-Zakharov and Bogatyrev 1963: 83).

Alisa Koonen, who was originally cast as Verochka, before being replaced by Korenyeva, was less contrite than Knipper and shortly left the Theatre to work with Mardzhanov and Aleksandr Tairov.[4,5,6] In her memoirs she refers to the special rehearsal-text which the actors were asked to use and which incorporated hieroglyphics to indicate changing moods. On the face of it, this was unexceptional. A question mark indicated 'surprise'; a question mark in brackets, 'hidden surprise'. A hieroglyph resembling an eye denoted 'attention' (the character observes) and a similar one in brackets meant that the character 'observes secretly'. A hieroglyph resembling an ear meant that the character 'listens' and one in brackets meant 'listens on the quiet'. A minus sign denoted a negation: 'I assert that this is not', a plus sign meant 'I assert, or confirm, that this is so'. There were also signs denoting increase of emotion and its abatement; one for a rise in energy and one for its fall.

However, the appearance of simplicity proved deceptive according to Koonen:

> The exercises associated with the 'system' turned out to be difficult all round. What was demanded was not simply the mechanical execution of the task, but also our inner participation. The first period of work took place around the table. Konstantin Sergeyevich dictated and we carefully noted down the symbolic designations of the various emotions and inner states. A large dash, for example, denoted stage apathy; a cross – the creative state; an arrow going up – transition from apathy to the creative state. An eye denoted the arousal of visual attention; a hieroglyph reminiscent of an ear – the arousal of aural attention. An arrow ending in a hook –

denoted spiritual cunning with conviction; an arrow going to the right – the need to convince someone of something. These and similar marks – a dash, dots, strokes, sharps and flats – were very numerous.

(Koonen 1985: 100)

Trying to get to grips with a role denoted by circles, arrows and strokes had the effect frequently of reducing Koonen to tears. But –

The comforting thing was I was not alone. Olga Leonardovna [Knipper], playing Natalya Petrovna, with all her tremendous stage experience also lived through her introduction to the 'system' with difficulty. After one performance she complained: 'I cannot act with Konstantin Sergeyevich. In our duet, he looks at me with such searching eyes that I can scarcely pronounce the words. And today, after one line, he suddenly hissed at me: "Relax your right leg, the heel is tense". I was so dumbstruck my leg started twitching and I almost forgot my lines.'

(101)

In his notebooks, under the heading 'Logic and Sequentiality of Feeling', Stanislavsky gives an account of a rehearsal of part of Act Four:

In order to depict simple, complex or compound emotion, it is necessary to understand its nature. I will take as an example today's rehearsal. Korenyeva and Boleslavskiy were rehearsing the scene between Vera and Belyayev from Act Four of *A Month in the Country*.[7] Korenyeva was to express torment, doubt, pain, hope, the despair of rejected love. Having split up the role into its component parts according to its main affective state in which the actor must live, we will receive the following formula:

(a) Vera enters, having just learned of Belyayev's (intended) departure. She is pale, distracted, in tears. It is understandable that a sense of feminine shame compels her to conceal her distracted state. The actress must enter in an affective state of heightened mood with rapid tempo and energetic rhythm of adaptability, selection and rapid changes of adjustment.

(b) Beginning with Vera's words, 'Aleksei Nikolaich, is it true

187

you wanted to leave?' [see Turgenev 1991: 98] as far as her line 'He doesn't love me!' [98] – this is a new large section, consisting of several smaller ones in which Vera presents herself as indifferent in order to conceal the point of her question, nudging Belyayev by means of her sly utterances into making a confession. The actress must live by means of cunning and rapidly changing adjustments, expressing an indifference which conceals a keen love.

(c) From the words, 'He doesn't love me!', down to 'And I don't blame her. I know she's a kind woman . . .' and so on, as far as 'Natalya Petrovna's in love with you, Belyayev' (99) – is a new section, in which the actress lives and is agitated by the fact that she is trying to explain her sensation of spiritual torment for herself and its gnawing spiritual pain.

(d) From the words, 'Natalya Petrovna is in love with you' down to 'Oh, she doesn't have to worry! And you can stay!' [100] – the actress lives with every possible means of convincing Belyayev of Natalya Petrovna's love. At first, Vera wishes to achieve the unexpectedness of revelation, then stubbornly convince him. All this is done to observe Belyayev at the moment when he comes to believe in Natalya Petrovna's love for him. She will know from his eyes whether he loves her or not.

(e) From the words, 'Really?', down to 'And really what am I – just a silly girl, while she's . . .' [100] – the actress lives in a state of self-concentration, trying to convince herself (with her own means) of that which Natalya Petrovna has conceived.

(f) From the words, 'And when all's said and done, who knows? Perhaps she's right' [100] – the actress assertively lives the feeling – *convince me.*

From all these pieces, taken together and logically linked together, the dramatic scene is made up.

(Stanislavskiy 1986: vol. 1 350–4)

In the actual score the scene takes up four pages of brief directorial notes numbered 41–79 (Kalashnikov 1988: 521–7/ Turgenev 1991: 97–101). Stanislavsky then goes on:

Dramatic *perezhivaniye* [the living-through of emotional experience] is a compositional whole. Separate parts of it should not be made up of drama itself [by 'drama' he presumably means something like 'isolated dramatic episodes']. It can be explained by this formula. Let us say that we define the dramatic scene as a composite whole by the letter O.

$$a + b + c + d + e + f = O.$$

Korenyeva, as all actresses do, did the following. She lived through all the separate sections correctly, but all of them were impregnated with drama. What we got was out-and-out drama. It was as if a delicately drawn and beautiful picture had been thickly covered with dark lacquer, as a result of which nothing was visible, apart from a general darkness. The formula achieved was thus:

$$O + O + O + O + O + O = O.$$

It is not possible to compare each component part of the whole with the whole itself composed of them.

(Stanislavskiy 1986: 353–5)

It is not hard to understand why the 'actress' was experiencing difficulty.

In the spring of 1909, Stanislavsky asked a student of the Art Theatre school to make a précis of Ribot's book 'The Logic of the Emotions' (*Psychologie des sentiments*), which had been published in Russian in St Petersburg in 1906. This was to provide the means to 'lay bare the souls of the actors', so as to enable the audience to attend to their inner thoughts and feelings. In his view, this could not be done by gestures and stage movement – only by 'invisible ray-emission' without dramatic voice projection, using the eyes and 'psychological pauses'. Everything had to be avoided which prevented an audience 'from perceiving the inner essence of the feelings and ideas which were being lived through emotionally' (Stanislavskiy 1988: 405–12). For what was to be an essentially static production, Stanislavsky sought the collaboration of a designer associated with The World of Art (Mir Iskusstvo) movement, M. V. Dobuzhinskiy, who also happened to be an expert on nineteenth-century interiors.[8] What Dobuzhinskiy came up with (notwithstanding the realistic appearances) was essentially semi-abstract and symbolic.

If the external world of nature was characterised by irregular forms and chaotic, even cataclysmic phenomena, the internal forms of these aristocratic settings betokened harmony, balance, symmetry. The settings were symptomatic of the 'classical' rather than the 'romantic' age, characterised by formal architectural perfection. These were 'idealised' environments which served to project an ideal of human perfectibility. The forms imposed themselves on the environment in a manner, unlike the relics of Ozymandias, which suggested their perennial permanence, defying the threat of natural erosion.

Stanislavsky may well have had in mind Peter the Great's construction of a neo-classical city on the site of a marshy swamp. As if to indicate this, tokens of that nature on which human will had been imposed were incorporated in the settings. Dominating the perfectly symmetrical half-circle of the room in Act One (reminiscent of an interior in Peter the Great's own Summer Palace) were two large, elaborately framed landscape paintings – one depicting a storm at sea with a shipwreck, the other the watery calm of a landscape with an erupting volcano in the background. These paintings would appear to have been introduced, not as ironic comment on the civilised proceedings, but as an indication of the way nature can be captured, tamed and converted into art – the painted equivalents of tiger-skin rugs or stuffed bears.

The theme of the production (it could be argued) became the need to live up to the ideal which the surroundings represented. If the survival of the house was related to the ravages of nature and the simple need for up-keep, then the survival of the values of those who inhabited these surroundings was related to the challenge represented by the turbulent times in which the production was staged. To this extent, the production was ideologically didactic. Those social elements which, like nature, threatened to destroy the culture which Dobuzhinskiy's settings represented, were necessarily identified as elemental and brutish. Just as nature needed to be subdued and turned into art, so the brutish beast in man had to be subdued and educated. The fact that St Petersburg itself had been built on the bones of those who died building it was neither here nor there. The city had to be built as an example of 'superhuman' achievement which it was ordinary humanity's task to emulate by transforming itself into a different order of species-being. It was this kind of transfigured example of human possibility which Stanislavsky's 'system' was designed to facilitate.

Mariana Stroyeva communicates something of the ideological, programmatic element in the production:

> For the last time in its history, the Art Theatre resurrected on its stage the poetry of the past with lyrical power. And in bidding farewell but not wishing to part it said, as it were, to its audience: look, there is something in that bygone perished time, something independent of time, which forever contains within itself marks of spiritual nobility. . . . In the frightening, 'uncomfortable' contemporary world, torn by contradictions, the theatre stubbornly sought a haven for the bright elegant harmony, the imperishable humanity and the 'beauty of man's inner world' [. . .] Having seen the play as a drama of misunderstood and repudiated spiritual heroism and moral nobility, as a drama of the destruction of refined aestheticism, Stanislavsky subjugated the whole external appearance of the production to the all-pervading tonality of the image of Rakitin.
>
> (Stroyeva 1973: 245–53)

Dobuzhinskiy sat in on all the preliminary discussions and rehearsals and, as he noted later: 'This symmetry and "equilibrium", which was so typical of Russian Empire-style interiors, answered Stanislavsky's intentions to create an atmosphere of calm and at the same time to lend to the external immobility of the actors an inner tension, as if to "nail" them in position' (Vinogradskaya 1971: vol. 2: 186).

Rehearsals began in earnest in August 1909, with analysis of the roles and the emotional through-line. Stanislavsky began to break the play down into sections, working on each separately and introducing ideas related to 'circles of attention', 'individual self-feeling' and 'feeling for the other'. At a rehearsal on 28 August he spoke of his intention to introduce a minute's silence on stage before curtain-rise so as to permit the performer 'to focus himself and enter into the circle' (199). The following day, in a letter to his wife, Nemirovich told her that Stanislavsky had cast aside his (Nemirovich's) literary plan and that the result would be 'the ruin of Turgenev' (Nemirovich-Danchenko archive no. 2172).

During September, Stanislavsky was enthusiastic about rehearsals, informing his correspondent, V. V. Kotlyarevskaya, that: 'Extremely interesting experiments are taking place in our theatre. My system works wonders and the entire company have gone for it with both hands' (Stanislavskiy 1954–61: vol. 7: 449). 'Do you remember my talking about creative concentration and circles of attention? I have developed this circle of attention in myself to such an extent that I carry it about with me day and night' (449). However, on 11 September, following a rehearsal of Act One conducted with his co-director Moskvin, his rehearsal diary records: 'Unsuccessful rehearsal. Nothing achieved' (Vinogradskaya 1971: vol. 2: 200). On 16 September, following a rehearsal in the presence of Nemirovich, he reported that the latter had been pleased with what he saw, 'even with Knipper, who acted worse in his presence. [...] We ... are happy and relieved and so have taken a two-day break' (Stanislavsky archive no. 545). In late September, he wrote describing work in progress:

> There will be no *mises-en-scènes*. A bench or divan at which people arrive, sit and speak – no sound effects, no details, no incidentals. Everything based on *perezhivaniye* and intonations. The whole production is woven from the sense-impressions and feelings of the author and the actors. How can this be noted down, how can the imperceptible means of the director's influence be transmitted to the actors? In its own way it is a kind of hypnosis, based on the mood feeling of the actors at the moment of work, on knowledge of their characters, their deficiencies and so on. In this play as in all others – this is the *only* work which is essential and worthy of attention.
>
> (Stanislavskiy 1954–61: vol. 7: 451)

In pursuit of this ideal, Stanislavsky began holding closed rehearsals in October. On his instructions, all the auditorium doors were to be closed and a notice hung on the main entrance announcing that a closed rehearsal was taking place. Not even Nemirovich was allowed in. Having transferred to the main stage, however, matters took a turn for the worse: 'it has not been rehearsal but poison. Everything has been lost. . . . It's a long time since I've experienced such torment, despair and loss of energy' (Stanislavsky archive no. 545). This feeling was substantiated by Nemirovich in a letter to his wife on 31 October:

> Today at last I was shown two acts of *A Month in the Country*. Moskvin and Stanislavsky have been rehearsing for over two months and have already held between 80 and 90 rehearsals and here they are, having prepared only two acts out of a total

of five. . . . I fear that Stanislavsky will prove quite bankrupt in the matter of production.

(Nemirovich-Danchenko archive no. 7164)

In a further letter of 1 November, he added:

One and a half months ago I was shown almost three acts in their entirety. Now there are only two of them. They also act worse than a month-and-a-half ago. What they have been doing with themselves all this time I can't for the life of me imagine! . . . The settings, the young man playing Belyayev, and Korenyeva are good; Stanislavsky himself is tolerable but Knipper is an utterly blank space.

There was also mention of the fact that Stanislavsky had considered replacing Knipper with Mariya Germanova but this, added Nemirovich, instead of helping matters, 'would finally kill Knipper' (7165).[9] He reported again on 7 November:

Yesterday, working on *A Month in the Country*, I came across a mood of hopelessness which seized all the participants, beginning with poor Knipper who wept, convinced as she has been for the past month, that she can't act the part and that it is isn't her kind of work.

(7169)

On 7 November, rehearsals were briefly suspended to give the cast a rest, which is when the exchange of letters between Knipper and Stanislavsky referred to above took place. When rehearsals were resumed on the 9th, Act Four was rehearsed for six hours, from noon to 6.00 p.m., without a break. Stanislavsky noted in his rehearsal diary: 'The fourth act was particularly tormenting as neither Knipper nor Korenyeva has the genuine temperament for this scene' (Stanislavsky archive no. 545). The rehearsal held on 17 November concentrated, exceptionally, on some of the minor characters –Lizaveta Bogdanovna and Shpigelskiy – of whom Stanislavsky had the following criticism to make (of their scene in Act Four):

You are acting liveliness, joy, excitement, that is you are acting the result. This is theatrical. In order to become genuinely joyful you have first of all to forget about joy. In his joy a person is lively and does everything nimbly, willingly, energetically. Perform your task – a mechanical one – deftly, i.e. quickly, resourcefully; run in lightly and take refuge from the rain. Look around you for somewhere to sit and settle yourselves, shake the rain from your dress, wipe your hands. In a word, remember to perform everything that is done when people escape from the rain and put their drenched clothes to rights, quickly, in sprightly fashion and with a will.

(Vinogradskaya 1971: vol. 2: 212)

After an unsuccessful rehearsal on 18 November, Stanislavsky was absent with chest pains and was suffering from loss of sleep. He called his doctor believing it to be angina. Following a run-through of the first four acts on 20 November, his alarm and despair increased as the first two acts were the only ones audible. Nemirovich came to Stanislavsky in his dressing room afterwards and declared that success was out of the question and 'God grant' they manage to get through the play on opening night. Stanislavsky was again unwell on 25 November following a rehearsal of Act Five on the 24th. He was also late for rehearsal on the 29th, as was Knipper.

By 4 December and the second dress rehearsal, which was given in the presence of an audience, matters had improved and Nemirovich began to predict success. 'All this was cheering', noted Stanislavsky (archive no. 545). Another open dress rehearsal was held on 7 December and the première was given on Wednesday 9 December with the following cast:

ARKADY SERGEYICH ISLAYEV, *a rich landowner*

N. O. Massalitinov[10]

NATALYA PETROVNA, *his wife*   O. L. Knipper

VEROCHKA, *a ward*   L. M. Korenyeva

ANNA SEMENOVNA, *Islayev's mother*   M. A. Samarova

LIZAVYETA BOGDANOVNA, *a lady companion*

E. P. Muratova

SCHAAF, *a German tutor*   N. N. Zvantsev[11]

RAKITIN, *a friend of the family*   K. S. Stanislavsky

BELYAYEV, *a student, Kolya's tutor*   R. V. Boleslavskiy

BOLSHINTSOV, *a neighbour*   I. M. Uralov

SHPIGELSKIY, *a doctor*   V. F. Gribunin

MATVEY, *a servant*   I. V. Lazaryev[12]

KATYA, *a maid*   L. I. Dmitrevskaya[13]

Three things appeared to strike critics most – firstly, that what had hitherto been considered a rather cumbersome play proved to be thoroughly stageworthy; secondly, that Dobuzhinskiy had provided remarkably beautiful settings; and thirdly, that Stanislavsky's performance as Rakitin was out of the ordinary. Critics were also delighted with the settings – the circular, blue drawing room in Act One with its mirror-waxed parquet floor and rosette motif in the centre, the symmetrically arranged, soft, striped furniture of genuine Karelian birchwood, and the sunlit parkland visible through the window. They remarked on the identical fire screens, placed on either side of the stage, which seemed to detach themselves from their surroundings as separate objects for aesthetic contemplation. The same was true of the two paintings, in the style of Karl Bryulov.[14] The semi-circular stage plan resembled a niche for sculpted groupings in which there were further niches in which classical-style urns had been placed.

For the garden scene in Act Two, a similar sense of symmetry prevailed. Behind a park bench in the centre of the stage, two seemingly identical trees forked upwards and over a pond. In the distance was a landscape of dwindling garden merging into meadow, enlivened by the dot of a church tower and the columns of a white pavilion. On a distant hillside, a white church with a blue cupola and gold spire was discernible, a field of ripening wheat, and the sails of a windmill on the horizon above which was a blue sky filled with fleecy clouds.

The setting for Act Three was a windowless sitting-room, dominated by a large circular stove extending the height of the room, with a central embrasure. Hanging on each wall of the V-shaped room, and standing out against the dark-green patterned wallpaper, were two large oval mirrors in identical dark frames. A white ceiling, richly ornamented in gold leaf, was complemented by a heavily patterned carpet in which circular flower motifs were prominent. These same motifs were taken up in the floral pattern of the scallop-shaped settee and in the chairs placed on either side of it. The symmetry was repeated in the plush red curtains covering the entrances at each downstage corner, running on rings along thick rails and extending from floor to ceiling.

The setting for Act Four, the *orangerie*, consisted of a large bare passageway with columns of chipped brick, built in something like the Venetian style which Shpigelskiy refers to, with a bare wooden ceiling, stained walls and round *oeil de boeuf* windows set high up. The main entrance was architecturally complicated, with lancet columns, rounded arches and with multi-coloured glass in narrow, half-oval apertures. In one corner were various garden implements, a stone urn, pieces of broken flower pot. In another was a green garden bench. Costumes fused organically with the settings in the stylised fashion of the 1840s. The image of the inhabitants was as if each had stepped out of a painting by either Viktor Borisov-Musatov or Konstantin Somov.[15,16] Even the least lavish settings were rendered attractive by the costuming – a yellow dress worn by Katya or a red one with black dots worn by Verochka. Rakitin's 'superb coat' in royal blue (christened a *paletot* by more ironical reviewers) was the subject of critical notices in itself (Grossman 1924: 153–5).

In Stanislavsky's performance there was an element of the passionless dandyism which an English audience might associate with a Wildean hero but which Russians saw as typical of the 1840s. 'Mr Stanislavsky plays Rakitin with unusual subtlety – very delicately and refinedly' (*Golos Moskvy* 1909: December: no. 283). 'In this Rakitin there is something of the young Turgenev and something of Alfred de Musset. . . . In him everything breathes elegance . . . as well as a genuine dandyism. . . . The gentleman reads . . . in unconstrained, easy-flowing pure French which harmonises with the entire picture of ancient Russian nobility' (*Rampa i zhizn'* 1909: no. 37).

> Mr Stanislavsky plays Rakitin almost without gesture, on a very few lustreless notes. This very much suits Rakitin, the aesthete, elegant in everything, both word and feeling, beautifully world-weary and condescendingly scornful of life. Perhaps there is also a slight grimace, as with all Russian lordly Childe-Haroldism. But the grimace has developed along with the face. Nevertheless the entire external reserve, both in intonation and gesture, does not conceal Rakitin's emotional feelings. These speak through his eyes.
>
> (*Rech'* 1909: 12 December)

The method employed in preparing the production score was quite different from earlier examples. To read the director's score of *A Month in the Country* is far less interesting than reading that of, say, *The Cherry Orchard*. This is largely because the former registers very little action and merely charts the thoughts and emotions which accompany the dialogue. It is worth remembering that the year 1909 was only three years after the experiments which Meyerhold was conducting at Komissarzhevskaya's theatre in St Petersburg. Indeed, the 'hardly palpable intonations' which Stanislavsky demanded from his actors appear reminiscent of Meyerhold's efforts to attain a form of stylised speech – like drops of water falling 'into a deep well' – which was a peculiar feature of his production of Maeterlinck's *Sister Beatrice*, in 1906 (Braun 1969: 54).

It also seems relevant to point to similarities between the static, formalised, sculpted groupings reminiscent of a bas-relief or frieze, characteristic of a Meyerhold production, and the similar groupings and foreshortened settings which characterised Stanislavsky's Turgenev production. Moreover, Dobuzhinskiy's designs incorporated many of those aspects of Symbolist staging deployed by Meyerhold in the spirit advocated by Georg Fuchs, in deliberately exploiting a reduction in stage-depth.[17] This afforded a shallow acting area against a plain or decorated background which had the effect of throwing action and gesture into relief. The setting also acted as a sounding-board for stylised speech patterns, employing monotonal and 'quasi-mystical' intonations. It also served, through its eschewal of perspective, to foreground the human image in one dimension.

It is perhaps symptomatic of the Turgenev production that critical comment related almost exclusively to Stanislavsky's attempt to introduce the basic elements of his 'system' into his own performance as Rakitin. There exists very little extant comment on the performances of the other characters and, unlike critical responses to the Art Theatre productions of Chekhov, little or no comment on the validity of Stanislavsky's interpretation of the play. Nobody appears to have expressed disquiet at the cuts or to have suggested that there might have been a different kind of production to the one he staged.

To the extent that Stanislavsky sought to root the production in the realistic psychology of human behaviour and, in Dobuzhinskiy's phrase, 'nail' the characters to the stage, the strategy is one to which T. S. Eliot's Prufrock would have had strong objections. This is precisely the 'modernist' complaint against the methods of this kind of forensic realism (sensing its kinship with naturalism) – that it seeks to 'formulate' life, to contemplate it 'wriggling on a pin'.[18] The countervailing insistence then has to be that 'the truth' (whatever that is) invariably escapes this kind of analytic scrutiny (in this connection, it is notable how many times in the score characters are described as 'observing' others with 'painful' intensity in order to pin down 'the truth'). Despite this, the production's ideological significance would appear to have evaded Stanislavsky's ostensible intentions and his efforts to pin 'meaning' to 'character'.

He may, in fact, be likened to Rakitin at the point in the score where the latter is described as 'a doctor' attempting to persuade

Natalya Petrovna of the need for a metaphorical 'operation' on her psyche. He performed this operation on the body of the play, by cutting into it, and on the psyches of the actors in persuading them of the need to undergo spiritual surgery in his own operating-theatre, during which everything superfluous would be cut away to leave only the bare bone of quintessential theatrical 'being'. The operation was a success, and the bone was laid bare. However, bone is made of matter not spirit, and proved in this particular instance to be a bone of contention.

15

SEASON TWELVE TO SEASON TWENTY: 1909–1917

The period after 1909 was one during which the work of designers associated with The World of Art movement began to dominate the stage of the Art Theatre. This was a phase in its history during which Alexandre Benois became a member of the company's directorate and acquired an influential voice in the staging of productions.[1] The period was also marked by a sense of directional uncertainty. Stanislavsky's path led him towards comedy and the past; Nemirovich continued to explore the path of tragedy and the present. These directions were marked by a seismograph of failure and success which defy obvious explanation.

In the season which saw Stanislavsky's public triumph with *A Month in the Country*, Nemirovich staged Andreyev's *Anathema* (2 October 1909) and Ostrovsky's *The Scoundrel* (11 March 1910), the latter being the rare (for him) production of a comic play. *Anathema* is a strangely hybrid piece in which Good, in the shape of the Jew, David Leiser, battles with Evil in the shape of a personified Devil, Anathema. It was the first of three attempts by Nemirovich to stage plays by Andreyev who, apart from Chekhov, Tolstoy and Gorky, seemed to him to be the one modern dramatist worth staging. The production was adjudged unsuccessful, despite a memorable performance by Kachalov in the main role, wearing costume and make-up which made him look hideously like William Blake's drawing of the ghost of a flea. The production also had striking sets by Simov, especially for the last scene before the gates of Heaven, dominated by the towering figure of an angel.

The production of the Ostrovsky play was chiefly memorable for Stanislavsky's comic portrayal of the decrepit official Krutitskiy, which long remained a favourite with audiences. However, Stanislavsky's performance, in its isolated moments of hilarious comic invention, appeared to run counter to the mood and feeling, not to say the 'ensemble', of the production as a whole. It is worth noting that he, who at this juncture was preoccupied with the application of the 'system' to the internal development of the artistic image, derived his image of Krutitskiy from the imaginative impression made by the *external* appearance of an old house overgrown with moss. The most memorable moments of his performance tended, consequently, to be those in which external effects predominated.

Six months of illness during preparatory work on *Hamlet* meant that the thirteenth season, 1910–11, belonged to Nemirovich. It proved to be one of the most remarkable in the Theatre's history and gave rise, in quick succession, to one of the best as well as one of the worst productions staged hitherto. The production of Semen Yushkevich's *Miserere*, on 17 December 1910, was greeted on opening night with catcalls and whistles – unheard of at the Art Theatre and partly attributable to its decision to make premières available to first-class season-ticket holders only.[2] The production of Hamsun's *In The Grip of Life* which followed, on 28 February 1911, was only marginally better received. The choice of plays had been something of an aberration, so much so that, during re-hearsals, when the actors protested at having to negotiate grossly inferior material, Nemirovich was forced to agree with them. The fact is, however, that these two productions followed in the wake of what was, probably, Nemirovich's most inspired work at the Art Theatre up until that point, if not the finest he ever staged in his life – a dramatisation of Dostoyevsky's *The Brothers Karamazov*, staged in two parts over two nights.

It was mounted in the remarkably short space of two months, and exploited the use of drapes on a revolving stage. Significantly, Nemirovich made a successful attempt to apply those elements of Stanislavsky's theory which he understood to the 'pieces' and 'problems' of a production which lent itself to detailed analysis of its fragmented sections with their violently contrasting moods. The twenty or so scenes, some lasting minutes and others an hour or more, were rehearsed with devotional intensity by Nemirovich and his assistants – Luzhskiy, and a newcomer to the theatre, Konstantin Mardzhanov. The success was phenomenal. Benois went so far as to describe the production as a 'sacred Mystery'. This elicited a polemical response from Meyerhold in the shape of one of his most famous essays – on the Russian *balagan*.[3] It also produced an outraged response in distant Italy from Gorky, who felt hostile in principle to what he took to be Dostoyevsky's fundamentally malign influence, even suspecting that one effect of a manifestly successful production might be an increase in the Russian suicide rate.

Principally, the production was a triumph for the actors, who seemed to have been freed, through the absence of scenery and through the undogmatic application of certain aspects of Stanislavsky's theory, to express themselves with an intensity which nobody could remember ever having experienced before and which, it was felt, only actors trained in an Art Theatre tradition devoted to high seriousness could ever hope to achieve. The production represented a highpoint in its fusion of the abstractly spiritual and the realistically social – something which was to be attempted, without similar success, in the Gordon Craig-inspired production of *Hamlet* in 1911, and which no other production in the history of the Art Theatre was to come near matching.

When the 'system' was next applied by Nemirovich – to a production of Tolstoy's *A Living Corpse* during the fourteenth season – it failed to prevent its coming to grief. But why, following the achievements of *The Brothers Karamazov,* was Nemirovich returning to something more like naturalistic melodrama (a question which might equally be asked of his decision to stage Andreyev's *Yekaterina Ivanovna* in 1912)? Apart from *Karamazov,* the most important production of this entire period was that of *Hamlet,* on 23 December 1911, which, whilst giving rise to disagreements between Craig and Stanislavsky resulting in compromise, was, nevertheless, one of the most interesting 'experimental' productions of the play ever staged.[4]

The main events of the fifteenth season, 1912–13, were the productions by Alexandre Benois of two Molière plays on the same evening – *The Forced Marriage* and *The Imaginary Invalid* – in the latter of which Stanislavsky played the part of Argan. Not only did Benois direct the productions but, as an expert in the art and iconography of seventeenth-century France, he also designed the settings. For some reason, however, he chose to model the sets on Flemish interiors, which had little connection with the style of French ones, and absolutely nothing to do with the theatre of Molière's day. One of the results was a lack of harmony between the everyday realism of the overall conception and the *commedia* spirit with which Stanislavsky went about interpreting Argan. It was a performance rich in comic detail but totally at odds with the production. Once again, here was the ironic spectacle of an actor devoted to the principle of ensemble, acting in a dimension which was completely antithetical to that of other members of the cast.

Following his success with *Karamazov*, Nemirovich hoped for something similar with his adaptation of Dostoyevsky's *The Possessed* which, as *Nikolay Stavrogin*, opened the sixteenth season on 23 October 1913. Unfortunately, the adaptation largely omitted the political dimension of the novel (the subject of a different production, according to Nemirovich). Unlike *Karamazov*, which used a narrator for those sections of the novel which were not in dialogue, this adaptation involved a reworking and reorganisation of the novel's structure. The production was also hampered by Dobuzhinskiy's 'atmospheric' settings which, with the exception of one or two scenes, appeared out of keeping, both tonally and spatially, with the novel's predominant moods. The Theatre's subservience to the priorities of The World of Art movement gave rise to a privileging of purely aesthetic elements, which did not cohere with the philosophical and dramaturgical *raison d'être* of the production as a whole.

There were only two productions of note between the seventeenth (1914–15) and the twentieth (1916–17) seasons – of Pushkin's *Little Tragedies*, on 26 March 1915, and of Dostoyevsky's *Stepanchikovo Village* (an adaptation of the novel) on 13 September 1917. Both, in different ways, seemed to reflect a sense of the crisis which had overtaken the Theatre. Never again, after 1917, did Stanislavsky attempt to act a new role. The failure of his efforts to apply the 'system' to his interpretation of Salieri, in Pushkin's *Mozart and Salieri*, and to the role of Rostanyev, in *Stepanchikovo Village*, proved experiences of a traumatic order. It could be argued that he spent the rest of his life trying to recover from these failures in seeking to develop and modify the 'system' – to the 'truth' and validity of which he remained dedicated.

It could also be argued that the Pushkin and Dostoyevsky productions also reflected a terminal crisis in the relationship between Nemirovich and Stanislavsky, who had temporarily re-established a degree of harmony following the success of *Karamazov*. With the debacle of *Mozart and Salieri*, in which Stanislavsky had sought, as Salieri, to render the murder of individual genius tragically sympathetic, his own self-criticism was devastating: 'I had neither voice nor diction, plasticity nor rhythm, nor a sense of tempo. I was a mere dilettante. . . . . What is important is that, after this production, I could say to myself: "I know that I know nothing'" (Stanislavskiy 1988: 449–56). Little is conceded to the possibility that he might have misconceived the role. Sadder still was the spectacle of Stanislavsky/Rostanyev standing in the wings with tears streaming down his face, unable to venture on stage for the dress rehearsal of *Stepanchikovo Village* (Guryevich 1948: 375). His conception of Rostanyev as a Don Quixote or Holy Fool clashed totally with Nemirovich's less sympathetic vision of the character as a kind of moral fanatic. The disagreement led, at the last minute, to Stanislavsky's removal from the role and Nemirovich's handing it to someone else. The vision of Stanislavsky weeping in the wings was, according to Serafima Birman and others, like witnessing 'the suffering of a mother who has given birth to a stillborn child' (Polyakova 1977: 329).[5]

16

CONCLUSION

An international symposium – *Stanislavsky in a Changing World* – was held in Moscow in 1989 at the height of the *glasnost* period. Those who addressed the conference included Peter Brook, Yuriy Lyubimov, leading Soviet Stanislavsky scholars, and other authorities from around the world.[1] Among the most interesting contributions were those given, seemingly impromptu and without notes, by Soviet theatre experts who, in the spirit of the times, dared to say what others had only been bold enough to think or state privately hitherto – namely, that Stanislavsky's reputation needed to be subjected to a form of *perestroika*. This 'reconstruction' needed to confront the possibility that Stanislavsky's work as a whole might be seen to be complicit with the ethos and ideology of the Stalinist period. Other, more considered, assessments were critical of his methods and stressed their limitations – none more so than that of the British scholar Peter Holland, who delivered a telling critique of the intellectual assumptions at the heart of the 1930 production score of *Othello*. The conference also contained more conventional evaluations of Stanislavsky, albeit less fulsome and hagiographic than audiences in the Soviet Union had come to expect.

The theatre which Stanislavsky returned to in the mid-1920s, following his successful American tour, was very different to the one he had left behind and where his last production – of Byron's *Cain* in 1920 – had been a response to revolution and civil war. The Art Theatre had been brought under state control. Some members of the company had stayed abroad; others had found it difficult to adjust to the new régime. The only independent productions which Stanislavsky staged during the 1920s were of Ostrovsky's *Burning Heart* (1926) and Beaumarchais's *The Marriage of Figaro* (1927).

Although his presence was both crucial and influential, his role on a production of Mikhail Bulgakov's *Days of the Turbins* (1926) was more that of artistic adviser, overall direction being in the hands of a member of the Theatre's younger generation, Il'ya Sudakov.[2,3] The same was true of his involvement in the preparation of a specifically 'Soviet' play – Vsevolod Ivanov's *Armoured Train 14–69* (1927).[4] As far as English-speaking readers are concerned, the most substantial record of his work during this period relates to the application of his acting theories to distinctly inferior work – *Merchants of Glory* by Marcel Pagnol and Paul Nivoix, and a historical melodrama, *The Sisters Gerard* (an adaptation of *Two Orphans* by Adolphe D'Ennery and Eugène Cormon).[5]

Following a severe heart attack in 1928, Stanislavsky virtually retired to his mansion, generously provided by the state and situated on the street which now bears his name and where the Stanislavsky Museum is currently housed. It was here that he rehearsed opera in a small, well-equipped theatre, and where he also rehearsed *Dead Souls*, *Molière* (Bulgakov's *A Cabal of Hypocrites*) and *Tartuffe*. It is interesting to note that much of his work between 1926 and 1938 was associated with Mikhail Bulgakov. It was at the Art Theatre's request that Bulgakov wrote *Days of the Turbins*, based on his own novel *The White Guard*. His second play, *Flight*, was about to be performed at the Art Theatre when it was banned, in 1929. Having obtained work at the Theatre in 1930, largely through the good offices of Stalin who liked the production of *Days of the Turbins*, Bulgakov adapted Gogol's *Dead Souls* for stage performance and had his own play *A Cabal of Hypocrites* staged there in 1936.[6] Moreover, Bulgakov's adulation of Molière, which also gave rise to a biography of the dramatist, may well have influenced Stanislavsky's decision to rehearse *Tartuffe*, work on which preoccupied him until his death.

Significantly, Bulgakov had little time for either Stanislavsky or his theories, which he thought were responsible for ruining or frustrating much of his own work in the theatre. Bulgakov's problems with the Soviet censorship simply served to compound these frustrations. However, the alterations which Bulgakov was forced to introduce into the stage version of *Days of the Turbins* had as much to do with disagreements with Stanislavsky as with the need to satisfy demands of the censor. His dramatisation of *Dead Souls*, which was a labour of love as far as Bulgakov was concerned, was rejected by Stanislavsky and then altered in the most high-handed fashion and the rehearsal and staging of *A Cabal of Hypocrites* were carried out in a manner totally inimical to the wishes of the author. Bulgakov's revenge took the form of his banned novel, *A Theatrical Romance*, in which Stanislavsky and the Art Theatre are subjected to a devastating lampoon. Even allowing for the exaggeration which is a necessary element of caricature, the parody appears uncomfortably close to the truth as Bulgakov experienced it.

The question is frequently asked whether or not Stanislavsky knew of what was going on in the Soviet Union during the late 1930s and, for reasons best known to himself, chose to keep his own counsel. After all (it is said) he lived through the so-called 'show trials' and 'purges' and was witness to the persecution of fellow artists, including Meyerhold (for whom he found work, staging opera, following the closure of the Meyerhold Theatre in 1938). It is also the case that Stanislavsky's theatrical theories and the practice of the Moscow Art Academic Theatre (as it became known – MKhAT) almost alone found favour with the régime, especially when, during the 1930s, a potentially 'idealist' element in the 'system' was modified through Stanislavsky's development of the so-called 'method of physical actions'. Theatres throughout the Soviet Union were invited to copy the example of the Art Theatre from about 1934 onwards – a tradition that persisted until the 1980s.

Did Stanislavsky have anything in common with the spirit of those reactionary times? As has been suggested, his earlier identification with the 'superman' or 'superior' type, mainly in his pre-1914 productions, could be said to have contained features which were complicit with a respectable form of fascism before that word acquired its post-war associations. This ideology, in its less emotive manifestations, characterised the outlook of many artists in the first half of the twentieth century and was inseparably linked with their idealism.

Faced with the irresolvable nature of the conflicts which the prospect of an inherently dualistic universe appeared to present, Stanislavsky attempted to resolve the dilemma through what might be termed his own brand of 'idealistic humanism'. The development of a theory, whose origins were born of a faith in the well-springs of some inner, quintessentially human, emotional truth, can be seen as part of an ideological offensive against the baser views of humankind which achieved their apotheosis in the theory and practice of a nineteenth-century naturalist movement which cast an absolute, reductionist shadow across past, present and future. The carnage of the First World War may be said to have provided a fitting tribute to that movement's deterministic hypotheses.

However, in order to wage this ideological war, it was necessary to abandon the realm of abstract idealism and descend from the mountain peaks to commence missionary work in the gullies of human reality. Stanislavsky's humanist offensive was at its most intense in the post-war, post-revolutionary period when it seemed most in tune with the spirit of a workers' state. However, during the 1930s, when work on his theory was at its height, its implicit ideology seemed at odds, both politically and artistically, with the social world which had evolved around him. However, for Stanislavsky, as for the Stalinists (with whom he otherwise had little in common), anything which appeared to contribute towards a sense of man's dehumanisation, to his being conceived in abstract terms – everything, in fact, which smacked of artistic modernism – was anathema. Hence, with supreme irony, Stanislavsky's own principles began at this historical juncture to converge with an official ideology of dogmatically promulgated 'socialist realism'. By 1937, this official humanist/realist ideological offensive against 'formalism', now running in grotesque tandem with the ideas of the officially 'canonised' Stanislavsky, had produced not only the 'saints' of a simplified universe but also the 'devils' of an essentially problematic world – the Kafkas, the Trotskys, the Meyerholds, the countless others, who could only be confronted in the crudest fashion by being either banned, exiled, imprisoned or killed.[7]

An insistence on the disjunction between the *actual* ideologies of Stanislavsky and Stalin should not be needed. However, the dualistic nature of a universe from which the former sought refuge, first in a spiritual idealism and then in a spiritual humanism, forced him to a position of compromise pitched on inherently unstable ground composed of versions of 'realism' and 'nature', which were themselves the source of the problem. Moreover, the road from the Ermitazh had terminated in a hermitage of an altogether unsuspected kind. The descent from the pinnacles of the abstract had led, not to the valley – and people and warmth and life, but to the equivalent of a secluded monastery – the mansion which Stalin provided and where Stanislavsky worked on his 'system'. A privileged, protected space provided by a dictator at state expense and located in the middle of Moscow now found its grotesque mirror-image in an exposed punishment cell, also provided by the dictator at state expense, but located ... in the middle of nowhere. It is a fine point whether 'Great Director' or 'Great Dictator' was the more authentic 'spiritual mountaineer' or 'engineer of human souls' at this precise historical juncture. Whatever he was, perhaps Stanislavsky needs to be seen as a hybrid of both, called, for the sake of convenience, 'Stalinslavsky' – a two-headed, mythical beast (their names were both pseudonyms) far removed from ordinary life – but who, even when considered separately as ordinary mortals – Alekseyev and Dzhugashvili – can be seen to have belonged to contiguous monastic orders and to have occupied adjoining, or adjacent, ideological cells.

As far as the fate of the Art Theatre is concerned, this had been sealed by the acquisition of the state-imposed title 'Academic', in 1920. Under extreme political pressure, the already shaky bases of the original Theatre were undermined still further. The 'Public-Accessible' now became the 'Academic' in every sense. The laurel wreath which was placed around the Theatre's brow, like that of Solness at the top of his spire, signalled both triumph and demise.[8] It is ironic that the effect of turning the Theatre into an Academy had the effect of rendering it even less distinguishable than before from the Imperial Theatres (which also became nationalised Academies) from whose gravitational orbit the Moscow Art Theatre had fought so long and so hard to break free.

NOTES

Part I: The Establishment of the Moscow Art Theatre

INTRODUCTION

1 The Moscow Art Theatre finally acquired its own, brand new, building on the occasion of its seventy-fifth anniversary in 1973. The seeds of the subsequent split were sown at this point, with the separate existence of two Moscow Art Theatres – the new one on Tverskoy Boulevard and the old one off Tverskaya Street (formerly Gorky Street) where it had been since 1902. The unofficial split came about in 1986 when Oleg Yefremov, who, in 1970, had been given the task of rejuvenating the Moscow Art Theatre, relinquished control of the new building. Tat'yana Doronina (whom Yefremov had invited in 1970 to join the company from Georgiy Tovstonogov's Leningrad Bolshoy Drama Theatre) assumed control of the new building in the name of the Theatre's more conservative wing. With the break-up of the Soviet Union, the older theatre, named after Gorky in 1932, rechristened itself in 'pre-Soviet' style after Chekhov, whilst the new building retained its association with the name of Gorky.

2 *Rabota aktera nad soboy* ('An Actor's Work on Himself') published in two separate parts in English translation as *An Actor Prepares* and *Building a Character.*

3 Among the worst years of Stalinist repression were those between 1934 (when the official ideology of 'socialist realism' was first promulgated) and 1941, when the invasion of Nazi forces signalled Russia's entry into the Second World War. Intense work on his theory preoccupied Stanislavsky during the critical period 1934–8, culminating in the publication of *Rabota aktera nad soboy* in 1938, the year of his death. These years saw the purges and the show trials, mass starvation as a consequence of collectivisation, mass deportations, the arbitrary arrest of millions of 'dissidents', the building of forced labour camps, the closure of theatres (including those of Meyerhold, Tairov and N. P. Okhlopkov), and the glorification of Stanislavsky and the Moscow Art

209

Theatre. Throughout the traumatic period of the 1930s, Stanislavsky lived and worked in a large mansion placed at his disposal by the Soviet government, apparently oblivious of everything which was happening around him.

4 M. N. Yermolova (1853–1928) – one of the great actresses of the nineteenth-century Russian theatre and synonymous with the finest traditions of the Imperial Malyy Theatre where she worked from 1871 until 1921. She has a theatre named in her honour situated on Tverskaya Street.

5 Ludwig Chronegk (1837–91) – director of the Meiningen Company from 1871 until his death, his skills as a company organiser and stage director were crucial to the company's success and its European renown.

6 Nemirovich-Danchenko wrote a long letter to Gorky on 19 April 1904 in which he spelt out the weaknesses, as he saw them, of Gorky's play (see Nemirovich-Danchenko 1979: 360–70).

7 The première of *The Seagull*, directed by Yevtikhiy Karpov and with Vera Komissarzhevskaya as Nina, was given at the Aleksandrinskiy Theatre in 1896. The première, which Chekhov witnessed, was certainly not a success but critical opinion of the actual production is inclined, these days, to redress the balance in favour of some of its virtues.

1 HISTORICAL BACKGROUND

1 St Petersburg, Petersburg, Petrograd and Leningrad are all names for the same city which has undergone many name-changes in its time and has recently reverted to St Petersburg (Sankt Peterburg) in honour of the saint rather than the tsar who founded it.

2 S. I. Mamontov (1841–1919) – powerful industrialist and philanthropist, founder of the Russian Private Opera in 1885, which played host to a number of remarkable designers and singers. The Mamontov estate at Abramtsevo, near Moscow, was maintained during the Soviet period as a cultural centre with strong international links.

3 V. A. Simov (1858–1935) – a well-known painter in his own right, Simov gained experience as a theatre designer with Mamontov's private opera company before becoming chief stage designer at the Art Theatre between 1898 and 1912 and then again from 1925 to 1935.

4 A. S. Suvorin (1834–1912) – journalist, publisher, editor of *Novoye vremya* ('New Time'), theatre critic, dramatist and theatre manager; probably best known as friend and correspondent of Anton Chekhov.

5 F. A. Korsh (1852–1923) – successful Moscow theatrical entrepreneur during the period 1882–1917.

6 P. M. Tret'yakov (1832–98) – textile manufacturer whose purchase of the best paintings by a nineteenth-century group of artists known as the *Peredvizhniki* (The Wanderers) became the basis of the art gallery in Moscow named after him.

7 S. I. Shchukin (1854–1937) – industrialist and art collector whose acquisition of Western European art, especially the work of French impressionists, became the core of many Russian galleries' and museums' holdings of work from that period.

NOTES

8 A. A. Bakhrushin (1865–1929) – businessman and entrepreneur who
founded, in 1894, the Theatre Museum in Moscow named after him
in 1918.

9 A. A. Brenko (1848–1934) – opened the first private theatre in Moscow,
the Pushkin, in 1880 (see MacLeod 1946: 62–6), not to be confused
with the present Pushkin Theatre, on Tverskoy Boulevard, which is the
former Kamernyy (Chamber) Theatre. The earlier Pushkin Theatre
was destroyed by fire.

10 V. A. Nyelidov (1869–1926) – an official at the office of the Imperial
Theatres in Moscow from 1893 to 1911 and director of their acting
companies between 1907 and 1909. He was the husband of O. V.
Gzovskaya, an actress at the Art Theatre between 1910 and 1917.

11 Reference here is to the cramped setting for Act Two of Gogol's *The
Government Inspector.*

12 P. P. Gnedich (1855–1925) – dramatist, translator, historian and chief
director of the Aleksandrinskiy Theatre from 1901 until 1908, when he
was succeeded by Meyerhold. Stanislavsky staged his plays at the Society
of Art and Literature and in the Art Theatre's first year.

13 C. J. Kean (1811–68) – son of Edmund Kean, he ran his own company
at the Princess's Theatre in London between 1850 and 1859 whose well-
rehearsed and well-costumed productions attracted the attention of
the Duke of Saxe-Meiningen, thus paving the way for many of the
innovations which the Meiningen troupe introduced.

14 H. Laube (1806–84) – dramatist and director of the Burgtheater in
Vienna, where he staged carefully rehearsed versions of plays by
Schiller and Eugène Scribe, amongst others. Wagner was amongst those
influenced by his pedagogy and practice.

15 A. N. Ostrovsky (1823–86) – probably Russia's greatest dramatist,
Ostrovsky's work had a very special connection with the Moscow Malyy
Theatre. In addition to being a prolific writer, he was also a great
advocate of stage reform. His best-known work is *Groza* ('The Thunder-
storm' or 'The Storm'), also known in an operatic version by Janacek as
Katya Kabanova.

16 K. L. Rudnitskiy (1920–89) – probably the most influential of Soviet
theatre critics in the post-war period, whose prolific output includes
pioneering studies of Meyerhold.

17 For Gogol's and Turgenev's ideas on theatre, see Worrall (1982:
31–48).

18 P. D. Boborykin (1836–1921) – dramatist and theatre critic responsible
for the promulgation of Zola's naturalist theories in Russia.

2 THE SOCIETY OF ART AND LITERATURE

1 A. F. Fedotov (1841–95) – actor, dramatist, director and teacher, his
principal claim to fame is his association with Stanislavsky in founding
the Society of Art and Literature in 1888 and in influencing the latter's
early ideas on directing.

2 G. N. Fedotova (1846–1925) – one of the great actresses at the Malyy

from 1862 to 1905 who had a special connection with the plays of Ostrovsky.

3 F. P. Komissarzhevskiy (1838–1905) – a famous lyric tenor and father of the better-known Fedor Komissarzhevskiy (1882–1954) and Vera Komissarzhevskaya (1864–1910). He influenced Stanislavsky both in his early career as a singer and his later acting career.

4 M. P. Lilina (real name Perevoshchikova, 1866–1943) – following her marriage to Stanislavsky in 1889, Lilina became a key member of the Art Theatre company and continued to act there until 1937.

5 V. V. Luzhskiy (real name Kaluzhskiy, 1869–1931) – a founder-member of the Moscow Art Theatre, he made an important contribution to its productions as both actor and director until his death.

6 A. F. Pisemskiy (1821–81) – novelist and writer of fifteen plays mainly about provincial Russian life, the most famous of which is *A Bitter Fate* (1859).

7 In accounts of this phase of Stanislavsky's history, the 'Okhotnyy' Club is sometimes referred to as the 'Hunting' Club, just as Turgenev's *Zapiski okhotnika* is translated both as *A Sportsman's Sketches* and *Sketches from a Hunter's Album*.

8 A. A. Sanin (real name Shenberg, 1869–1956) – staged crowd scenes at the Society of Art and Literature before joining the Art Theatre as co-director and actor. He left in 1902 to work independently as a director before rejoining the Theatre from 1917 to 1919 and then emigrating in 1922. Sanin was briefly involved in attempts to translate George Bernard Shaw's *Pygmalion* into Russian for performance at the Malyy.

9 A. R. Artem (pronounced Artyom, real name Artem'yev, 1842–1914) – trained as an artist before becoming an actor in his late-forties. A noted character actor, he was especially renowned for his interpretation of roles in Chekhov, Gorky and Turgenev.

10 M. A. Samarova (real name Grekova, 1852–1919) – an actress both at the Society of Art and Literature and then at the Art Theatre until 1919.

11 V. F. Komissarzhevskaya (1864–1910) – one of the most remarkable actresses of the late nineteenth century, who worked with both Stanislavsky and Meyerhold and who, for a time, ran her own experimental theatre in St Petersburg.

12 N. E. Efros (1867–1923) – one of the best critics and historians of the Russian theatre at the turn of the century and one of the Art Theatre's principal supporters; author of monographs on the Theatre itself and on individual productions.

13 L. M. Leonidov (real name Vol'fenzon, 1873–1941) – joined the Art Theatre in 1903 and became a stalwart of the acting troupe. His great successes included Lopakhin in *The Cherry Orchard* (1904), Dmitriy Karamazov in *The Brothers Karamazov* (1910) and Othello (1930).

14 M. V. Lentovskiy (1843–1906) – entrepreneur, theatre manager and playwright. His extraordinary career is chronicled in Andrew Donskov: *Mixail Lentovskij and the Russian Theatre*, Michigan: Russian Language Journal, 1985.

15 Erckmann-Chatrian, pseudonym of French novelists Emile Erckmann (1822–1899) and Louis-Alexandre Chatrian (1826–1890).

NOTES

3 THE CREATION OF A NEW THEATRE

1 F. O. Shekhtel' (1859–1926) – architect and graphic artist, designer of railway stations as well as private homes, he was responsible for the Russian pavilion at the Glasgow International Exhibition (1901), the Ryabushinskiy Mansion in Moscow (1900–2) – later Gorky's home and now his museum – as well as the 1902 conversion of the Lianozov Theatre into the Moscow Art Theatre's second, permanent home. He specialised in art deco and art nouveau styles.

2 Ya. V. Shchukin (1856–1926) – entrepreneur and theatre-owner who hired the Ermitazh to the Moscow Art Theatre between 1898 and 1902.

3 N. N. Sinel'nikov (1855–1939) – director, entrepreneur and theatre manager.

4 P. M. Medvedyev (1837–1906) – entrepreneur and provincial theatre-owner; director of the Aleksandrinskiy Theatre from 1890–1893.

5 V. N. Davydov (real name Goryelov, 1849–1925) – acted at the Aleksandrinskiy Theatre in St Petersburg from 1880 until 1924 with spells elsewhere. He was the original Ivanov in Chekhov's play at the Korsh Theatre (1887).

6 Ye. P. Karpov (1857–1926) – director at the Aleksandrinskiy Theatre from 1896 to 1900 and then again from 1916 to 1926, his main claim to fame is as director of the first production of Chekhov's *The Seagull* in 1896.

7 P. M. Pchel'nikov (1851–1913) – director of the Moscow Office of the Imperial Theatres from 1882–1898.

8 O. L. Knipper-Chekhova (1868–1959) – the Art Theatre's leading lady and wife of Anton Pavlovich Chekhov, her whole life was spent working at the Theatre.

9 V. E. Meyerhold (born Karl Theodore Kazimir Meyergold, 1874–1940) – a founder-member of the Art Theatre company who left in 1902 to become a theatre director. After spells with Komissarzhevskaya in St Petersburg, where he subsequently became artistic director of the Aleksandrinsky Theatre, he became leader of the theatrical avant-garde after the 1917 revolution and ran his own theatre successfully, albeit controversially, from 1923 until 1938. He was arrested during the 'purges' and died in prison.

10 I. M. Moskvin (1874–1946) – a principal actor at the Art Theatre from the day of its inception to the end of his life.

11 *Lubok*: a form of popular woodblock print illustration (frequently hand-coloured) introduced into Russia in the eighteenth century, often depicting scenes from folklore with a comic or satiric purpose.

12 S. T. (Savva) Morozov (1862–1905) – factory-owner and philanthropist whose money saved the Art Theatre from premature closure in its difficult first years.

13 A. P. Lenskiy (real name Verbitsiotti, 1847–1908) – one of the finest tragic actors of the nineteenth-century Russian theatre, much admired by Meyerhold and others. He was a member of the Malyy company from 1876 until his death.

14 V. A. Telyakovskiy (1860–1924) – Head of the Moscow office of the

Imperial Theatres from 1898 to 1901 and director of the Imperial Theatres as a whole from 1901 to 1917. He took the bold step of installing the 'radical' Meyerhold as artistic director of the Aleksandrinskiy Theatre – a post which he held from 1908 to 1917.

15 M. G. Savitskaya (1868–1911) – a graduate of Nemirovich's class at the Philharmonic School, she remained at the Art Theatre until her death.

16 M. L. Roksanova (real name Petrovskaya, 1874–1958) – one of Nemirovich's favourites whom he hoped to groom for stardom but who acted disappointingly. Her spell at the Theatre was short-lived, ending in 1902.

17 E. M. Munt (1875–1954) – a graduate of the Philharmonic School and Meyerhold's sister-in-law.

18 A. L. Zagarov (real name Fessing, 1877–1941) – a graduate of Nemirovich's acting classes, he stayed with the Art Theatre until 1906.

19 L. V. Aleyeva (real name Nyedobrovo, no dates available) – acted at the Art Theatre from 1898 to 1900.

20 I. A. Tikhomirov (1872–1908) – one of Nemirovich's pupils; he acted at the Art Theatre from 1898 to 1904.

21 M. F. Andreyeva (real name Yurkovskaya; married name Zhelyabushakaya, 1868–1953) – apart from acting at the Art Theatre from 1898 to 1906, with a short break from 1904 to 1905, Mariya Andreyeva's main claims to fame are as mistress to Maksim Gorky (this caused a scandal when Gorky visited the United States in her company) and as founder, with Aleksandr Blok, of the Grand Dramatic Theatre (the Bolshoy Dramaticheskiy teatr) in Petrograd, after the revolution.

22 G. S. Burdzhalov (1869–1924) – a stalwart of the company from 1898 until his death, he was involved in setting up the Art Theatre's Fourth Studio in 1921.

23 A. L. Vishnyevskiy (real name Vishnyevyetskiy, 1861–1943) – a childhood friend of Chekhov's in Taganrog and a member of the Art Theatre company for forty-five years.

24 M. E. Darskiy (real name Psarov, 1865–1930) – left the Art Theatre at the end of its first season disillusioned with Stanislavsky who, in turn, disliked his acting.

25 V. F. Gribunin (1873–1933) – a member of the company for thirty-five years.

26 S. N. Sud'binin (1867–1944) – a member of the company from 1898 to 1904; he became a sculptor in later life.

27 A. I. Adashev (real name Platonov, 1871–1934) – as well as acting at the Theatre until 1913, he established his own acting school where Vakhtangov received his early training before joining the Art Theatre and setting up his own studio.

28 V. A. Lanskoy (real name Solyanikov, 1871–?) – had been a ballet dancer before joining the Art Theatre troupe where he stayed for one season.

29 Alla Nazimova (1879–1945) – was instrumental in introducing Stanislavsky's acting methods to America from 1906 onwards but had left the Art Theatre without ever experiencing the 'system' at first hand.

30 V. S. Kalinnikov (1870–1927) – composer and music teacher at the

Moscow Philharmonic School before becoming conductor of the Art Theatre orchestra, a post he held for one year only.

31 Ya. I. Gremislavskiy (1864–1941) – principal make-up artist at the Art Theatre for forty-three years.

32 G. D. Ryndzyunskiy (1873–1937) – assistant in the Art Theatre administration 1898–9 and then secretary to the directorate 1899–1902. In addition to the published record of the first year's work (1899), he also kept a detailed record of the Theatre's work during its second season. Unfortunately, it is hand-written and virtually illegible even to Russian eyes.

33 *Guverner* – a vaudeville by V. A. D'yachenko (1818–76)

34 The director's score of *The Seagull* was published in Russia in 1938: S. D. Balukhatyy (ed.) *'Chaika' v postanovke Moskovskogo Khudozhestvennogo teatra, rezhisserskaya partitura K. S. Stanislavskogo*, Leningrad-Moscow: Iskusstvo. For a translation, by David Magarshack, of the complete text and Balukhaty's introduction, see Balukhaty (1952).

4 THE HERMITAGE THEATRE ON CARRIAGE ROW

1 Of the 815 seats, 440 (54 per cent) cost more than one rouble, 275 (34 per cent) cost between fifty kopecks and one rouble and 140 (12 per cent) cost less than fifty kopecks. The total number of seats sold during the first season was 104,320, which broke down as follows: more than one rouble – 51,250 (48.5 per cent); between fifty kopecks and one rouble – 34,266 (32.5 per cent); less than fifty kopecks – 19,804 (19 per cent).

2 Entry to the theatre was by means of a *kontramark* (theatre pass), the issue of which was organised by the scholastic institution in question, presumably on a 'first-come, first-served' basis.

3 Those productions on offer were *The Merchant of Venice* (27 December), *Despots* (3 January), *Late Love* and *Feminine Curiosity* (6 January) and *The Mistress of the Inn* (10 January). This was part of an arrangement which the Theatre reached with a workers' organisation called The Society for People's Recreation. However, 'officialdom' decreed that the only theatrical fare suitable for workers was the Ostrovsky play, *Late Love*, and the arrangment with the Society petered out. This failure to attract a working-class audience is also attributable to officialdom's dislike of cheap morning productions, especially on Sundays, as a sizeable gathering of working people in any one place was considered to constitute a likely 'threat to public order'. The play *Feminine Curiosity* by Aleksey Yakovlev (1773–1817) was one of a number of short plays which were staged at the Sporting Club during the first season.

4 Kh. S. Zolotov (no dates available) – assistant director at the Art Theatre 1898–9.

5 N. G. Aleksandrov (1870–1930) – joined the Art Theatre from the Society of Art and Literature and stayed with the company until his death.

6 A. S. Solov'ev (1869–1950) – worked at the Society of Art and Literature

before becoming director's assistant and rehearser of crowd scenes at the Art Theatre from 1898 to 1903.

7 Many of these items are displayed in the Stanislavsky Museum in Moscow.

8 L. A von Fessing (1848–1920) – remained in post as the Theatre's superintendent until 1920.

5 ACTORS, SALARIES, CONDITIONS OF SERVICE

1 P. O. Morozov (1854–1920) – one of the first to establish theatre criticism as a serious discipline in Russia. He also wrote dramatic biographies.

2 A. S. Kosheverov (1874–1921) – remained at the Theatre until 1902.

3 V. V. Charskiy (real name Chistyakov) (1834–1910) – worked mainly in the provinces on tour and, occasionally, performed in the capitals.

4 Fessing – A. L. Zagarov (see C N Chapter 3, Note 18).

5 B. M. Snigirev (stage name Snyezhin, 1875–1936) – one of Nemirovich's students at the Philharmonic School who worked at the Art Theatre between 1898 and 1902 before rejoining the company briefly for two years in the 1920s and then again in 1932. These last two spells were spent working in the archival section of the Theatre's museum.

6 S. M. Tarasov (1868–?) – worked at the Theatre during its first season.

7 M. P. Nikolayeva (real name Grigor'yeva, 1869–1941) – actress at the Society of Art and Literature and lifelong member of the Art Theatre.

8 Ye. M. Rayevskaya (real name Iyerusalimskaya, 1854–1932) – acted at the Art Theatre from 1898 until her death and was a founder-member of the Fourth Studio in the 1920s.

9 V. N. Pavlova (1875–1962) – acted at the Art Theatre from 1898 to 1919 before emigrating to Germany.

10 V. I. Kachalov (real name Shverubovich, 1875–1948) – joined the Art Theatre in 1900 and stayed with the company all his life. An extremely gifted actor with a very fine voice, he created a number of memorable roles from Trofimov to Brand and Chatskiy. His versatility even ran to interpreting the part of the peasant partisan leader, Vershinin, in Vsevolod Ivanov's *Armoured Train 14–69* (1927).

11 There was no way that the Art Theatre could have competed with the Imperial Theatres, during its first years, in terms of actors' salaries. Actors at the latter could earn as much as 7,000 roubles a year plus perks. Even provincial actors could earn considerable sums at the turn of the century – between 6,800 and 8,500 roubles a season of about eight-and-a-half months' duration. It was also possible for leading actors to make substantial sums by touring. Komissarzhevskaya grossed nearly 50,000 roubles on tour between 1902 and 1904 (see Andreyeva 1961).

12 I. M. Uralov (1872–1920) – acted at the Art Theatre from 1907 to 1911.

13 A. G. Koonen (1889–1974) – joined the Art Theatre School in 1906, graduating to minor roles on the Art Theatre stage. A protégée of Stanislavsky, it was a great disappointment to him when Koonen

decided to leave in 1913. It was whilst working at the Free (Svobodnyy) Theatre, in 1913, under Konstantin Mardzhanov that she met her future husband, Aleksandr Tairov, with whom she went on to found the Kamernyy Theatre in 1914, where she acted until its closure in 1949.

14 V. V. Kotlyarevskaya (? –1942) – one of Stanislavsky's regular correspondents, she worked at the Aleksandrinskiy Theatre from 1898 to 1918 before emigrating to Rumania.

6 SAVVA MOROZOV AND THE LIANOZOV THEATRE

1 Chamberlain Lane (Kamergerskiy pereulok) is situated towards the lower end of what was Gorky Street (which has now reverted to its former name of Tverskaya Street). The narrow road on which the theatre is situated is today called Proyezd Khudozhestvennogo teatra (Art Theatre Passage). The street also used to be referred to as Gazyetnyy pereulok (Newspaper Alley) as it was in two sections – the first, 'Gazyetnyy' leading into 'Kamergerskiy'.

2 A. A. Stakhovich (1856–1919) – adjutant to the Governor-General of Moscow and a senior shareholder in the Moscow Art Theatre from 1907 to 1919; he was also one of the founders of the Theatre's Second Studio.

3 Ye. N. Goryeva (1859–1917) – actress and entrepreneur.

4 L. V. Sobinov (1872–1934) – a lyric tenor and briefly (1917–18 and 1921) director of the Bolshoy Theatre.

5 A. S. Golubkina (1864–1927) – studied in Moscow and Paris, concluding her training under Auguste Rodin. Her favourite themes were of either man or woman awakening to consciousness, revealing 'both the soul of man and those elemental forces within him which unite the souls with the soul of nature, the earth and the cosmos' (D. A. Sarabianov, *Russian Art: From Neo-classicism to the Avant-Garde*, London: Thames & Hudson, 1990 (p. 294).

6 K. N. Nyezlobin (real name Alyab'yev, 1857–1930) – theatre owner and director who ran his own theatre in Moscow from 1909 to 1917.

7 M. A. Chekhov (1891–1955) – nephew of the dramatist and an actor and teacher at the Art Theatre from 1913. He was closely associated with Yevgeniy Vakhtangov and the work of the First and Third Studios, especially following Vakhtangov's death in 1922. Shortly after taking charge of the Second Moscow Art Theatre in 1928, Chekhov felt obliged to leave the country permanently as increasing pressure was put on his artistic freedom. Settling briefly in the Baltic States and then in England, where he taught and staged plays at Dartington Hall, he finally left for America at the outbreak of the Second World War. The theatre studio which he established in Ridgefield, Connecticut, was short-lived and Chekhov moved to Hollywood where he worked as a teacher and film actor. Influenced by the Russian Symbolists and the theosophical thought of Rudolph Steiner, his writings on the art of theatre were published in English and in Russian after his death.

8 N. L. Tarasov (? –1910) – entrepreneur and MAT shareholder,

organiser with N. Baliyev of Die Fledermaus (The Bat) Cabaret Theatre, known in Russian as Letuchaya Mysh'.

9 N. F. Baliyev (1877–1936) – co-founder with Tarasov of Die Fledermaus (The Bat) Cabaret Theatre (1908–22), which developed from the so-called 'cabbage parties' (*kapustniki*), home-grown evening entertainments which Stanislavsky describes in *My Life in Art*. Baliyev met Stanislavsky during the company's European tour, in 1906, returning to Moscow and performing for a short while (1906–11) in the company's productions. He emigrated in 1920.

10 I. A. Sats (1875–1912) – composer, conductor, and Head of the Art Theatre Musical Section from 1906 until his death.

Part II: The Moscow Art Theatre Repertoire 1898–1917

7 FIRST SEASON: 1898–1899

1 Giles Fletcher, The Elder (1548–1611) – poet, author and diplomat. Graduate of Eton and King's College, Cambridge, he was elected to parliament in 1583 and sent as ambassador to Russia in 1588. He concluded an alliance between Tsar Fedor and Elizabeth I and secured better trade conditions for the English Muscovy Company. In 1591 he published *Of the Russe Commonwealth*.

2 It is difficult to get a sense of the vivid colours of this production which can, perhaps, best be gauged from a painting by Andrey Khudyakov of the setting for the scene in the Kremlin Palace in Act One and which is included in Sayler (1925), facing page 28.

3 Simov's painting in the manner of V. V. Vereshchagin, called *The Disgrace of Metropolitan Filipp*, painted in 1895 and with its vivid portrayal of a provincial crowd, provides a good indication of his manner.

4 I. F. Krasovskiy (stage name Krovskiy 1870–1938) – acted at the Society of Art and Literature and then at the Art Theatre for one year. Spent his remaining time at the Malyy Theatre.

5 N. P. Khmelev (1901–45) – joined the Art Theatre Second Studio in 1919 and was a member of the Art Theatre company proper from 1924 onwards.

6 V. O. Klyuchevskiy (1841–1911) – appointed to the Chair of History at Moscow University in 1879, his *Kurs russkoy istorii* ('A History of Russia') is considered a landmark in world historiography. His study of Peter the Great (Macmillan, 1958) is also of great importance.

7 S. A. Tolstaya (1844–1919) – wife of Leo Tolstoy.

8 P. M. Yartsev (1871–1930), theatre critic, director and dramatist.

9 S. Glagol' (real name Goloushev, 1855–1920) – writer, painter and theatre critic.

10 See Balukhaty (1952), Jones (1986), Henry (1965) and Braun (1982).

11 One of Chekhov's criticisms of Stanislavsky's interpretation of Trigorin was precisely the fact that he wasn't sufficiently ordinary and 'down-at-

heel', dressed in checked trousers, with holes in his shoes and carrying crude home-made fishing rods. (See Stanislavskiy 1958: 93–4).

12 A. I. Urusov (1843–1900) – lawyer, critic and translator who, like the Malyy actor/director and childhood friend of Nemirovich, Prince Sumbatov-Yuzhin, did not take his title too seriously.

13 M. I. Pisaryev (1844–1905) – after a career in the provinces, he settled at the Aleksandrinskiy Theatre in 1885 and was husband of the famous actress P. A. Strepetova who acted at the same theatre from 1881 to 1890.

14 A special programme was produced for this production, which attempted to explain the conventions of Greek theatre performance to audiences likely to be unfamiliar with them.

8 SECOND SEASON: 1899–1900

1 Verse translations of the play can be found in Alexis K. Tolstoi, *The Death of Ivan the Terrible*, trans. Alfred Hayes, London: Kegan Paul, Trench, Trubner & Co. Ltd, 1926, and in George Rapall Noyes (ed. and trans.) *Masterpieces of the Russian Drama* (2 vols) vol.2, New York: Appleton & Co./Dover Publications, 1933/1961.

2 S. V. Vasil'yev – a Moscow choir master.

3 V. L. Yuren'yeva (1876–1962) – acted at the Second Moscow Art Theatre from 1930 to 1936.

4 A. R. Kugel' (1864–1928) – who wrote under the pseudonym 'Homo novus' was, together with Efros, among the best-known theatre critics in Russia during the early years of this century. His openness to innovation and his hostility to naturalism made him one of the Art Theatre's most implacable foes, although an accommodation was reached in 1926 when the Theatre staged his play *Nicholas I and the Decembrists*. He founded the Crooked Mirror (Krivoye zerkalo) Cabaret Theatre in 1908 which he headed until his death. He also edited the influential journal *Teatr i iskusstvo* ('Theatre and Art') from 1897 to 1918.

5 Yu. D. Belyayev (1876–1917) – theatre critic and dramatist.

9 THIRD SEASON: 1900–1901

1 I. I. Ivanov (1862–1929) – literary historian, theatre researcher and critic.

2 For accounts of the production of *Three Sisters* see Worrall (1990), Munk (1966) and R. L. Jackson (ed.) *Chekhov: A Collection of Critical Essays*, New Jersey: Englewood Cliffs, 1967, pp. 121–35.

3 L. N. Andreyev (1871–1919) – short-story writer and dramatist, whose Symbolist plays were very popular in Russia between 1900 and 1917. He is best known in the West for his extravaganza, set in a circus, *He Who Gets Slapped* (1914). He was also an excellent theatre critic and, together with S. Glagol', wrote a monograph on Art Theatre productions under the pseudonym 'Dzhems Linch' (James Lynch).

10 FOURTH SEASON: 1901–1902

1 P. M. Yartsev (1871–1930) – theatre critic, director and dramatist.
2 I. N. Ignatov (1858–1921) – theatre critic and theatre historian.
3 S. A. Naydenov (real name Alekseyev) (1868–1922) – his first play *Vanyushin's Children* (1901) is probably his best and is frequently revived in Russia.

11 FIFTH SEASON: 1902–1903

1 V. P. Verigina (1882–1974) – a graduate of the Art Theatre School she acted at the theatre from 1902 to 1904 before joining Meyerhold at Komissarzhevskaya's theatre in St Petersburg. Her memoirs give interesting accounts of productions of the time (see Verigina (1974)).
2 N. N. Litovtseva (1878–1956) – a graduate of Nemirovich's at the Philharmonic School and wife of Kachalov, she remained at the Art Theatre for fifty years, from 1901 to 1951.
3 A. P. Kharlamov (1876–1934) – a graduate of Nemirovich's school he acted at the Art Theatre between 1898 and 1903 (with breaks).
4 E. P. Muratova (1874–1921) – a graduate of Nemirovich's school, she joined the theatre in 1901 and remained there until her death.
5 M. A. Gromov (? –1918) – joined the company in 1899 and stayed until 1906.
6 N. A. Baranov (no dates available) – a former choir-singer, he was with the company from 1899 until 1903.
7 A. A. Blok (1880–1921) – one of Russia's greatest twentieth-century poets, who also produced some interesting short plays in verse, in particular *Balaganchik* ('The Fairground Booth' or 'Puppet Show') staged memorably by Meyerhold at Komissarzhevskaya's theatre in 1906 (see Braun (1969)).
8 For a translation of Stanislavsky's score for this scene, see Cole and Chinoy (1964).
9 Satin's speech on 'Man', which rather incongruously lists Napoleon (of 1812 infamy) alongside Mahomet in the pantheon of human greatness, assumed special significance during the Soviet period as a socialist-humanist paean to the potential of common humanity.
10 K. P. Pyatnitskiy (1864–1938) – one of the founders and directors of the Znaniye Publishing House with which Gorky was associated.

12 SIXTH SEASON: 1903–1904

1 Sergey Diaghilev (1872–1929) – ballet impresario, closely connected with The World of Art movement via its magazine *Mir iskusstva*, he is probably best known for his commissioning of ballet scores, in particular Stravinsky's *Petrushka* and *The Rite of Spring*. His 'Russian seasons', staged abroad before 1917, made both Diaghilev and his company's principal male dancer, Vaslav Nijinsky, world famous.
2 L. A. Sulerzhitskiy (1872–1916) – a name unaccountably missing from

NOTES

some theatrical encyclopedias – joined the Art Theatre in 1905 and
became someone in whom Stanislavsky placed unique faith as a teacher
and transmitter of his ideas. Together with Vakhtangov, to whom
Stanislavsky was also very close, they set up the First Studio. Sulerzhitskiy
met an untimely death in a boating accident which, coupled with
Vakhtangov's early death from cancer in 1922, were blows to Stanislavsky's hopes from which, some say, he never fully recovered.

3 Andrey Bely (real name Boris Bugayev) (1880–1934) – poet, novelist
and leading member of the Russian Symbolist movement who was
influenced by the theosophical writings of Rudolph Steiner. Best
known outside Russia for his experimental novel *Peterburg* (first version
1916), a work considered by Vladimir Nabokov to be comparable in
significance to James Joyce's *Ulysses*. Bely's remarks on *The Cherry
Orchard* can be found in Senelick (1981: 89–92).

4 A. I. Pomyalova (real name Val'ts, 1862–?) – was a ballet dancer but
had done some acting before she joined the Art Theatre – the first time
from 1898 to 1905, and then again from 1906 to 1909.

5 The scene in question can be found in Michael Frayn's introduction
to his own translation of the play (see Chekhov 1995 lvii–lviii).

6 S. V. Khalyutina (1875–1960) – actress and teacher, graduate of
Nemirovich's Philharmonic School class, she acted at the Theatre from
1898 until 1950.

7 F. D. Batyushkov (1857–1920) – philologist and man of letters who was
briefly put in charge of the Petrograd theatres in 1917 by the
Provisional Government.

8 L. Ya. Guryevich (1866–1940) – theatre historian, theatre critic, and
author of a number of books and articles devoted to the Art Theatre,
she assisted Stanislavsky closely during the Soviet period and was
instrumental in getting him to revise and publish *My Life in Art* in its
Russian-language version.

9 K. D. Bal'mont (1867–1942) – Symbolist poet who spent a lot of time
in the West; he was also a prolific translator and wrote essays on Western
European literary culture.

10 A. V. Amfiteatrov (1862–1938) – dramatist and critic who wrote under
the English pseudonym 'Old Gentleman'.

13 SEASON SEVEN TO SEASON TEN: 1904–1908

1 I. (Ye. F) Armand (1875–1920) – born Elisabeth d'Herbenville in Paris,
she married a Russian and joined the Bolsheviks in 1905. Aleksandra
Kollontay, a friend of Lenin and his wife Nadezhda Krupskaya, gives
the impression in her novel *A Great Love* that Armand might have been
Lenin's mistress, although there is no solid evidence for this. Armand
was prominent in the Women's Movement and is buried in the Kremlin
wall alongside prominent revolutionary figures.

2 Nemirovich made many changes to the text, introducing cuts and
alterations, transposing scenes and introducing 'confidants' to react to
some of the long monologues.

3 Soon after writing the score for Act Three of *Ghosts*, Stanislavsky saw a production of *A Month in the Country* on 12 March 1905 with Mariya Savina as Natalya Petrovna – which may be when he decided to stage the play himself.

4 A. S. Griboyedov (1795–1829) – author of one remarkable verse play, just about every line of which has entered Russian proverbial speech. A rare English production of this Russian classic was given, in a version by Anthony Burgess, entitled *Chatsky*, at the Almeida Theatre, London in 1993. Griboyedov died young having had the misfortune to be sent as ambassador to Persia, where he was killed by a hostile crowd.

5 M. S. Shchepkin (1788–1863) – a serf entertainer who became one of the greatest actors of the nineteenth-century Russian stage with the same kind of importance for realistic innovations in acting and staging as David Garrick had for the eighteenth-century English stage. He was a personal friend of Gogol, Turgenev and Ostrovsky.

6 Having left the Art Theatre in 1902, Meyerhold was invited back by Stanislavsky in 1905 to engage in experimental work on non-naturalistic productions. For this purpose, Stanislavsky acquired small premises on Povarskaya Street and lent Meyerhold younger members of the company to assist with his work on plays by Maeterlinck and other Symbolist dramatists. However, because of the actors' lack of experience and the disruption caused by the insurrectionary events of that year, Stanislavsky concluded that the work was unsuccessful and ceased to subsidise it any further. Meyerhold continued his experiments, very successfully, at Komissarzhevskaya's theatre in St Petersburg between 1906 and 1908.

7 G. V. Plekhanov (1857–1918) – a collaborator of Lenin's until he broke with him to join the Mensheviks in 1903, Plekhanov played a unique role in converting the Russian intelligentsia to Marxism and, apart from his political essays, wrote interestingly on art and literature from a Marxist perspective.

8 S. V. Yablonskiy (real name Viktorovich, 1870–1953) – journalist and critic closely associated with the newspaper *Russkoye slovo* ('The Russian Word'). He emigrated in 1920.

9 V. E. Yegorov (1878–1960) – a member of The World of Art movement; he worked at the Art Theatre from 1906 to 1911.

10 N. P. Ul'yanov (1875–1949) – theatre designer who also worked with Meyerhold at Komissarzhevskaya's theatre 1905–6.

14 SEASONS ELEVEN AND TWELVE: 1908–1909

1 For a discussion of Stanislavsky and the French psychologist Théodule-Armand Ribot, see 'Emotional Memory' in E. Bentley (ed.) *The Theory of the Modern Stage*, Harmondsworth: Penguin, 1968.

2 The First Studio was created by Stanislavsky in collaboration with Vakhtangov and Sulerzhitskiy as an intimate theatre where exploratory work on his 'system' might be furthered. Formed in 1912, the first production was of Herman Heijerman's *Op Hoop van Zegen* ('The Good

Hope'/'The Wreck of "The Hope"'), followed by Vakhtangov's production of Hauptmann's *Das Friedensfest* ('Reconciliation'/'The Festival of Peace').

3 P. A. Markov (1897–1980) – Head of the Literary Section of the Moscow Art Theatre between 1925 and 1949, Markov was an extremely influential figure during politically turbulent times, as well as a very fine theatre critic.

4 L. M. Korenyeva (1885–?) – acted at the Art Theatre from 1904 until 1958).

5 K. A. Mardzhanov (real name Mardzhanishvili, 1872–1933) – worked as assistant director at the Art Theatre from 1910 to 1913 before leaving to found the short-lived Svobodnyy (Free) Theatre in Moscow in 1913 where he staged operetta. Having staged a memorable production of Lope de Vega's *Fuente Ovejuna* in 1919, Mardzhanov went on to become the leading theatrical light in Soviet Georgia where the second State Georgian Theatre was named after him in 1933.

6 A. Ya. Tairov (1885–1950) – director and founder, together with Alisa Koonen of the Moscow Kamernyy (Chamber) Theatre in 1914 and which he headed until shortly before his death. For an account of his career, see Worrall (1989).

7 R. V. Boleslavskiy (real name Strzhesnitskiy, 1887–1937) – worked at the Art Theatre between 1908 and 1918 both at the main house and at the First Studio where he acted and directed. He emigrated to the United States after the revolution, where he and Mariya Uspenskaya (1887–1949) together founded the American Laboratory Theatre, teaching the Stanislavsky 'system' to Lee Strasberg, among others. His book, *Acting – The First Six Lessons*, was published in 1949.

8 M. V. Dobuzhinskiy (1875–1957) – studied law before taking up art, his first collaboration with The World of Art was as magazine and book illustrator. His work at the Art Theatre included designs for a Turgenev Evening of three plays (1912) and for Dostoyevsky's *The Possessed* (staged as *Nikolay Stavrogin*, 1913). He moved to Lithuania in 1924, finally settling in the USA in 1939. He collaborated with Michael Chekhov on a production of Dostoyevsky's *The Possessed* both at Dartington Hall in Devon and in Ridgefield, Connecticut, during the late 1930s and early 1940s.

9 M. N. Germanova (real name Krasovskaya, 1884–1940) – a graduate of the Art Theatre's own school in 1902 she remained at the theatre until 1919 when she emigrated.

10 N. O. Massalitinov (1880–1961) – member of the Art Theatre from 1907 to 1919 and, from 1925, a director of the Bulgarian National Theatre.

11 N. N. Zvantsev (1870–1923) – member of the Art Theatre troupe from 1903 to 1911 and then again from 1921 to 1923; he also worked as a director at the Nyezlobin Theatre between 1913 and 1918.

12 I. V. Lazaryev (1877–1929) – had two spells at the Art Theatre, 1902–3 and 1909–20.

13 L. I. Dmitrevskaya (1890–?) – worked at the Art Theatre from 1906 to 1924.

14 K. P. Bryulov (1799–1852) – Italian born, he came to Russia as a child before returning to Italy later. His most important work is considered to be the large canvas *The Last Day of Pompeii* (1833) which took him six years to complete. He was also an excellent portrait painter. Sir Walter Scott, Pushkin and Gogol all thought highly of his work.

15 V. E. Borisov–Musatov (1870–1905) – Symbolist painter of the Moscow school who also worked in Paris in the 1890s where he was strongly influenced by Puvis de Chavannes.

16 K. Somov (1869–1939) – a member of The World of Art movement who combined an enthusiasm for the work of Aubrey Beardsley with a taste for the old masters, especially Vermeer. Among his finest paintings is a portrait of Aleksandr Blok (1907). He died in Paris.

17 G. Fuchs (1868–1949) – founder of the Munich Artists' Theatre in 1908, his book *Revolution in the Theatre* made a strong impact on Meyerhold and other Russian avant-garde theatre practitioners.

18 The quotation, from T. S. Eliot's 'The Love Song of J. Alfred Prufrock', runs:

> And I have known the eyes already, known them all—
> The eyes that fix you in a formulated phrase,
> And when I am formulated, sprawling on a pin,
> When I am pinned and wriggling on the wall,
> Then how should I begin
> To spit out all the butt-ends of my days and ways?

15 SEASON TWELVE TO SEASON TWENTY: 1909–1917

1 Alexandre Benois (real name A. N. Benua, 1870–1960) – a leading figure of The World of Art movement, he worked with both Stanislavsky and Diaghilev, designing sets for the first performance of Stravinsky's *Petrushka* (1911). His last work in the Soviet Union, before emigrating, was for a production of *The Marriage of Figaro* at the Leningrad Bolshoy Drama Theatre.

2 S. S. Yushkevich (1868–1927) – a protégé of Gorky's, many of whose plays have Jewish themes. He emigrated to France in 1920.

3 Meyerhold's essay 'The Fairground Booth' can be found in Braun (1969).

4 For a full account of the Craig–Stanislavsky *Hamlet*, see Senelick (1982).

5 S. G. Birman (1890–1970) – actress and director, she worked at the Art Theatre from 1911 to 1913, then, from 1913 to 1936, at the First Studio and at the Second Moscow Art Theatre. She also made film appearances, none more famous than in Sergey Eisenstein's *Ivan the Terrible* in which she played the tsar's aunt Yefrosinya Staritskaya.

16 CONCLUSION

1 Yu. P. Lyubimov (1917–) – one of the most interesting and innovative post-war Russian theatre directors who founded the Taganka Theatre

NOTES

in 1964 and whose best work was achieved there in a ten-year period until the mid-1970s. He also staged a number of operas and plays abroad, not always successfully, including some in England during the 1980s.

2 M. A. Bulgakov (1891–1940) – worked as director's assistant at the Art Theatre from 1930 to 1936 where some of his plays were performed. He is best known outside Russia for his 1926 play *The Days of the Turbins* (*Dni Turbinykh*), which is based on his 1920s novel *The White Guard*, under which title it is often performed in English, and for *The Master and Margarita* (first published in the Soviet Union 1966–7), a novel which combines elements of the Bible and the Faust legend with contemporary fantasy in the style of Gogol. An adaptation of his satirical novel about the Art Theatre, *A Theatrical Romance*, was staged at the National Theatre, London, in 1991 under its English title, *Black Snow*.

3 I. Ya. Sudakov (1890–1969) – joined the Second Studio in 1916, graduating to the Art Theatre in 1924 where he remained until 1937, rejoining the company from 1946 until 1953.

4 V. V. Ivanov (1895–1963) – prose writer and dramatist, his *Armoured Train 14–69*, which began life as a short story, was the first 'Soviet' play to be staged at the Art Theatre. Ivanov also wrote other civil war plays and dramas with historical themes.

5 See Gorchakov (1954/1956).

6 J. V. Stalin (real name Iosif Vissarionovich Dzhugashvili, 1879–1953) – General Secretary of the Communist Party of the Soviet Union from 1922 until his death, he originally trained for the priesthood.

7 Kafka's work was the target of hostile criticism at the First Soviet Writers' Conference in 1934. Trotsky (real name Lev Davydovich Bronshteyn, 1879–1940) was forced into exile in 1929 and murdered by a Soviet agent in 1940. Meyerhold was arrested in 1939 and executed in prison in 1940.

8 The central character in Ibsen's *Masterbuilder* – an architect who, encouraged to climb as high as he can build, falls from the spire of his own house, as he attempts to crown the building's pinnacle with a laurel wreath.

225

BIBLIOGRAPHY

References to archive material is to that held by the Moscow Art Theatre itself. The initials MAT refer to the pre-revolutionary Moscow Art Theatre, the Russian equivalent of which is MKhT (Moskovskiy Khudozhestvennyy teatr). The initials MKhAT have no English equivalent and refer to the Moscow Art Academic Theatre (Moskovskiy Khudozhestvenny akademichiskiy teatr) which became the Moscow Art Theatre's official title after 1920.

Aganbekyan, A. (1939) *Moskovskiy Khudozhestvennyy teatr, 1898–1938. Bibliografiya*, Moscow-Leningrad: VTO.

Amiard-Chevrel, C. (1979) *Le Théâtre Artistique de Moscou (1898–1917)*, Paris: CNRS.

Andreyeva, M. F. (1961) *Perepiska. Vospominaniya. Stat'i. Dokumenty. Vospominaniya o M. F. Andreyevoy*, Moscow: Iskusstvo.

Anisimov, A. V. (1984) *Teatry Moskvy*, Moscow: Moskovskiy rabochiy.

Aseyev, B. N. and Obraztsova, A. G. (1976) *Russkiy dramaticheskiy teatr*, Moscow: Prosveshcheniye.

Balukhaty, S. D. (ed.) (1952) *'The Seagull' Produced by Stanislavsky* (trans. D. Magarshack), London: Dennis Dobson.

Bassekhes, A. (1960) *Khudozhniki na stsene MKhAT*, Moscow: VTO.

Bazilyevskaya-Solov'eva, I. (1951–2) 'Doktor Shtokman na stsene MKhT' in *Yezhegodnik Moskovskogo Khudozhestvennogo teatra*, Moscow: Izd. MKhAT.

Belyayev, Yu. (1902) *Aktery i p'yesy*, St Petersburg.

Benedetti, J. (1982) *Stanislavski: An Introduction*, London: Methuen.

—— (1988) *Stanislavski*, London: Methuen.

—— (ed) (1991) *The Moscow Art Theatre Letters*, London: Methuen Drama.

Berkovskiy, N. (1969) 'Stanislavskiy i estetika teatra' in B. Zingerman (ed.) *Teatral'nyye stranitsy*, Moscow: Iskusstvo.

Braun, E. (ed.) (1969) *Meyerhold on Theatre*, London: Methuen.

—— (1982) 'Stanislavsky and Chekhov' in Braun, E. *The Director and the Stage: From Naturalism to Grotowski*, London: Methuen.

Chekhov, A. P. (1926) *The Letters of Anton Pavlovich Tchehov to Olga Leonardovna Knipper*, London: Chatto & Windus.

—— (1963) *Sobraniye sochinenii*, (12 vols), vol. 9 *P'yesy 1880–1904*, Moscow: Gos. Izd. Khud. Lit.

BIBLIOGRAPHY

—— A. P. (1974–83) *Polnoye sobraniye sochinenii i pisem* (30 vols) Moscow: Izd. Akad. Nauk.

—— (1995) *The Cherry Orchard*, trans. with an intro. by Michael Frayn, London: Methuen.

Cole, T. (ed.) (1955 rev. edn 1971) *Acting – A Handbook of the Stanislavski Method*, New York: Crown Publishers/Bonanza Books.

Cole, T. and Chinoy, H. C. (eds) (1964) *Directors on Directing*, London: Peter Owen/Vision Press.

Danilov, S. S. (1948) *Ocherki po istorii russkogo dramaticheskogo teatra*, Leningrad-Moscow: Iskusstvo.

Doroshevich, V. M. (1962) *Rasskazy i ocherki*, Moscow: Iskusstvo.

Durylin, S. N., Grabar', I. E. and Markov, P. A. (eds) (1955) *K.S. Stanislavskiy – Teatral'noye nasledstvo. Materialy, pis'ma, issledovaniya*, Moscow: Izd. Akad. Nauk.

Edwards, C. (1966) *The Stanislavsky Heritage*, London: Peter Owen.

Efros, N. E. (1918) *K. S. Stanislavskiy, opyt kharakteristiki*, Petersburg: Gostip.

—— (1919) *Vishnevyy sad v postanovke MKhAT*, Petrograd: Svetozar.

—— (1923) *'Na dne' Gor'kogo v postanovke MKhAT*, Moscow: GIZ.

—— (1924) *Moskovskiy Khudozhestvenny teatr (1898–1923)*, Moscow-Petrograd: GIZ.

Fel'dman, O. (1967) *'Boris Godunov' v Khudozhestvennom teatre,'* in V. Frolov (ed.) *Voprosy teatra, sbornik stat'yei i materialov*, Moscow: VTO.

Flanagan, H. (1929) *Shifting Scenes of the Modern European Theatre*, London: Geo. G. Harrap.

Freydkina, L. V. (1945) *Vl. I. Nemirovich-Danchenko*, Moscow: Iskusstvo.

Gorchakov, N. M. (1954/1956) *Stanislavsky Directs*, New York: Funk & Wagnalls/Minerva Press.

Gorky, M. (1949–56) *Sobraniye sochinenii* (30 vols), Moscow: Goslitizdat.

—— (1966) *Letters*, Moscow: Progress.

—— (1973) *The Lower Depths* (trans. K. Hunter-Blair and J. Brooks), London: Methuen.

Grossman, L. (1924) *Teatr Turgeneva*, Petersburg: Brokgauz-Efron.

Guryevich, L. Ya. (1948) *O Stanislavskom – sbornik vospominaniy*, Moscow: VTO.

Henry, P. (ed.) (1965) A. P. Chekhov, *Chaika*, Letchworth: Bradda Books.

Izralyevskiy B. (1965) *Muzyka v spektaklyakh Moskovskogo Khudozhestvennogo teatra. Zapiski dirizhera*, Moscow: VTO.

Jones, D. R. (1986) 'Konstantin Stanislavsky and *The Seagull*: The Paper Stage', in *Great Directors at Work*, Berkeley: University of California.

Kalashnikov, Yu. S. (ed.) (1988) *Rezhisserskiye ekzemplyary K. S. Stanislavskogo* (6 vols), vol. 5, *1905–1909*, Moscow: Iskusstvo.

Kholodov, E. G. (ed.) (1987) *Istoriya russkogo dramaticheskogo teatra* (7 vols, 1977–87), vol. 7, Moscow: Iskusstvo.

Khudozhestvenno-Obshchedostupnyy teatr v Moskve, Mysli i vpechatleniya zritelya (1901) Moscow: Tov. tip. A. I. Mamontova.

Kirichenko, E. (1973) *Fedor Shekhtel'*, Moscow: Stroyizdat.

Kitchin, L. (1960) 'Chekhov Without Inhibitions – The Moscow Art Theatre in London, 1958' in *Mid-Century Drama*, London: Faber & Faber.

Kleberg, L. and Nilsson, N. A. (1984) *Theater and Literature in Russia 1900–1930*, Stockholm: Almqvist & Wiksell International.

Knebel', M. (1967) *Vsya zhizn'*, Moscow: VTO.
Knipper-Chekhova, O. L. (1934) *Perepiska s Chekhovym* (2 vols), vol. 1 (1899–15.9.1901), Moscow: Mir.
—— (1936) *Perepiska s Chekhovym* (2 vols), vol. 2 (26.10.1901–10.10.02), Moscow: Mir.
—— (1972) *Vospominaniya i stat'i. Perepiska s A. P. Chekhovym* (2 vols), vol. 1 (1902–5), Moscow: Iskusstvo.
—— (1972) *Perepiska. Vospominaniya ob O. L. Knipper-Chekhovoy* (2 vols), vol. 2 (1896–1959) Moscow: Iskusstvo.
Koonen, A. (2nd edn 1985) *Stranitsy zhizni*, Moscow: Iskusstvo.
Krymova, N. A. (1971) *Stanislavskiy – rezhisser*, Moscow: Iskusstvo.
Kugel', A. (1934) *Russkiye dramaturgi*, Moscow: Mir.
Lenskiy, A. P. (1935) *Stat'i, Pis'ma, Zapiski*, Moscow-Leningrad: Academia.
Lilina, M. P. (1960) *Ocherki zhizni i tvorchestva*, Moscow: VTO.
Litovtseva, N. N. (1949) 'Iz proshlogo Moskovskogo Khudozhestvennogo teatra' in *Yezhegodnik MKhAT za 1943*, Moscow-Leningrad: Izd. MKhAT.
MacLeod, J. (1946) *Actors Cross the Volga*, London: Geo. Allen & Unwin.
Magarshack, D.(1950) *Stanislavsky: A Life*, London: MacGibbon & Kee.
Markov, P. A. (1976) *V Khudozhestvennom teatre – kniga zavlita*, Moscow: VTO.
Marshall, N. (1957, 3rd edn 1975) 'Stanislavsky and the Moscow Art Theatre' in *The Producer and the Play*, London: Davis-Poynter.
Matskin, A. (1969) 'Pyat' Chekhovskikh rolyey' in B. Zingerman (ed.) *Teatral'nyye stranitsy*, Moscow: Iskusstvo.
Melik-Zakharov, S. and Bogatyrev, S. (eds) (1963) *K. Stanislavsky 1863–1963*, Moscow: Progress.
Meyerkhol'd, V. E. (1976) *Perepiska 1896–1939*, Moscow: Iskusstvo.
Mikhal'skiy, F. N. and Rogachevskiy, M. L. (1974) *Moskovskiy Khudozhestvennyy teatr v sovyetskuyu epokhu*, Moscow: Iskusstvo.
Miller, A. I. (1931, reissue 1966) 'The Moscow Art Theatre and the Soviet Theatre of Russia' in *The Independent Theatre in Europe 1887 to the Present*, New York–London: Benjamin Blom.
Moore, S. (1960, rev. edn 1965) *The Stanislavski System*, New York: Viking Press.
—— (ed.) (1973) *Stanislavski Today*, New York: American Centre for Stanislavski Theatre Art.
Morgan, J. V. (1984) *Stanislavski's Encounter with Shakespeare – The Evolution of a Method*, Michigan: UMI Research Press.
Moskovskiy Khudozhestvennyy teatr (1955), vol. 1 (1898–1917), Moscow: GIII.
Moskovskiy Khudozhestvennyy teatr v illyustratsiyakh i dokumentakh (1938) *(1898–1938)*, Moscow: Izd. MKhAT.
Moskovskiy Khudozhestvennyy teatr, istoricheskiy ocherk yego zhizni i deyatel'nosti (1914) (2 vols), vol. 1 (*1898–1904*), vol. 2 (*1905–14*), Moscow: Rampa i zhizn'.
Munk, E. (ed.) (1966/1967) *Stanislavski and America: An Anthology from the Tulane Drama Review*, New York: Hill & Wang/Fawcett World Library.
Nemirovich-Danchenko, V. I. (1952 and 1954) *Teatral'noye naslediye* (2 vols), Moscow: Iskusstvo.

BIBLIOGRAPHY

—— (2nd Eng. edn 1968) *My Life in the Russian Theatre*, London: Geoffrey Bles.

—— (1973) *Vl. I. Nemirovich-Danchenko o tvorchestve aktera* (ed. V. Ya. Vilenkin), Moscow: Iskusstvo.

—— (1979) *Izbrannyye pis'ma* (2 vols) (1879–1943), vol.1 (1879–1909), vol. 2 (1910–43), Moscow: Iskusstvo.

—— (1980) *Vl. I. Nemirovich-Danchenko – Retsenzii. Ocherki. Stat'i. Interv'yu. Zamyetki. 1877–1942*, Moscow: VTO.

—— (1984) *Nyezavershennyye rezhisserskiye raboty – 'Boris Godunov', 'Gamlet'*, Moscow: VTO.

—— (1989) *Rozhdeniye teatra – Vospominaniya, stat'i, zamyetki, pis'ma*, Moscow: Pravda.

Nyekhoroshev, Yu. I. (1984) *Dekorator Khudozhestvennogo teatra Viktor Andreyevich Simov*, Moscow: Sovyetskiy khudozhnik.

Nyelidov, V. A. (1931) *Teatral'naya Moskva (sorok lyet Moskovskikh teatrov)*, Berlin-Riga: Globus.

Orlov, Yu. M. (1989) *Moskovskiy Khudozhestvennyy teatr – Novatorstvo i traditsii v organizatsii tvorcheskogo protsessa*, Rostov-on-Don: Rostovskoye knizh. izd.

Ostrovskiy, A. N. (1973–80) *Polnoye sobraniye sochinenii* (12 vols), Moscow: Iskusstvo.

Pichkhadze, L. A. (ed.) (1978) *Moskovskiy Khudozhestvenny Akademicheskiy teatr – k 80-letiyu teatra*, Moscow: Iskusstvo.

Pitcher, H. (1979) *Chekhov's Leading Lady: A Portrait of the Actress Olga Knipper*, London: John Murray.

Polyakova Ye. I. (1969) 'Stanislavskiy-Dobuzhinskiy-Benua' in B. Zingerman (ed.) *Teatral'nyye stranitsy*, Moscow: Iskusstvo.

—— (1972) *Stanislavskiy – akter*, Moscow: Iskusstvo.

—— (1977) *Stanislavskiy*, Moscow: Iskusstvo.

—— (1982) *Stanislavsky*, Moscow: Progress.

Pozharskaya, M. N. (1970) *Russkoye teatral'no-dekoratsionnoye iskusstvo, kontsa XIX–nachala XX vyeka (1895–1907)*, Moscow: Iskusstvo.

Radishcheva O. A. and Belov, G. P. (1987) *Moskovskiy Khudozhestvennyy Akademicheskiy teatr. Iz istorii stroitel'stva i restavratsii zdaniya teatra*, Moscow: Izd. MKhAT.

Rostotskiy, B. I. and Chushkin, N. N. (1940) *'Tsar Fedor' na stsene MKhAT*, Moscow: VTO.

Rudnitskiy, K. L. (1969) *Rezhisser Meyerkhol'd*, Moscow: Nauka.

—— (1989) *Russkoye rezhisserskoye iskusstvo* (2 vols), vol. 1 (1898–1907), Moscow: Nauka.

—— (1990) *Russkoye rezhisserskoye iskusstvo* (2 vols), vol. 2 (1908–1917), Moscow: Nauka.

Ryndzyunskiy, G. D. (1899) *Khudozhestvenno-obshchedostupnyy teatr. Otchet o deyatel'nosti za pervyy god (14.VII.1898–28.II.1899)*, Moscow: A. A. Levenson.

Sayler, O. M. (1920/1922) *The Russian Theatre*, New York: Little, Brown & Co/Brentano's.

—— (1925) *Inside the Moscow Art Theatre*, New York: Brentano's.

Senelick, L. (ed.) (1981) *Russian Dramatic Theory from Pushkin to the Symbolists*, Austin: University of Texas.

—— (1982) *Gordon Craig's Moscow 'Hamlet'*, Westport, Connecticut–London: Greenwood.

—— (ed.) (1991) *National Theatre in Northern and Eastern Europe*, Cambridge: Cambridge University Press.

Shaykevich, V. A. (1968) *Dramaturgiya Ibsena v Rossii. Ibsen i MKhAT*, Kiev: University of Kiev.

Shestakova, N. A. (1989) *Proyezd Khudozhestvennogo teatra, 3*, Moscow: Moskovskiy rabochiy.

Sibiryakov, N. N. (1974, rev. edn 1988) *Mirovoye znacheniye Stanislavskogo*, Moscow: Iskusstvo.

Slonim, M. (1963) *Russian Theater from the Empire to the Soviets*, London: Methuen.

Smelyanskiy, A. (1993) *Is Comrade Bulgakov Dead? Mikhail Bulgakov at the Moscow Art Theatre*, London: Methuen.

Sobinov, L.V. (1970) *Pis'ma*, vol. 1, Moscow: Iskusstvo.

Solov'eva, I. N. (1979) *Nemirovich-Danchenko*, Moscow: Iskusstvo.

—— (ed.) (1983) *Rezhisserskiye ekzemplyary K. S. Stanislavskogo* (6 vols), vol. 3 (1901–4), Moscow: Iskusstvo.

—— and Shitova, V. V. (1985) *K. S. Stanislavskiy – Chelovyek. Sobytiya. Vremya*, Moscow: Iskusstvo.

Stanislavski, C. (1924/1967) *My Life in Art* (trans. J. J. Robbins), Harmondsworth: Penguin Books.

Stanislavski, C. (1948/1963) *Stanislavski Produces 'Othello'*, London: Geoffrey Bles.

—— (1958, rev. edn 1981) *Stanislavski's Legacy* (ed. E. R. Hapgood), London: Eyre Methuen.

Stanislavsky, K. (1964) 'Production Plan for *The Lower Depths*, A Scene from Act II' in T. Cole, and H. C. Chinoy (1964).

Stanislavskiy, K. S. (1938) *Rabota aktera nad soboy*, Moscow–Leningrad: GIKhL.

—— (1954–61) *Sobraniye sochinenii* (8 vols), Moscow: Iskusstvo.

—— (1962) *Moya zhizn' v iskusstve*, Moscow: Iskusstvo.

—— (1986) *Iz zapisnykh knizhek* (2 vols), vol. 1 (1888–1911), vol. 2 (1912–38), Moscow: VTO.

—— (1987) *Stanislavskiy repetiruyet* (ed. I. Vinogradskaya), Moscow: STD.

—— (1988) *Sobraniye sochinenii* (9 vols), vol. 1, Moscow: Iskusstvo.

—— (1990) *Moe grazhdanskoye sluzheniye Rossii* (ed. M. Lyubomudrov), *Vospominaniya. Stat'i. Ocherki. Rechi. Besyedy. Iz zapisnykh knizhek*, Moscow: Pravda.

—— (n. d.) *My Life in Art* (trans. G. Ivanov-Mumjiev), Moscow: Foreign Language Publishing House.

Stroyeva, M. N. (1955) *Chekhov i Khudozhestvennyy teatr*, Moscow: Iskusstvo.

—— (1973) *Rezhisserskiye iskaniya Stanislavskogo* (2 vols), vol. 1 (1898–1917), Moscow: Nauka.

—— (1977) *Rezhisserskiye iskaniya Stanislavskogo* (2 vols), vol. 2 (1917–38), Moscow: Nauka.

Styan, J. L. (1981) *Modern Drama in Theory and Practice* (3 vols), vol. 1 *Realism and Naturalism*, Cambridge: Cambridge University Press.

Surkov, E. D. (ed.) (1961) *Chekhov i teatr. Pis'ma, fel'yetony, sovremenniki o Chekhove*, Moscow: Iskusstvo.

Kniga o Novom teatre (1908), St Petersburg: Shipovnik.

Tolstoy, A. K. (1922) *Tsar Fyodor Ivanovitch*, trans. Jenny Covan, London: Brentano's.

—— (1959) *P'yesy*, Moscow: Iskusstvo.

Tolstaya, S. A. (1978) *Dnevniki* (2 vols), vol. 1, Moscow: Iskusstvo.

Toporkov, V. O. (1979) *Stanislavski in Rehearsal: The Final Years*, New York: Theatre Arts Books.

Turgenev, I. (1991) *A Month in the Country* (trans. R. Freeborn), Oxford/ New York: Oxford University Press.

Tynan, K. (1961) 'The Russian Theatre' in *Curtains*, London: Longman.

Varneke, B. V. (1971) *History of the Russian Theatre*, New York: Hafner.

Verigina, V. P. (1974) *Vospominaniya*, Leningrad: Iskusstvo.

Vilenkin, V. Ya. (ed.) (1986) *Rezhisserskiye ekzemplyary K. S. Stanislavskogo* (6 vols), vol. 4 (1902–05), Moscow: Iskusstvo.

Vilenkin, V. Ya. and Solov'eva, I. N. (eds) (1980) *Rezhisserskiye ekzemplyary K. S. Stanislavskogo*, (6 vols), vol. 1 (1898–9), Moscow: Iskusstvo.

Vinogradskaya, I. N. (1971) *Zhizn'i tvorchestvo K. S. Stanislavskogo* (4 vols), vol. 1 (1863–1905), Moscow: VTO.

—— (1971) *Zhizn'i tvorchestvo K. S. Stanislavskogo* (4 vols), vol. 2 (1906–15), Moscow: VTO.

—— (1973) *Zhizn'i tvorchestvo K. S. Stanislavskogo* (4 vols), vol. 3 (1916–26), Moscow: VTO.

—— (1976) *Zhizn'i tvorchestvo K. S. Stanislavskogo* (4 vols), vol. 4 (1927–38), Moscow: VTO.

Vinogradskaya, I. N. and Solov'eva, I. N. (eds) (1981) *Rezhisserskiye ekzemplyary K. S. Stanislavskogo* (6 vols), vol. 2 (1898–1901), Moscow: Iskusstvo.

Vsevolodskiy, V. (Gerngross) (1929) *Istoriya russkogo teatra* (2 vols), vol. 2 Leningrad/Moscow: Tea-Kino-Pechat'.

Williams, R. (1968) '*The Seagull*, by Chekhov' in *Drama in Performance*, London: C. A. Watts.

Worrall, N. (1982) *Nikolai Gogol and Ivan Turgenev*, London: Macmillan.

—— (1989) *Modernism to Realism on the Soviet Stage: Tairov – Vakhtangov – Okhlopkov*, Cambridge: Cambridge University Press.

—— (1990) 'Stanislavsky's Production of Chekhov's *Three Sisters*', in Russell, R. and Barratt, A. (eds) *Russian Theatre in the Age of Modernism*, London: Macmillan.

Yablonskiy, S. (1909) *O teatre*, Moscow: Sytin.

Yarmolinsky, A. (ed.) (3rd edn 1973) *Letters of Anton Chekhov*, New York: Viking Press.

Young, S. (1948 reprint) *Immortal Shadows: A Book of Dramatic Criticism*, New York: Charles Scribner/Hill & Wang.

Yuren'yeva, V. L. (1946) *Zapiski aktrisy*, Moscow/Leningrad: VTO.

Yuzovskiy, Yu. (1959) *Maksim Gor'kiy i ego dramaturgiya*, Moscow: Iskusstvo.

Zagorskiy, M. B. and Stepanova, N. L. (1952) *Gogol' i teatr*, Moscow: Iskusstvo.

INDEX

56, 71, 85, 86, 93, 101, 108;
production of *Antigone* 108–10,
112, 128, 152
Sats, I. 81, 160
Savitskaya, M.G. 43, 59, 61, 109,
122, 137, 166, 168
Scandinavian saga 177
Schiller, F. 21; *Fiesco* 22–3; *Love
and Intrigue* 26; *The Maid of
Orleans* 22; *The Robbers* 35
Schopenhauer, A. 130
Shakespeare, W. 13, 21, 86, 88,
153; *As You Like It* 21; *Hamlet* 35,
68, 69, 200, 201; *Julius Caesar*
21, 22, 61, 80 (production of
152–4); *King Lear* 35; *The
Merchant of Venice* 22, 32, 46, 47,
53, 54, 85 (production of 97,
99, 103–4, 105, 113, 114, 122);
Othello 29, 35, 102, 183, 201;
Twelfth Night 102, 114; *The
Winter's Tale* 21
Shamshin, A. 33
Shchepkin, M.S. 170
Shchukin, S.I. 14
Shchukin, Ya.V. 32, 49, 74
Shekhtel', F.O. 32, 73, 74, 76, 78,
79
Shelyaputinskiy Theatre (New
Imperial Dramatic Theatre) 42,
52, 121
show trials 206
Simov, V.A. 14, 44, 46, 55, 60, 64,
71, 80, 86, 89–90, 94, 95, 107,
108, 116, 126, 134, 160, 165,
180, 199
Sinel'nikov, N.N. 34
Slavic Bazaar restaurant 36
Smith, Sir Thomas 89
smutnoye vremya 86
Snigirev, B.M. 60
Sobinov, L. 73, 122
socialist realism 9, 207
Society of Art and Literature 6, 22,
24–31, 33, 36, 38, 39–40, 41, 43,
44, 54, 103, 114; theatre school
25, 65
Society of Russian Dramatic
Writers/Stage Authors 52, 65

Sokolov, A. 19
Solov'ev A.S. 55
Solovtsov Theatre 153
Somov, K. 196
Sophocles 108; *Antigone* 44, 46, 47,
52, 53, 54, 56, 57, 60, 85, 105,
108 (production of 108–10)
Soviet Union 9, 206; former Soviet
Union 13
Sporting (Hunting) Club 27, 28,
37, 41, 53, 54, 56
Stakhovich, A.A. 71, 82
Stalin, J.V. (I.V. Dzhugashvili) 204,
205, 207, 208
Stanislavsky (Alekseyev), K.S.
passim: assumes role as
principal director of the
Moscow Public-Accessible Art
Theatre 43; attitude towards
Morozov 69, 70, 78; business
experience 32–3; composition
of *The Seagull* production score
47; contribution to *When We
Dead Awaken* 126; directorial
debut 26; early disagreements
with Nemirovich-Danchenko
37–8; early rehearsal methods
29; ethnographical interests 29,
46, 86, 121, 132, 168; first
meeting with Nemirovich-
Danchenko 35–6; first plans for
a professional theatre company
30; first preparation of a prompt-
book 28; heart attack and
illness 205; influence of
Fedotov and Komissarzhevskiy
24; letter to Chekhov *re The
Cherry Orchard* 158; *My Life in
Art* 69, 102, 112, 131, 134, 175,
182, 183; naming the new
theatre 50; on tour with the
Malyy 28; operatic
performances with the Musical
Dramatic Circle 24;
performance as Anany Yakovlev
26–7; performance as Argan
201–2; performance as Astrov
115–16, 120; performance as
Brutus 153; performance as